Russians in Hollywood, Hollywood's Russians

Russians

in Hollywood,
Hollywood's Russians
Biography of an Image
Harlow Robinson

NORTHEASTERN UNIVERSITY PRESS ★ Boston

Published by

UNIVERSITY PRESS OF NEW ENGLAND

Hanover & London

NORTHEASTERN UNIVERSITY PRESS
Published by
University Press of New England,
One Court Street, Lebanon, NH 03766
www.upne.com
©2007 by Northeastern University Press
Printed in the United States of America

5 4 3 2 1

Title page photograph: *Doctor Zhivago* cast members walking down the Moscow
street set with director David Lean. Courtesy of the Margaret Herrick Library,
Academy of Motion Picture Arts and Sciences.

Continued on page 316

For my dear

Hollywood friends

JOHANNA DEMETRAKAS

and

KATE AMEND

Contents

Acknowledgments

Every book is the product of many hands, and this one is no exception. Over the long period of time (yes, longer than anticipated, I confess) it has taken to bring this project to completion, I have been sustained by a galaxy of individuals and institutions. My colleagues in the Department of Slavic Languages and Literatures at the University at Albany, State University of New York (where I taught from 1980 to 1996), encouraged me during the early stages, and the SUNY Faculty Research Awards Program gave me a deeply appreciated early grant for essential research in Germany and Russia. Northeastern University, where I have been a faculty member since 1996, has provided many different kinds of assistance, including a sabbatical leave and a two-year research leave granted to me as the Matthews Distinguished University Professor for 2004–2006. The Matthews Professor program was created through the generosity of George Matthews and his wife, Kathleen. At Northeastern I have also received valuable advice and encouragement from my colleagues in the Cinema Studies Program, Profs. Inez Hedges, Gerald Herman, and Kathy Howlett, and from the faculty members in my home Department of History. Graduate students in the Department of History performed invaluable work as my research assistants.

In cities on several continents, I have been fortunate to meet a number of highly qualified and helpful specialists. In Berlin, I was given expert assistance in the collections of the Stiftung Deutsche Kinemathek by Gerrit Thies. In Los Angeles, the members of the remarkably knowledgeable, professional, and helpful staff of the Margaret Herrick Library of the Academy of Motion Picture Arts and Sciences, and particularly Research Archivist Barbara Hall, gave me many helpful suggestions. At the Department of Special Collections at UCLA, Supervisor of Reader Services Jeffrey Rankin was a patient and discerning guide. Jennifer Miller of the Film and Television Archive at UCLA efficiently organized screenings of rare films. Madeleine F. Matz, Reference Librarian in the Motion Picture, Broadcasting, and Recorded Sound Division of the Library of Congress in Washington, D.C., arranged for me to see numerous films in that collection and identified important reference sources. In New York, I was grateful for the extensive collections and expert staff of the New York Public Library's Library of the Performing Arts at Lincoln Center. Ellen Scaruffi, former Curator of the Bakhmeteff Collection at the Library of Columbia University, discovered and generously shared with me relevant materials from various sources.

Along the way, just when I needed the encouragement, numerous colleagues affirmed the importance of this project and offered suggestions and advice. Prof. Richard Stites provided personal and professional inspiration through his enthusiasm and example. Prof. Cathy Portuges, Prof. Emeritus Louis Menashe, and Brian Harvey generously read the manuscript and offered insightful and constructive comments.

At UPNE, Phyllis Deutsch and Richard Pult helped me with conception, organization, and structure, and expertly steered the manuscript through the innumerable stages from manuscript to book.

To my life partner and husband (thank you, Massachusetts), Robert Holley, I express my love and gratitude for patience and faith, for taking me to Los Angeles in the first place, and for providing—again—invaluable editorial and computer assistance.

All photos except figures 1, 7, 8, 10, 11, and 13 are reproduced courtesy of the Margaret Herrick Library, Academy of Motion Picture Arts and Sciences. Figures 10 and 11 are reproduced courtesy of the Special Collections of the UCLA Libraries.

Russians in Hollywood, Hollywood's Russians

Introduction
Meeting Doctor Zhivago

"I once asked a Russian whether the Russians
behaved as they did in my film. 'No,' he answered,
'they do not, but they should.'"
Josef von Sternberg, *Fun in a Chinese Laundry*[1]

Like many members of my generation, I received my first enduring images of Russia from the movies and television. In 1965, my parents took me and a school friend, both of us in those early teenage years when it is socially unacceptable for boys to get excited about anything except sports, to the Elmwood Cinema in Elmwood, Connecticut, to see the just-released David Lean epic *Doctor Zhivago*. That was in the days when big, serious films had overtures and intermissions, and *Doctor Zhivago* was nothing if not serious and big, with a super-sized running time of 192 minutes and a balalaika-spiked Oscar-winning score by Maurice Jarre that contained a hit tune ("Somewhere My Love") that saturated the airwaves for months. I was enthralled.

The cinematically constructed Russia of angelic Lara and handsome Yuri and brooding Strelnikov and evil Komarovsky—full of waltzes, wars, gigantic hydroelectric dams, endless train trips, ice palaces, flowering Siberian fields, and humorless revolutionaries equipped with dramatic facial scars—seduced me utterly and forever. Lean's desperately romantic and passionate film, released at a moment when the United States and the USSR (more or less synonymous, incorrectly, in the American popular consciousness with Russia) were locked in the deadly nuclear competition of the Cold War, sent me on a quest for deeper knowledge of things Russian. I began to read the novels of Dostoyevsky and, a few years later, began studying Russian, taking the first steps on a lifelong crusade to conquer and penetrate that most challenging and rewarding of languages. *Doctor Zhivago* humanized Russia for me, transporting me far beyond the small faded New England clock city where I had spent my life to date to a vivid and exciting world that on the screen loomed so much more real and important than my own. There was Russia right on the screen just a few hundred feet away, alluring and seemingly attainable. I could almost reach out and touch it.

This Russia affected me emotionally in a way I had never been affected before, erasing whatever vague fear I had absorbed from school textbooks or daily newspaper and television news stories about the evil Commies in Moscow and their dangerous comrades in nearby Cuba who together were building missiles with which to attack us. We talked in school about building fallout shelters. Those stories seemed abstract and remote, but Dr. Zhivago's was immediate and full of very recognizable feelings. No wonder Vladimir Ilych Lenin, scheming godfather of the USSR, had once called the cinema "the most important of all the arts." For it conveys the illusion of reality like no other medium ever invented. Images seen on the screen have a way of overwhelming and superseding all others. The ability of film to shape public opinion has also been widely recognized by American politicians, including (to name only one prominent example) Senator Joseph McCarthy and members of the Un-American Activities Committee of the House of Representatives in the early 1950s, who combed through movies in search of evidence of overt and hidden pro-Communist (and therefore pro-Russian) messages.

At the time, I knew nothing about Boris Pasternak, the genius upon whose poetic and complex novel the movie *Doctor Zhivago* had been based (much too loosely for the taste of many critics, including Brendan Gill of the *New Yorker,* who called the film a "grievous disappointment"), who had died just five years earlier, engaged to the bitter end in an exhausting life-and-death struggle with Soviet totalitarian censorship. I do not believe I knew then that the novel had never been published in the USSR, or that its appearance abroad had gravely endangered Pasternak's already precarious existence, or that Pasternak had been awarded the Nobel Prize for Literature to the deep chagrin of the Soviet government. Indeed, I knew next to nothing about the Russian Revolution or Communism. Of those artists and matters I would come to know later. But such is the awesome power of the moving visual image, the vivid sense of its undeniable reality, its ability to establish immediate and direct emotional connection, that none of this mattered during my first intimate encounter with Russia at the Elmwood Cinema. It was the people and their stories in *Doctor Zhivago,* and the hypnotic beauty of the musical and visual synthesis achieved by a great director working with some of the greatest actors of the time, that removed all barriers of geography, history, and ideology. How awful could Russia be if such people as Julie Christie and Omar Shariff lived there?

In time, I came to recognize how artificial, inaccurate, and manipulative was the image of Russia presented in *Doctor Zhivago,* and in other films about Russia that emerged from Hollywood. I came to understand that a feature film was *not* the same as reality, and discovered that *Zhivago* was filmed in Spain and in studios, not on the streets of Moscow and the steppes of Siberia. For the great majority of Americans, however, the image of Russia and the USSR presented in mainstream Hollywood films acquired enormous power and authority, particularly in the absence of consistently reliable alternative information on a country that because of historical and political events of the twentieth century occupied such a privileged and unusual position in the American psyche.

Hollywood films about Russia were fated to play a special role, because for most of the twentieth century, Russia/USSR was the primary "other" in the American consciousness, the ideological and military enemy, with vast and terrifying resources, by the middle of the century capable and apparently desirous of blowing us all off the planet. It is also a most curious historical coincidence that the Bolshevik Revolution of 1917 (which led to the establishment of the world's first Socialist/Communist society, one of whose avowed goals was to overthrow world capitalism, headquartered in the United States) occurred precisely at the moment when the American film industry was entering a rapid period of development, moving westward from New York toward Hollywood (farther away from Russia, even more abstract viewed from the palm-lined avenues of Los Angeles). The overthrow of the Romanov dynasty and the creation of the USSR was one of the biggest and most shocking stories of the century, so it is hardly surprising that films about Russia constituted a significant part of the output of the Hollywood studios from the very beginning of their existence.

The increasing importance of the Soviet-American relationship, especially after World War II, and its centrality in American foreign policy, ensured that films about Russia would continue to occupy a privileged position in Hollywood production, given the studios' need to make movies of a topical nature. Not surprisingly, many of these feature films about Russia engaged in a vigorous (and sometimes humorous) defense of capitalism, as we shall see. Who were the men who ran the Hollywood studios, after all, but some of the most successful capitalists that the system had ever produced?

Further complicating and enriching this phenomenon was the presence in the Hollywood film industry from its earliest days of a large number of émigrés from both pre- and post-Revolutionary Russia. Some of them anti-Soviet and some pro-Soviet in their ideological leanings, they participated (as directors, actors, composers, writers, designers, cameramen) in the making of many of the films that presented Russia and the USSR to the American audience. These Russians also worked, of course, on many other films that did not deal with Russia, joining other émigrés (from Hungary, Germany, Austria, France, England, Sweden, Czechoslovakia, Poland, and so on) in the amazing ethnic melting pot that Hollywood became.

It is this double story—of the history of the evolution of the American cinematic image of Russia, and of the participation of Russians in the Hollywood film industry—that I propose to tell in the pages that follow.

★   In *The Kaleidoscopic Lens: How Hollywood Views Ethnic Groups*, Randall M. Miller has noted the enormous power of cinema as a transmitter of cultural values to a very wide audience. "Hollywood movies became a major transmitter of 'assimilationist' values and helped to reinforce a narrow conception of American life to which all groups were expected to conform."[2] Because Hollywood movies were made (for the most part) by studios and producers eager to attract the largest possible audiences and to maximize profit, social attitudes—including the representation of "non-Americans"—had to remain within the range of what was perceived to be generally acceptable at any given moment in the "common culture." Whether Hollywood films, whose primary goal has been to entertain rather than to educate (the reverse of the paradigm existing in the nationalized state-subsidized Soviet cinema) have shaped public attitudes and prejudices or merely reflected them is a question that has been long debated by critics, scholars, and historians.

The answer seems to consist in a combination of these two forces (depending upon the courage and personal convictions of the producers and artistic staff for any given film), but there is general consensus that films can be viewed as a relatively reliable barometer of social attitudes, as "handbooks of social behavior."[3] The making of films is a collective enterprise, so the product tends to exhibit collective values. Important, too, is the fact that the medium of the cinema grew from lower-class roots and was aimed (especially in its early history) at a lower-class broad audience, not an elitist one. Thus, the values system presented could not conflict too sharply with that of the audience, or the film would not be commercially successful. One of the resulting paradoxes was that Hollywood's perceived commercial necessity of presenting the dominant-group worldview on screen often worked against the interests of the many members of ethnic groups working in the film industry: "Participation of ethnic minorities in the movie industry did not and does not guarantee fair treatment of ethnic groups in movies."[4] This observation also holds true for the Russians.

As an upholder and enforcer of in-group values, Hollywood cinema has always required outsiders. These outsiders, usually members of some minority group (ethnic, racial, religious, sexual, ideological) are subjected to stereotyping, a process by which members of the in-group make negative generalizations about members of the out-group, thereby marginalizing and denigrating them. As Richard Dyer has written, stereotypes are "those who do not belong, who are outside of one's society. . . . This is the most important function of the stereotype: to maintain sharp boundary definitions, to define clearly where the pale ends and thus who is clearly within and who clearly beyond it."[5] Stereotypes support the status quo and existing power relationships within society, reinforcing the dominant ideology. Whether they be derived from Latino, black, gay, or Communist outsider identity, stereotypes confirm the audience's confidence in its insider status, creating a bond of complicity between the filmmakers and the audience in their shared superiority. The stereotype presents the "other," needed by an individual to complete his or her sense of self, as noted by cultural critic Mikhail Bakhtin.

Stereotypes can be especially powerful when they project "others" with whom members of the audience are unlikely ever to come into contact in the course of daily life. This applies in great measure to the stereotype of the Russian/Soviet Communist in the period before the collapse of the USSR in 1991. Very few Americans had ever met a Russian or a Communist, which made it easier for them to be stereotyped and marginalized. In addition, the prevailing ideological message from the mainstream common culture (in the media, for example) about Russia and Russians was predominantly negative (with a few exceptions, as we shall see, especially where ballet dancers were concerned), since they were closely identified with the military (and later, nuclear) threat posed to the security of the United States by the USSR. The fact that only a tiny number of Americans had ever traveled to the USSR also contributed to the ease with which Russians could be marginalized and stereotyped. Stereotypes of Russians in Hollywood cinema differed from other ethnic stereotypes because they were not based on racial factors (skin color), and because they contained a strong element (in the case of post-Revolutionary characters) of fear rather than the usual ridicule or condescension. In the case of films dealing with espionage, Russians were particularly dangerous because as educated white people they could "pass" for members of the in-group; their "otherness" was in many ways invisible, unless revealed by English spoken with a strong Russian accent, which became one of the features of the Hollywood Russian stereotype ("*dah-link*").

★   Before World War I, the American relationship with Russia and Russian culture was rather distant. The Russian empire lay far away, and there were few issues of mutual interest or conflict. Trade was relatively limited; hemp was imported for shipbuilding to Salem and Boston, where a Russia Wharf still stands. Russian-American relations tended to depend on the state of American relations with Great Britain and France and their fluctuating relations with Russia. The most important territorial issue concerned the Russian colonization of Alaska, the Pacific Northwest, and northern California, explored and thinly settled by subjects of the Tsar in the decades after the Russian victory over Napoleon in 1812. In the end, however, Tsar Alexander II chose to focus his efforts on Central Asia (where Russia faced off directly against the British), sold Alaska to the United States in 1867 for $7,200,000, and gave up further claims to Russia's possessions in North America.

It was World War I that transformed the Russian-American relationship. When the United States declared war on Germany on April 6, 1917, America for the first time became an ally of Russia in a major global conflict, united with the armies of Russia, France, and Britain against Germany, Hapsburg Austria, and the Ottoman Empire. By then, however, Russia was in economic and political chaos, the long-ruling Romanov dynasty having only recently been forced from power (on March 3, 1917) in the incredible aftermath of the February Revolution of 1917. The United States government initially greeted the removal of Tsar Nicholas II from power with enthusiasm, since it appeared that a parliamentary/democratic regime more congenial to American principles had replaced him. The Bolsheviks, including Lenin, were regarded in the United States as German spies and agents who were being sent to Russia to undermine the Russian war effort. There was fear that the new Provisional Government headed by the socialist lawyer Alexander Kerensky would pull Russian troops back from the front, but Kerensky insisted on continuing the increasingly unpopular and poorly managed Russian war effort.

The new radical Bolshevik regime headed by Vladimir Ilych Lenin, established when the October Revolution of 1917 overthrew Kerensky and the Provisional Government, did take Russia out of the war. An armistice was declared in late October 1917, and in early 1918 the separate Treaty of Brest-Litovsk was signed with the Central Powers. Suddenly, the United States had not only lost an ally in the Great War, but had also gained an avowed ideological enemy, the world's first socialist regime, created on the virulently anti-capitalist foundation of the teachings of Karl Marx as interpreted by Lenin. The fervent religious quality of Soviet Communism, and its frankly international ambitions, scared and obsessed Americans, provoking a highly emotional reaction. A long and relatively tranquil era in Russian-American relations had come to an end. In large part, the twentieth century would be about the Russian-American ideological and military conflict.

It is notable and important that the creation of the USSR in late 1917, and the resulting emigration of so many Russian theater people with the talents sought after in the film business, coincided almost exactly with the establishment of the film industry in Los Angeles. In the aftermath of World War I, two new utopias promising a better life had emerged at opposite ends of the earth: the world's first socialist society in Russia, and the "dream factory" of Hollywood. Both offered unprecedented opportunities for self-invention (and reinvention).

This process of personal and cinematic reinvention has been described by numerous gifted writers, including Neal Gabler in his seminal *An Empire of Their Own: How the Jews Invented Hollywood*. Gabler focuses on the numerous Hollywood magnates who rose from the humblest of immigrant origins in Eastern European Jewish communities to occupy a position of enormous power, influence, and wealth as the creators and owners of the major American film studios. Most of the resourceful self-made men Gabler writes about (Samuel Goldwyn, Louis B. Mayer) grew up in territories controlled until the end of World War I either by Russia or Austro-Hungary. As new immigrants to the United States, they eventually gravitated to the entertainment business, where class and ethnic origin were less important than in other fields. They moved into the film business as it was growing rapidly into a democratic and highly lucrative form of popular entertainment, and were instrumental in creating a new world of fantasy and glamour in the new city of Los Angeles in the 1920s and 1930s. In the process, they also reinvented themselves, often shedding spouses they had wed in more rustic surroundings and who proved incapable of keeping up. It was these enterprising outsiders to American culture who had the vision and discipline to see the enormous commercial potential of cinema and who became the original Hollywood insiders.

A significant number of the Russian émigré actors (Gregory Ratoff, Mikhail Rasumny, Lewis Milestone, Anatole Litvak) treated in the pages that follow were, like the moguls discussed by Gabler, of Jewish origin. Because most of them left Russia after the Russian Revolution, and for political or ideological reasons rather than religious ones, I have chosen to identify them primarily as Russian, not Jewish. Jews as a group enthusiastically supported the Bolshevik Revolution, since the Bolsheviks promised to wipe out the anti-Semitism that was an important ingredient in the Orthodox Christian theocratic structure supporting the Romanov dynasty. The Soviet Communist Party leadership even included a number of Jews, notably Leon Trotsky (whose real name was Bronstein). After the Bolshevik Revolution, religious practice was effectively banned, since Communism regarded religion of any kind as "the opium of the masses." Instead, Lenin and his associates promoted a secular Communist identity that transcended religious and ethnic difference. The Jewish/Russian émigré actors who arrived in the United States in the 1920s were not seeking freedom from anti-Semitism. Rather, they were seeking greater creative and financial opportunities, as well as artistic freedom.

For my purposes, I also treat as "Russian" those actors and directors who came to Hollywood from non-Russian ethnic groups within the Tsarist or Soviet empire but considered themselves culturally Russian because they received their training in Russia and worked in the Russian language.

Among these the most prominent example is director Rouben Mamoulian, an Armenian who studied in Moscow. At the same time, I have limited my discussion to first-generation émigrés to the United States. Actors such as Natalie Wood, who were born in the United States of Russian parents, have not been included.

★   When I first began working some years ago on what has become this book, I was intending to tell only the story of the Russian émigrés who worked in and around the Hollywood film industry. In researching their lives and careers, however, I became increasingly interested in how Russia and the USSR had been represented on screen in mainstream feature films. This seemed a bigger and more substantial narrative, and one that had not yet been told. In the end, I decided to combine these two stories into a work of cultural and group biography.

Substantial attention has been paid to the history of the contribution of various émigré groups to Hollywood film. Notable examples are such volumes as John Russell Taylor's *Strangers in Paradise: The Hollywood Emigrés, 1933–1950,* John Baxter's *Hollywood Exiles,* and Otto Friedrich's *City of Nets: A Portrait of Hollywood in the 1940s.* In all of these, however, the Russians are considered very briefly and cursorily, grouped together with the Austrian/Germans. The present volume is the first that considers Russian émigrés in the Hollywood cinema as a separate group.

Similarly, despite the proliferation of so-called "representation studies" in recent years, the image of Russians in American movies has been notably understudied by scholars and film historians. Books examining how the members of various ethnic, national and other groups (Italians, Hispanics, Asians, blacks, gays and lesbians, Jews) have been portrayed in Hollywood films can be found in large numbers on the shelves of most libraries. One of my favorite examples of this genre is Vito Russo's groundbreaking *Celluloid Closet: Homosexuality in the Movies,* which served as an inspiring model as I worked on my own book. The absence of a similarly comprehensive historical and cultural study of the film image of Russians is all the more surprising in view of the important and special role that Russian/Soviet characters have played in a wide variety of Hollywood genres (war, epic, spy, romance, comedy, adventure, historical melodrama) since the very beginnings of the American film industry. Michael Strada and Harold Troper were the first to explore this territory in their worthy and important 1997 book *Friend or Foe? Russians in American Film and Foreign Policy, 1933–1991* (Scarecrow Press). Their approach is not cultural or aesthetic, however, but primarily political and ideological, with a particular emphasis on foreign policy. Moreover, the authors do not treat films released before 1933 or after 1991. Nor do they deal at all with the participation of Russian émigré actors in the creation of the Hollywood image of Russia/USSR, or with other aspects of film production, such as music.

Unlike Strada and Troper, I have not attempted to provide an encyclopedic overview of all of Hollywood's "Russia films." I have intentionally chosen films that I consider representative of major trends and eras, which possess particular artistic or political significance—and which speak to me most persuasively. For making these choices I am happy to accept responsibility, even as I anticipate that some readers might not always agree with my selections and omissions. *Chacun à son goût.*

All dates are given in New Style, according to the western calendar introduced in the USSR (replacing the so-called Old Style) in 1918. All translations from Russian are mine unless otherwise indicated.

Romanovs and Revolution

"Sitting in Hollywood, we had to make oranges grow in Greenland."
Boris Pilnyak, *Okay: An American Novel*

In the years immediately following the 1917 Bolshevik Revolution, many creative artists in all fields (writers, composers, painters, actors, directors) chose to leave behind the economic and political chaos that was making life in Russia so difficult, seeking refuge elsewhere. Many of these émigrés believed they were leaving Russia only temporarily, and anticipated that they would return after the situation there had settled down. Even some of those who supported the fragile new socialist regime led by Vladimir Lenin thought it highly likely that he would be overthrown, and went abroad to bide their time.

In their search for places more conducive to creative work, the members of the Russian creative class dispersed all over the globe. Some went to Harbin, in China, not far from the Russian border. Some (including many theater people) went to Berlin, where a large and thriving Russian community developed in the 1920s, until the rise of Hitler sent them looking for safer havens. Many went to Paris, which by the 1930s had become the center of the Russian émigré intellectual community. Some went to Buenos Aires. Some went to New York and San Francisco, both already possessing large and well-established Russian émigré communities. And a few even went to Los Angeles.

At the time, Los Angeles was a small city on the edge of a forbidding desert, known for its mild climate and for the film industry that was beginning to move there from New York, but still regarded as a frontier town devoid of European culture and comforts. By the end of World War I, the future of the American movie business was happening in Los Angeles, and those who sought to succeed in that arena were establishing residence there.

Among them was Russian silent film actress Alla Nazimova. She had come to America even before the Russian Revolution. Born in 1879 in Yalta, a resort town on the Crimean Black Sea coast, Nazimova studied in Moscow with Vladimir Nemirovich-Danchenko, co-founder of the Moscow Art Theater, and began her theatrical career in Russia as a stage actress, in such vehicles as *Camille*. In 1905 she was brought to New York with a touring troupe and stayed, learned English, and achieved fame on Broadway—her most famous role was as the title character in Ibsen's *Hedda Gabler*.

In 1916, Nazimova made her first film, and soon became a much sought-after actress in the silent cinema. In late 1918, not long after she was signed to a highly lucrative contract by Metro Pictures, Nazimova bought a Spanish-style house at 8080 Sunset Boulevard, since Metro was moving its operations from New York to a new lot on Cahuenga Boulevard. Transformed by Nazimova into a hotel called The Garden of Alla, in 1927 after her film career had failed, this house was a legendary site for wild parties, attended by a colorful assortment of guests, including members of Nazimova's lesbian entourage and of the growing Russian émigré community working in the film industry. Particularly memorable were domestic performances given there by legendary Russian operatic bass Fyodor Chaliapin (in 1923, 1924, and 1925) and by the Russian ballerina Anna Pavlova (in 1924).

It was here, also, that a young Russian composer named Sergei Prokofiev (1891–1953) spent a few evenings on his first visit to Los Angeles in late 1920. Already well established as one of the most important composers of his generation by the time of the Bolshevik Revolution, Prokofiev chose to leave Russia in spring of 1918 (only temporarily, he believed), and had been trying to establish himself as a composer and pianist in the United States, based in New York. When he came to Los Angeles for several recitals, he was charmed not only by the pleasant climate ("I am smiling along with the California countryside"), but by the presence of a vital Russian artistic community that greeted him with open arms. He recorded his impressions in his diary.

December 21, 1920. This morning I arrived in Los Angeles, that famous and warm little corner of the world. Even three or four years ago, hardly anyone knew anything about it, but now Los Angeles has been catching up to San Francisco in the size of its population. . . . My friend Dagmar

FIGURE 1.

Sergei Prokofiev. Program for Prokofiev's
official American debut at Aeolian Hall in New York City in
November 1918. Prokofiev on a street in New York.

Godowsky [daughter of Polish pianist/composer Leopold Godowsky] "is also here, so, in short, the three weeks which I will spend here among the palms, the sun and the beautiful women, will be a real carnival. After gloomy Chicago, and then intense concertizing, this looked very pleasant to me.[1]

On New Year's Eve, Prokofiev went to a party given by the Godowskys, where he saw many members of the film community in high spirits.

There were about 50 people in four small rooms, almost all of them in costume, with most of the men dressed as women and the women as men, two saxophones were wailing along with a drum, and everyone was dancing with abandon, getting all tangled up in the streamers that covered the floor. It was something like the last scene of *Petrouchka,* where Stravinsky has written in the score: "Shrovetide reaches its climax." It was impossible to recognize anyone underneath the makeup and wigs, and I didn't know anyone there except Dagmar. They were for the most part "stars" from the cinema, since Dagmar has been acting in films for a year already, and Los Angeles is the film capital. Most of the women were incredibly attractive, some were frozen in their beauty, but others instead were indulging in the merriment with a complete lack of caution.

At this party, Prokofiev was introduced to Nazimova, "who in Russia was a mediocre actress, but here is a *movie-star,* one that all American knows."[2] In fact, Prokofiev encountered Nazimova at the height of her fame. Her latest film, *Billions,* in which she played a Russian princess involved with an American poet who inherits a fortune, had just opened and was another in a string of critical and box-office failures that sank her Hollywood career not long after it had started.[3]

Over the next few weeks, Prokofiev attended several parties at Nazimova's house. One was a costume party, and the guests were instructed to appear dressed as Apaches. On January 13, 1921, the date on which the Old Russian New Year was celebrated according to the Orthodox calendar, Prokofiev gave a concert, and was feted afterward at Nazimova's:

Nazimova has a charming little house, along with a small and pleasant group of film people and artists. The evening—or rather, the night— passed very agreeably, everyone got a bit drunk, and I danced with Maria

Baranovskaya. [Baranovskya was an actress who had studied with director Vsevolod Meyerhold in Russia, and was married to the Russian pianist Alexander Borovsky.] At twelve midnight the lights were extinguished, we shouted "hurrah," someone sang "God Save the Tsar," and then the "*Marsellaise.*" We finally agreed upon the "Glory" chorus from Glinka's opera *A Life for the Tsar,* which I predicted would become the new Russian national anthem. At five a.m. we went out into the garden, where it was warm and smelled so fresh—and enjoyed California.[4]

Prokofiev would return to Los Angeles on several other occasions in the future, and maintained close epistolary relationships with several members of the Russian émigré community, although he never did work in the American film industry, despite invitations from Gloria Swanson and Walt Disney. Instead, he decided in 1936 to return to the USSR.

Prokofiev's description of the confusion over what anthem should be sung to celebrate the Russian New Year in 1921 reflects the cultural and political uncertainty experienced by Russian émigrés living in Los Angeles after the Bolshevik Revolution. After 1918, communication with Russia became very difficult, and travel to the USSR almost impossible because of the Civil War that raged there until 1921. Meanwhile, the film industry was growing at an incredibly rapid pace, drawing money and talent to Los Angeles.

For many of the Russians who had left home and now found themselves in what was beginning to look (as the 1920s went on and the Soviet regime became more entrenched) like permanent exile, their new life was confusing and difficult. As scholar George Martin Day writes in a 1934 study on how the Russian émigré community was adjusting to life in Hollywood,

> Like the ancient Hebrew exiles in Babylonia, these Russians of Hollywood, often homesick and grieving for the Russia that once was, are a scattered remnant in a strange land. They still live in the past, idolize and idealize it, and are fearful lest their children grow up and forget the culture traditions of old Russia. Former officers in the Czar's army are now proprietors of restaurants and cafes, are raising poultry and vegetables, or are earning a precarious living in motion pictures; ex-generals have begun life over again as janitors, elevator operators, and cobblers.[5]

Actor Leonid Kinskey, famous for his role as the ebullient bartender Sascha in *Casablanca,* later described the special atmosphere among the Russians on the fringe of the film business during this period:

> The Russian aristocracy who reached Hollywood had no profession. They only had manners and good clothes. And so they became extras. There were people called "dress extras." They had full dress, dinner jackets. These people were getting more money, naturally. Now, I was reprimanded by one of the assistant directors because I was talking to extras all the time. And I was talking to extras because they were *amazing* people. They were Russian aristocracy, German aristocracy. Very interesting people to talk to, in comparison to our junk, you know, other actors.[6]

The suffering and privations they had experienced in escaping Russia did give the Russian émigrés a certain sense of confidence, however, a belief that whatever challenges this new world presented would be minor compared to those they had already endured. For many of these Russians, taking small parts in films was nothing more than a way to pay the rent; they viewed this work as a means to accumulate capital to undertake other economic activities, such as opening stores and restaurants. More than a few high-ranking officers of the Tsar's army, now impoverished vagabonds blacklisted in Soviet Russia, were cast in silent films.[7] German expatriate director Josef von Sternberg, who was friendly with many members of the Hollywood Russian community, even turned the story of one such officer into a brilliant film, *The Last Command* (1928). Emil Jannings won an Academy Award for his portrayal of a Tsarist general come face-to-face in Hollywood with a former revolutionary, now a rising young film director, whom he tried to execute years before in Russia. The director takes his revenge by casting him in the humiliating role of his own life story, and the general dies on the set. (The Swiss-born German-speaking Jannings had played another Russian role, that of Dmitri Karamazov, in a 1920 film of *The Brothers Karamazov.* Like Nazimova, Jannings, with his thick accent, did not survive the transition to the talkies.)

Not long after they arrived in Hollywood in the 1920s, the Russian émigrés created a lively and close-knit community with bookstores, cafes, stores, and even a Russian Orthodox church at 656 Micheltorena Street. This church became a spiritual center for the Russian community. What distinguished the Russians from other Hollywood émigrés (the Hungarians, French, British, Germans, Swedes, Poles, Czechs) was that they were unable to return to their homeland. They had to create a new permanent home in Los Angeles. For all émigrés in Hollywood, in the words of historian John Russell Taylor, the important thing was "making an impression, projecting an image, demonstrating early on that you can do the work."[8] For Russians, this was perhaps even more important.

Of course Hollywood not only welcomed but needed immigrants—and not only Russians. To a large extent, the film industry was built by men who had not long before arrived in the United States from areas in Eastern Europe formerly dominated by the Austrian-Hungarian and Russian empires, both of them destroyed by World War I. Unfettered by the class system of the old world and energized by the huge financial rewards possible under capitalism, these producers relished the opportunity to create something new according to their own rules. This new world was attractive for actors, too. In the days of silent cinema, until the late 1920s, it didn't matter if actors and actresses had strong accents speaking English, or if they didn't speak English at all. What mattered is whether they could act, whether they looked good on screen, and whether (like Nazimova) they were already popular on stage and could attract their fans to the cinema.

In these very early days of Hollywood, Russian performing artists were also very much in vogue. Russian ballet dancers had been winning over American audiences, beginning with Anna Pavlova before World War I, and later with the Ballets Russes of Serge Diaghilev, which toured America beginning in January 1916. (Many Americans aspiring to a career in dance even changed their names to Russian ones, such as Nazimova's soulmate Natacha Rambova, a dancer in her youth and later a designer, born in Salt Lake City with the name Winifred Shaughnessy.)

Pianist and composer Sergei Rachmaninoff arrived in New York in November 1918, at the height of his fame, and made enormous sums of money in the coming years from his American appearances. Fyodor Chaliapin (whose son Fyodor Chaliapin, Jr., later worked in Hollywood as a successful film actor) made celebrated appearances at the Metropolitan Opera in the title role of Mussorgsky's opera *Boris Godunov* in late 1921. On Broadway, Nikita Balieff (1877–1936) in early 1922 staged the hit cabaret-style revue *La Chauve-Souris* (The Bat), featuring seven actors formerly associated with Konstantin Stanislavky's Moscow Art Theater. The arrival in the

United States of the Moscow Art Theater itself in early 1923 only heightened the Russia-mania. The box-office receipts for the MAT were the
largest ever recorded for any dramatic company performing on Broadway
in any language, including English. Over the next sixteen months, the
MAT gave 380 performances of thirteen productions in twelve American
cities—in Russian![9]

Stanislavsky, co-founder with Vladimir Nemirovich-Danchenko of the
MAT, was overwhelmed by the reception he and his company encountered
in the United States. "We have never had such a success in Moscow or anywhere else. . . . No one seems to have had any idea what our theatre or actors are capable of. I am writing all this . . . not in self-glorification, but
just to give you an idea at what an embryonic state stage art is here and how
eagerly they snatch up everything good that is brought to America."[10] The
respect in which Stanislavsky was held in the United States explains why
actors who appeared with the MAT, or who had received training with
MAT's teachers in Russia, were so attractive to Hollywood film directors
and producers, eager, especially in the early days of the industry, to acquire
artistic credibility. Numerous members of the MAT company who toured
America (Akim Tamiroff, Maria Ouspenskaya, Olga Baclanova, Vladimir
Sokoloff) also chose to remain, and eventually gravitated to Hollywood,
where they became accomplished character actors. And Stanislavsky's
psychologically based approach to acting, or the "Method," as it became
known, became extremely influential among American film actors and
directors.

★   In the years after World War I, Hollywood attracted not only Russians
like Nazimova with established reputations, but also youngsters with little
or no experience. Among those was Lewis Milestone (1895–1980). His is
a classic rags-to-riches American tale, leading from humble boyhood in
the Russian province of Bessarabia, to Germany, New York, and finally
Hollywood, where he signed with Howard Hughes in 1926 and rose to become one of the most respected directors of his generation. Milestone's
adaptation of Erich Maria Remarque's novel *All Quiet on the Western Front*
(1930) won the young director his second Oscar, and is still regarded as
one of the most powerful anti-war films ever made. Later he made several
films based on novels of John Steinbeck (*Of Mice and Men, The Red Pony*)
and even the original *Ocean's Eleven* (1960).

As a boy in Kishinev, the capital city of Bessarabia, a territory populated mainly by Jews and Rumanians but historically controlled by Russia, Milestone (he later changed his name from the original Lev Milstein) witnessed the terrible 1903 pogrom against the Jewish population. The environment of his childhood, Milestone later told Donald Chase, was "as repressive as can be imagined today."[11] In a scene reminiscent of the stories of Odessa writer Isaac Babel, Milestone remembered that after the second Kishinev pogrom in 1905, "you'd look outside and it seemed as if a snowstorm was in progress. It was feathers from feather beds. They would tear them up; this thing went on for days."[12] Despite the repression and prejudice, Milestone, whose father ran a clothing store, found a way to express his creativity, becoming involved in theater, in tiny "bit" parts. In the theater, he saw performances by important guest stars such as the comedian Victor Petipa (son of the choreographer Marius Petipa) and Gregory Ratoff. (Ratoff also eventually ended up in Hollywood as a director and actor.) Milestone's family was planning for him to become a pharmacist, but he wanted desperately both to work in the theater and to leave Russia, so he pleaded with them to give him the money to go to Hamburg and the United States, where his aunt lived. After a few adventures with friends in Germany, he set sail from Hamburg, like thousands of other emigrants from Eastern Europe, in late 1913. Milestone's decision to leave Germany was a wise one: "Had I not gone to the States when I did, Germany, because of my Russian citizenship, would have made me a prisoner of war."[13]

Still a teenager, Milestone settled in New York and found work as a society photographer's assistant. When the United States entered the war against Germany, however, he decided to enlist, and volunteered to join the Motion Picture Section of the Photographic Section of the Army Air Corps. Through this assignment he met many film people, including directors Wesley Ruggles, Richard Wallace, Victor Fleming, and Joseph von Sternberg. "I didn't know it then but that was my entrance into the world of motion pictures."[14] Milestone even appeared as an actor in the some of the propaganda films made by his unit.

When the war ended, Milestone (like Nazimova) decided to move to Hollywood "because everything was out here as far as motion pictures went."[15] After a month in Los Angeles, he found a job working as an assistant editor for independent producer J. D. Hampton, receiving $20 a week. He learned the art of editing there and in several other studios ("I supplemented my income by getting into crap games") so well and so quickly that he was given his first film to direct by Jack Warner in 1925. In 1927, Milestone directed the comedy *Two Arabian Nights,* with Mary Astor. The Russian émigré actor Michael Visaroff (1892–1951) played the role of a Russian ship captain. In 1929, *Two Arabian Nights* was awarded the Oscar for best director, in the first Academy Awards competition ever held. Less than two years later, at age 35, Milestone won two Oscars—for best picture and best director—for *All Quiet on the Western Front,* capping a remarkably rapid rise from the streets of Kishinev.

Because of his difficult early life, Milestone, or "Milly" as he was affectionately known in the film business, developed strong self-reliance and confidence, qualities that served him well as Hollywood grew in the 1920s and '3os. He gained a reputation for driving a hard bargain even with the most intimidating producers, for his plain-talking independence and toughness, for his love of jokes. His friends included many other Russian émigrés in the film industry. With actor Akim Tamiroff he enjoyed a particularly close creative relationship, casting him in both *The General Died at Dawn* (1936) and *Ocean's Eleven* (1960).

Just how many Russians there were at all levels of the film industry in the early 1920s is clear from a story Milestone liked to tell about his early days working for J. D. Hampton. One of his duties was to pick up daily rushes from a film lab. The lab was run by a Russian émigré named Joe Aller. "I was always amused because when I came in I heard nothing spoken but Russian, but they didn't know that I was Russian and that I could understand everything they were saying." (Having arrived in the United States at the age of 18, Milestone was able to acquire fluency in English much more easily than those who came as adults.)

> I used to raise hell just to tease them, and as I came in I'd hear them say in Russian, "Here's that little son-of-a-bitch again—give him the stuff and get rid of him." One day after this had been going one for a little while, I came in there whistling a very famous revolutionary tune called *Warszawianka,* a Polish composition. The root of the word was Warszawa, or Warsaw. Suddenly they all stopped and listened. Then Joe came over and said, "Where the hell do you know that from?" So I answered him in Russian, "You idiot—what do you think I am?" Well, then they cheered, and by the next day I couldn't get any service at all. "You can wait," they

said. "You bullied us for some time, so now you can wait." That was when Joe and I became really close, when he found out we had a common background.[16]

★ Even as Russians were coming to Hollywood to work in the film industry off-screen, producers and directors were turning frequently to Russian subjects on-screen. A favorite theme was the tragic fate of the Russian aristocrats who had been displaced by the Bolshevik Revolution. By far the most dramatic and seductive story was that of Tsar Nicholas II and his family, the last Romanovs to rule Russia, who had been executed in the basement of a house in Ekaterinburg in July 1918. Their glamorous and doomed lives, and their involvement with Grigori Rasputin—the monk who, because of his apparent abilities to ease the suffering experienced by their hemophiliac son and heir Aleksei, gained unprecedented personal access to the Empress Alexandra—provided ample material for many screenplays from the early days of silent film. In nearly all of them, the Romanovs, including Tsar Nicholas II, are portrayed in a highly romanticized fashion, mourned as the victims of the Revolution rather than criticized for their ineffectual, passive, and irresponsible leadership.

As early as 1917, shortly after the assassination in St. Petersburg of Rasputin by outraged aristocrats in December 1916, huge crowds turned out in the United States to see *Rasputin, the Black Monk*, with British vaudevillian Montague Love in the title role. At least two more films featuring Rasputin appeared in 1918: *The Fall of the Romanoffs* (starring Edward Connelly) and *The Legion of Death* (directed by Tod Browning). The extremely sympathetic portrayal of the Romanovs in these early films, made during World War I, reflects American hostility toward the newly created Bolshevik regime—its stated goal was to destroy capitalism—and American fear that Lenin would take Russia out of the war against Germany. Also stressed in most of the American films made about the Romanovs is their piety, in contrast to the anti-religious savagery of their persecutors.

Fascination with the Russian royal family endured into the sound era. One of the most impressive of the many "Romanov projects" was *Rasputin and the Empress*, released in 1932, produced by Irving Thalberg for Metro-Goldwyn-Mayer and directed by Richard Boleslawski. Boleslawski (1889–1937) was a Pole born in Poland (with the real name Boleslaw Ryszard Szrednicki) when it was part of the Russian Empire, and he studied at the

Moscow Art Theater before and during World War I. After coming to the United States, Boleslawski was very active as an interpreter and teacher of Stanislavsky's acting techniques in New York and later Hollywood. Because of his friendship with Ethel Barrymore, who carried enormous clout, Boleslawski was chosen to replace the original director, Charles Brabin, for this high-profile film starring all three of the Barrymores (John, Ethel, and Lionel) in their only screen appearance together. Then a grande dame of the Broadway theater, Ethel received $100,000 for the role of Empress Alexandra. Lionel got the juicy part of Rasputin, and John was the dashing Prince Paul Chegodieff, whose character was based on the real assassin of Rasputin, Prince Felix Youssoupoff.

The script by Charles MacArthur is extremely sympathetic to the Romanovs. True, Prince Chegodieff does grow impatient with the inability of the Tsar (Ralph Morgan) to face up to what is really happening in Russia. Producer Irving Thalberg also sought advice from screenwriter Lenore Coffee (she had worked on the 1926 romantic peasant-and-princess drama *The Volga Boatman*, directed by Cecil B. DeMille). "Rasputin didn't succeed because he was so clever," Coffee reportedly told Thalberg. "It was because they were all so damned stupid."[17] During shooting, Ethel Barrymore insisted that Alexandra be shown in a positive light, repeatedly scolding the production staff that "I knew Her Majesty personally!"[18] A Russian émigré named Mercedes de Acosta was employed as a researcher, although there was little attempt to preserve historical accuracy. She did warn warn Thalberg, however, that the scene in which the supporting character of Princess Natasha was apparently raped at a drunken party was potentially offensive to the real Prince Youssoupoff, since this character was based on his wife. Her instincts were correct; Youssoupoff did eventually bring a suit against MGM for libel, and reportedly received a settlement of $750,000.[19]

With an enormous budget (for the time) of $1 million, *Rasputin and the Empress* was one of the major movie events of the year, and proved highly successful at the box office. Lionel Barrymore clearly relished the role of Rasputin, and the intensely physical scene of his murder by his brother John still makes for entertaining viewing today. In his direction, Boleslawski makes repeated use of archival documentary footage of street protests and rallies, in a manner strongly reminiscent of the montage fiction/documentary style of the films of Sergei Eisenstein (especially

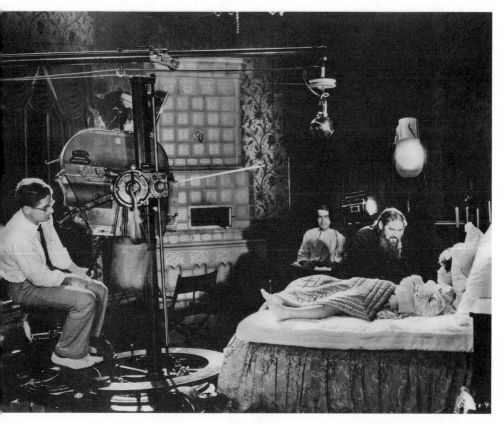

FIGURE 2.

Rasputin and the Empress. MGM 1932. Lionel Barrymore (center) as Rasputin at the bedside of Tsarevich Alexei (Tad Alexander). Courtesy of the Margaret Herrick Library, Academy of Motion Picture Arts and Sciences.

October, or *Ten Days That Shook the World*). The political and historical message of *Rasputin and the Empress* is reactionary, seeking personal explanations for history: it was all that awful Rasputin's fault. Nicholas and Alexandra are rational, noble, admirable people attempting to maintain dignity amid a sea of vulgarity and violence. In the last sequence, Nicholas politely hands to a surly guard a packet of projected reforms for Russia, asking him to convey them to the new leaders in the hope that they might help. "I am only thinking of Russia," he says. Then he and his family are escorted to the train that will take them away from Petrograd. In the final frames, they are taken into a cellar and only have time to cross themselves before they are shot against the wall. In the final shot, we see a Russian cross floating against a sky and hear a choir singing the anthem "God Save the Tsar." The concluding Christian message confirms the righteousness and innocence of the royal family.

"An engrossing and exciting pictorial melodrama" is how the *New York Times* accurately described *Rasputin and the Empress.* Significantly, there are no Russians among the major actors, and no attempt to use Russian accents. The diction and costume melodrama atmosphere are squarely British upper crust, which serves to make the viewer feel closer to the Romanovs, to regard them as familiar and worthy of respect. Ethel Barrymore plays Alexandra as a kind of queen mother. As for the rest of Russia out there beyond the tea sets and champagne and drawing rooms, it is crude, unpredictable, and dangerous—just the way most Americans thought about the USSR in 1932.

★   Nearly forty years later, in 1971, another epic about the Tsar and his family hit the screen, *Nicholas and Alexandra,* released by Columbia. Based on the best-selling book of the same title by Robert Massie, it draws heavily on personal diaries and letters and also treats the last of the ruling Romanovs for the most part with sympathy and compassion. The Russian Revolution is viewed as a kind of annoying inconvenience in the life of tender, devoted attachment led by the shy and isolated royal couple. For casting, producer Sam Spiegel and director Franklin Schaffner went to veteran British stage actors Michael Jayston and Janet Suzman to play the leading roles, and asked British composer Richard Rodney Bennett to write the musical score. The resulting atmosphere is stuffy and somewhat moribund, lacking in authenticity and spontaneity.

FIGURE 3.

Nicholas and Alexandra. Columbia 1971. Michael Jayston as Tsar Nicholas II and
Janet Suzman as Alexandra. Courtesy of the Margaret Herrick Library,
Academy of Motion Picture Arts and Sciences. Gift of Rush Hinsdale from
collection of Whitney Williams.

In 1971, at the height of the Cold War and as the stagnant and vulgar reign of Leonid Brezhnev dragged on in the Kremlin, the film reflects a certain nostalgia for good taste, good manners, and fine china. Suzman and Jayston do manage to convey how the intense emotional codependence of the royal couple, and their refusal to understand how fundamentally the world had changed, doomed not only their country but their innocent family and fellow aristocrats as well. With her barely controlled hysteria (especially over the health of her only son and heir Aleksei) and whiny neediness, Suzman shows how Alexandra was able to manipulate and frustrate her husband. After he has agreed to abdicate, ending more than three hundred years of Romanov rule in Russia, Jayston as Nicholas appears in his wife's bedroom and drops abjectly to his knees, collapsing in tears as he tries to choke out the words, "I didn't want to. . . . I didn't mean to . . . ," as she looks on in condescending horror at the weakling she both needs and despises. It is a powerful and profoundly sad scene.

Nicholas and Alexandra manages to trivialize one of the great historical and social transformations of the twentieth century; the brief interpolated scenes with key figures like Lenin and Trotsky and Count Witte (Laurence Olivier) seem disconnected and undigested into the narrative. No Russian actors are used in significant roles, and no Russian accents. It is the design and clothes (particularly those worn by Suzman, luxurious muffs and capes and hats) that create the strongest impression, and these were the aspects of the production rewarded by the Oscar voters: *Nicholas and Alexandra* won for Art Direction and Costume Design.

★   The last scene of *Nicholas and Alexandra* (like the last scene of *Rasputin and the Empress*) depicts the basement assassination of the couple and their five children (four girls and one sickly boy). For many years after the real murder in July 1918, however, persistent rumors circulated that one of the daughters—Anastasia—had somehow miraculously survived the slaughter and escaped abroad. Numerous women claiming to be Anastasia surfaced in Europe and America, including one particularly convincing imposter, Anna Anderson, who even persuaded surviving members of the Romanov family of her authenticity. Only the rise of *glasnost* in the Soviet Union (which led to investigation of many crimes committed by Lenin and his colleagues in the early years of the USSR) and the collapse of Communism in 1991 finally made it possible to prove that Anastasia had in fact been murdered in Ekaterinburg, when the remains of the family were located outside the city and DNA testing was subsequently performed.

During the decades before this proof was established (and even afterward), the character of Anastasia and her supposed survival and subsequent life inspired scores of fictional tales, in the form of stories, novels, plays, and films. The Anastasia story was especially appealing to American audiences, who as democrats both derided and envied the tradition of aristocracy that underlay European society. In the Anastasia narrative also reside strong elements of the Cinderella rags-to-riches story, one of the most enduring and productive of all fictional narratives. Anastasia's search for identity represents a universal quest for belonging to which audiences can easily respond. It didn't take long for Hollywood to recognize the box-office potential of the Anastasia industry. In the 1928 film *Clothes Make the Woman,* Eve Southern plays an Anastasia who (like the general played by Emil Jannings in *The Last Command*) ends up in Hollywood where she is cast in the role of her own life and is accidentally shot by the same man (now also an actor) who saved her from the fate suffered by her family in Ekaterinburg.

Perhaps the most accomplished of the numerous films about Anastasia (including a very popular animated version released in 1997 that makes no attempt *whatsoever* to incorporate historical truth) was made in 1956 with an all-star cast featuring Yul Brynner (a megastar after his appearances on Broadway in *The King and I*) and Ingrid Bergman. Another Russian émigré directed—Anatole Litvak (1902–1974).

Born in Kiev, Litvak later reportedly lived in a brothel in Petrograd before fleeing Russia for Germany in 1925. He started his film career there before moving on (ahead of the Nazis) to France and England. By the late 1930s he was in Hollywood, where he quickly established himself among the leading directors in town. His second film, *Tovarich* (starring Charles Boyer and Claudette Colbert), was a stylish romp about Russian aristocrats living in impoverished masquerade in Paris. Litvak adapted quickly to the high life in Hollywood, with a spectacular house on the beach in Malibu and a taste for gambling. In the words of screenwriter Arthur Laurents, who worked with Litvak as screenwriter on *Anastasia* and other projects, "Tola," as he called the director, "did everything in his own style . . . his clothes were never casual nor was he."[20] It used to annoy Laurents that the supremely confident Litvak, who spoke English with a "French-Russian accent he couldn't hear," was forever correcting the dialogue in his scripts.[21]

For *Anastasia*, Laurents adapted a play with the same title by Marcelle Maurette that had opened a successful Broadway run in late 1954. The plot bears a strong resemblance to Bernard Shaw's *Pygmalion* (and to the musical *My Fair Lady*, which opened on Broadway in early 1956, the same year *Anastasia* was released). Anastasia (Bergman), who goes by the name Anna Koreff, adrift in Paris and suffering from amnesia or trauma, plays the Eliza Doolittle to the Henry Higgins character of former Tsarist general Bunin (Yul Brynner), who sees in her the chance to strike it rich by convincing the surviving Romanovs she is the real thing, leading to the release to her (and him) of some of the enormous fortune held for the family in European banks. So Bunin undertakes to coach Anastasia (or whoever she is, he doesn't really care) in the ways of the Russian royal court, hoping that the Dowager Empress Maria Fyodorovna (Helen Hayes), will declare Anna her granddaughter and heir. Bunin is assisted in this effort by his comic sidekick, Boris Chernov, played by the marvelous Akim Tamiroff, reveling in his thick Russian accent, the asset he once called his "golden goose." ("We're not doing this for art, we're doing this for money," he declares.) Another minor role, that of the giggly and highly emotional Baroness von Livenbaum, lady-in-waiting to Maria Fyodorovna, is played to the tearful hilt by Martita Hunt: "I am all of Chekhov's three sisters rolled into one."

Laurents's well-crafted screenplay, with its felicitous mixture of humor, sadness, and mystery, serves the stellar cast very well, and helps to make *Anastasia* a much more absorbing and respectable film than it has any right to be. Bergman conveys the confusion and desperation of an amnesiac trying to recall her past without ever overplaying, while Brynner, with his hard and military bearing, provides just the right contrast to her softness. As is the case with Garbo, another Swedish actress cast in several prominent Russian film roles, Bergman's unusual intonation in spoken English generates the impression of vague foreignness that would have been difficult for an American actress to achieve. In the end, romance triumphs. Even though they have succeeded in convincing Maria Fyodorovna that Anna is really Anastasia (the clincher is Anna's nervous cough, which the Dowager Empress remembers from her childhood), Bunin and Anna are so in love that they run away from all the attention just so they can be alone together. Bergman won her second Oscar for her only Russian role.

★   Besides Nicholas, Alexandra, and Anastasia, the other member of the Romanov clan who attracted the most attention from Hollywood was Catherine II ("The Great"), whose long reign (1762–1796) brought Russia onto the stage of the great European powers. But it was not so much for Catherine's intelligence or territorial acquisitions that she caught the fancy of directors and producers—rather it was the legend of her active and adventurous love life. Not long after she arrived in Hollywood, Polish émigré Pola Negri, later made infamous for her histrionics at the funeral of Rudolf Valentino, took the role of Catherine in *Forbidden Paradise* (1924), a comedy directed by Ernst Lubitsch, another recent arrival in California, with whom she had already collaborated in Berlin. (Having grown up in Poland when it was still part of the Russian Empire, Negri had direct and brutal personal experience of Russian autocracy—her father was sent to a Siberian prison camp.) Other film Catherines were Louise Dresser in Clarence Brown's *Eagle* (1925), Paule Andral in Raymond Bernard's *Tarakanova* (1928), Elisabeth Bergner in Paul Czinner's *Catherine the Great* (1934), Suzy Prim in Fedor Ozep's *Tarakanova/Betrayal* (1938), Tallulah Bankhead in *A Royal Scandal/Czarina* (1946), and Jeanne Moreau in a 1967 film version of Bernard Shaw's play *Great Catherine: A Thumbnail Sketch of Russian Court Life in the XVIII Century (whom Glory still adores)*.

But the Greatest of all screen Catherines was Marlene Dietrich, who took the role in *The Scarlet Empress,* a classic 1934 film directed for Paramount by Josef von Sternberg. Sternberg's fondness for Russian subjects and actors has already been noted. Before coming to *The Scarlet Empress,* he had directed *The Last Command,* and worked with Russian émigré actress Olga Baclanova in *The Docks of New York.* Sternberg's film treats only the early part of Catherine's life—her girlhood in Germany, selection as bride for the deranged Peter III (successor to the Russian throne occupied by his aunt, Empress Elizabeth), her difficult transition to life in the Russian court, and her collaboration in a plot to murder Peter III and take the throne herself. The primary source for the screenplay (by Manuel Komroff) is Catherine's diary, and Sternberg's main interest was in her amorous adventures, as indicated by the original title (later changed because of objections from the Production Code Administration): *Her*

FIGURE 4.

The Scarlet Empress. Paramount 1934. Marlene Dietrich as Catherine
the Great. Courtesy of the Margaret Herrick Library,
Academy of Motion Picture Arts and Sciences.

Regiment of Lovers. The eventual title, *The Scarlet Empress,* creates obvious association with other "scarlet" ladies in history and literature, and was designed to titillate.

From the outset, Sternberg intended the film to make a bold visual statement, "a relentless excursion in style."[22] By this time, Sternberg and Dietrich were an experienced team, having collaborated on some of the most notable films of recent years: *The Blue Angel, Morocco, Dishonored, Shanghai Express, Blonde Venus.* So closely linked had the two become creatively that Sternberg liked to say that "Miss Dietrich is me—I am Miss Dietrich."[23]

In the role of Catherine, Dietrich (at Sternberg's urging) stresses her ability to manipulate those around her through sexual allure and sophistication. The focus is on sexual affairs, not affairs of state. The Russia constructed by Sternberg and art director Hans Dreier is a dark and violent place, where the ruling royals live in lodges hewn from logs, their doors decorated with wild-eyed icons that spy and judge and frighten. In a fantasy sequence near the beginning of the film, the girl Catherine (still a German princess named Sophia) is being told of (or imagining) the brutality of Russia, a gallery of horrors that includes Peter I personally beheading a row of subjects with an ax, and a human body hung upside down and used as a bell clapper, slapped from side to side. (Bells are an important image throughout the film, symbolizing Russian power and spirituality. In the film's last scene, it is Catherine's delirious ringing of the bells that signifies her sole ascent to the throne of the Empire.) At the end of this sequence, Sternberg inserts one of the intertitles that appear sporadically throughout, showing his nostalgia for the silent-film conventions that he had left behind only a few years before: "Russia—a vast empire that had built its foundations on ignorance, violence, fear and oppression." In the minds of most Americans, and of the European émigrés who were flooding the Hollywood studios, this description applied not only to the Russia of Catherine's day, but also to the present.

One of the most obvious and egregious of the many historical errors and distortions in Sternberg's film is the setting of the entire action in Moscow. By 1744, when Catherine arrived in Russia, its new capital of St. Petersburg, established in 1703 by Tsar Peter I as Russia's "window on the west," was, although still under construction, already a large and important city, and most of the political activity—including the coup that overthrew Peter III and put Catherine on the throne in 1762—took place there. Designed by Italian architects and built in European style to compete with the great capitals of Europe, St. Petersburg stood in stark contrast to older and more conservative Moscow.

To Sternberg, however, the exaggerated expressionist image of Russia as backward and Byzantine, all logs and secrecy and onion domes, was more appealing both visually and artistically. The reigning Empress Elizabeth (played with marvelous take-no-prisoners irascibility by Louise Dresser, using a New York accent) is frequently shot from below, dwarfed by a looming throne carved in the shape of an eagle; other pieces of furniture are also made in the form of animals in distorted poses. Gargoyles protrude from the walls, creating a sense of sinister surveillance. A bony skeleton serves as a centerpiece at a banquet—a warning to those who might stray or overeat? So elaborate is the design concept that it at times overwhelms the actors, turning them into mere props. In many key scenes, dialogue is eliminated, most notably in the lavish sequence of Catherine's wedding to Peter III, where Dietrich works wonders with her facial expressions, photographed through a white veil, demonstrating the skill the future monarch has gained at mastering and masking her true emotions (sexual and otherwise) in order to achieve political goals.

Always intensely interested in music, Sternberg used fragments from compositions by Tchaikovsky (particularly the fateful recurrent fanfare from the Fourth Symphony), Mendelssohn (in the wedding scene, in total disregard of the Russian Orthodox ban on instrumental music during services), Rimsky-Korsakov, and Wagner—and even added some music he wrote himself. The film's final sequence, Catherine's assumption of sole power as Empress on horseback, riding up the stairs of the palace to the bells with mounted cavalrymen all around her, is scored (anachronistically) with excerpts from Tchaikovsky's *1812 Overture*. Sternberg had no interest in historical accuracy; his goal was to create a cinematic *gesamtkunstwerk* with his favorite diva at the center. As Carolly Erickson, biographer of Catherine II, has written of *The Scarlet Empress*, "Hollywood mythmaking reduces Catherine's life—and an important era in Russian history—to a dark fairy tale in which a charming innocent, forced to marry a troll and pitted against a wicked court, uses her beauty and her wiles to overturn the forces of evil. But the factual story of Catherine's life was more compelling than any myth, its flawed heroine all the more admirable for enduring and ultimately transcending the sordid cruelties of the Russian court."[24]

The high style of *The Scarlet Empress* did not go over well with audiences or most critics. Unfortunately for Sternberg, his Catherine film ended up in direct competition with another, *Catherine,* released in England in early 1934, just three months before *The Scarlet Empress* opened there to scathing reviews. Its American release was no more successful. While impressed by the production design, critics found the performances mannered and wooden, almost a parody rather than the announced comedy—and indeed, today, *The Scarlet Empress* could justifiably be described as "campy." As an image of Russia, the film was too obviously exaggerated and personal to be taken seriously, but it nonetheless reinforced stereotypes about Russian life as harsh and crude, and Russian rulers as willful, selfish, over-sexed and utterly contemptuous of their subjects—who once again receive precious little screen time here.

The year after he made *The Scarlet Empress,* Sternberg tackled another Russian subject: a screen version of Fyodor Dostoyevsky's novel *Crime and Punishment.* The novels of Fyodor Dostoyevsky were not as popular with Hollywood filmmakers as those of Leo Tolstoy. Their intense psychological concerns were less obviously translatable to the film medium, and they dealt for the most part with the grimy lower and middle classes, not the more picturesque aristocracy. A silent version of *Crime and Punishment* had been made in 1917. For the leading role of Raskolnikov, the student who kills a merciless pawnbroker to test his theory of moral superiority, Sternberg chose the Hungarian émigré Peter Lorre, already famous for his roles in Fritz Lang's *M* (as a child murderer) and Hitchcock's *Man Who Knew Too Much.*

Of filming *Crime and Punishment,* von Sternberg admitted perceptively that, "At best it can be no more than a film about a detective and a criminal, no more related to the true text of the novel than the corner of Sunset Boulevard and Gower is related to the Russian environment."[25] And indeed, the film tells us absolutely nothing about Russia in the nineteenth century. It is shot almost entirely in interiors, and the characters wear clothes of the 1930s, so the story becomes more universal and contemporary. There is no attempt at Russian accents or color, and no Russian music—in fact the dominant musical motif is the opening bars of Beethoven's Fifth Symphony. In contrast to the much more theatrical and manic

Scarlet Empress, von Sternberg here focuses on the psychological aspects of the story, and uses a claustrophobic, gloomy, dimly lit visual style. He also minimizes the violence of the story, even in the scene of Raskolnikov's murder of the pawnbroker, which is filmed from the criminal's perspective to minimize the depiction of the pawnbroker's terror.

★ It is not surprising that Hollywood producers, who valued entertainment and escapism because it sold tickets, were more interested in making films about the Romanovs than about the Revolution that overthrew them. The Romanovs were royalty, and royalty was very much in vogue on screen, especially in the 1920s and early 1930s. But making entertaining, commercially viable films about the Russian Revolution, such a serious and chaotic and disastrous event in such a distant and isolated place, was another matter altogether. How was it possible to present the ideological and historical complexities of an event so recent, and whose causes and repercussions were still poorly understood? And how could it be done in a manner that would draw audiences to movie theaters?

After President Woodrow Wilson sent American troops to Russia in July 1918 to fight against Lenin's Bolshevik government in the Civil War, relations between the United States and the new Russia became extremely tense and hostile. Russia's borders were effectively closed to American visitors, and news of what was happening there was sparse and unreliable. With the establishment of the Comintern in March 1919, an association centered in Moscow of Communist Parties all over the world whose goal was the overthrow of capitalist regimes, the American perception of Russia became only more negative. That same year, the formation of the Communist Labor Party and of the Communist Party in the United States led to the first Red Scare, a campaign to intimidate and even arrest American Communists. Increasingly, Communists became equated with Russians in the American popular imagination.

A number of the feature films Hollywood produced about the Russian Revolution personalized the event by involving an American character in Russia. In the comedy espionage genre, *Bullin' the Bullsheviki* (1919) deals with an American woman named Lotta Nerve who goes to the Russian town of Killemoff to destroy Bolshevism. In another film made the same year, *Common Property,* an American woman married to a Russian and living in Saratov is rescued by the American cavalry. Star-crossed stories of peas-

ants and aristocrats were also popular, such as *Mockery* (1927), starring
Lon Chaney as a peasant who comes to the aid of a Countess during the
Revolution.

Along with von Sternberg's *Last Command,* one of the most memorable
and artistically successful films of the 1920s representing life in revolutionary Russia is *Tempest* (1928), starring John Barrymore. This well-shot
and entertaining peasant-princess love story has a complex and tangled
history that involves some of the most prominent figures in Hollywood at
the time, as well as one of the most important people in the history of
modern Russian theatre: the director Vladimir Nemirovich-Danchenko
(1858–1943). Although he receives no credit on screen in the final version,
it was Nemirovich-Danchenko, co-founder with Konstantin Stanislavsky
of the Moscow Art Theater, who originally developed the idea for the script
of *Tempest.*

Nemirovich-Danchenko was brought to Hollywood at the invitation of
powerful producer Joseph M. Schenck, recently appointed as President of
United Artists. Born in Rybinsk, Russia, and still able to speak Russian
fluently, Schenck (1878–1961) had met Nemirovich at a performance by
Nemirovich's Musical Studio of the Moscow Art Theater in Chicago, during its 1926 American tour, and had extended an invitation to the great
master of the theater (then in his late sixties) to come and work in his
studio, to do "anything you want."[26] When Nemirovich shortly after had
a falling out with his partner Stanislavsky, who was threatening to evict
the Musical Studio from its Moscow home, he suddenly decided to remain abroad and to accept Schenck's proposal. Nemirovich arrived in Los
Angeles in late September 1926, in the company of his secretary Sergei
Bertenson.

At the time, Russian theater and film people were enjoying something
of a vogue in Hollywood. Numerous American film people had been visiting Russia (then enjoying a relatively free cultural period during the New
Economic Policy). Douglas Fairbanks and Mary Pickford had made a triumphant tour there in 1926, and had brought back glowing reports on theatrical and film activity. When Nemirovich-Danchenko met John Barrymore, for whom Schenck wanted him to write a screenplay, the charming
Barrymore was ecstatic in his praise: "But you know this is just like having
the gods descend from Olympus to us here in Hollywood! We need you so
much, and there is so much you can teach us! When I heard that you were

Nemirovich-Danchenko, at first I thought that you couldn't really be the real one, maybe his brother or something. I couldn't believe it!" As Bertenson observed in his diary, Barrymore "is drawn with unusual force to everything Russian in art."[27]

As time went on, however, Nemirovich and Bertenson became increasingly disillusioned with the way they were treated by Schenck, Barrymore, Fairbanks, and other Hollywood power brokers. Nemirovich, who had never worked in the cinema before, tried repeatedly to develop story ideas, but Schenck and his associates found them too "artsy" and insufficiently commercial. One of Nemirovich's suggestions was a film about Emilian Pugachev, much celebrated in Russian literature and song. This charismatic Russian peasant rebel led a massive uprising in 1773–1774 that nearly overthrew Catherine II before he was finally caught, brought to Moscow in a cage, and hung. For Schenck, however, the project was inappropriate because it had a tragic ending. "The public will not sympathize with a hero who perishes," Schenck told Nemirovich. "If it were possible for Catherine II, entranced by how handsome Pugachev is when she sees him in the cage at the end, to forgive him and grant him freedom—that would be much better!"[28] For the highly cultivated, deeply educated, and subtly refined gentleman Nemirovich to hear such judgments was shocking and painful. He found the tyranny of the Hollywod "happy ending" oppressive and cheap. Changes made by MGM to the tragic ending of Tolstoy's novel *Anna Karenina* for a touring version (shown in provincial theaters) of the 1927 film *Love*, starring Greta Garbo and John Gilbert, particularly annoyed Nemirovich: Anna enters a monastery rather than committing suicide, and is reunited with her lover Vronsky after the death of her husband Karenin.[29]

By February 1927, Nemirovich and Bertenson were feeling depressed and isolated in Hollywood.

> Nothing new or interesting has happened. Barrymore is silent, and we have not heard anything from Schenck either. What nonsense this all is: here Vladimir Ivanovich has been living in Hollywood for five months now, having been invited here, according to the newspapers, "for the improvement of the business of cinema." But they aren't giving him anything to do, and before his very eyes they have mutilated his script for *Resurrection* and are about to kill the *Anna Karenina* project. And he

is powerless. What sort of scandal would there be all over Russia if Belasco [David Belasco, playwright, author of *Madame Butterfly* and many other plays] were living in Moscow and no one bothered to ask him for advice about the production of an American play?[30]

While in Hollywood, Nemirovich-Danchenko was invited to numerous parties and receptions with the Hollywood elite, including the screening of Cecil B. DeMille's *King of Kings* at the grand opening of Graumann's Chinese Theater. But Nemirovich was not taken in by the glamour and glitz. He saw that the big stars constituted only a tiny percentage of the actors in Hollywood, and that many others, including numerous Russian émigrés, were desperately poor. In a letter to his sister-in-law Elena Tizengauzen written on August 11, 1927, he warned her not to allow her son-in-law to come to Hollywood in search of fame.

This stream heading towards Hollywood, these dreams of getting established here are creating such an oversupply that many people are on the brink of starvation. The only reason they are not starving is that it's not hard to find a job in a restaurant—washing dishes, sweeping the sidewalk and so on. I personally know *very many* such actors who have managed to stay alive with such work. What they call "extras" here—those who make up the crowd or the atmosphere in a film—number in the tens of thousands. They run around looking for a place to get a job. Then they get something for seven or even ten dollars a day. So? In two or three days they are waiting and searching again, often for months at a time. When they work they are treated like animals. Actually this whole business is set up in a most disturbing way, it's a form of speculation. Maybe they will organize a union and figure something out, but the papers are already full of warnings: "Don't go to Hollywood!"[31]

Feeling useless and restless, and eager to return to the work of the Moscow Art Theater Musical Studio back home, Nemirovich left Hollywood himself just before Christmas 1927, without having brought a single script idea to the screen. He was the first of several prominent Soviet film and theater people brought to Hollywood in the late 1920s and early 1930s with great fanfare and expectations by the major studios; all returned home without producing any completed work.

After Nemirovich returned to Russia, one of the screenplays he had tried to develop for United Artists was finally made into a film, but only in drastically changed form—*Tempest*. From the beginning, this project was intended primarily as a vehicle for John Barrymore, one of Hollywood's leading romantic male stars, and was set in Russia around the time of the 1917 Revolution, involving a soldier who becomes a revolutionary and then betrays his political ideals for love. In the course of developing the script with Nemirovich, Barrymore and Schenck demanded repeated changes to make the part for Barrymore more heroic, and to strengthen the romantic story line. In the original concept, entitled *Homeland*, Nemirovich saw Russia as the hero of the film, but Schenck and his associates told him in no uncertain terms that a film with symbolic pretensions could not be commercially successful in America. As the product of Russian and Soviet training and institutions, Nemirovich did not grasp the commercial aspect of writing for films in Hollywood, and had great difficulty in fulfilling the producers' requirements. There were rumors that Barrymore had grown disenchanted with Nemirovich-Danchenko's work, and that he did not want to perform in the "Bolshevik screenplay of the Bolshevik Danchenko."[32] The start of production was repeatedly delayed.

Finally, Russian émigré director Viktor Tourjansky (1891–1976), who was born in Kiev and had been working in Europe, was engaged to direct the picture, although the original idea had been for Nemirovich to direct himself. By November 1927, Tourjansky was supplemented by two others: Lewis Milestone and Sam Taylor. They made further changes in the screenplay, "all to please Barrymore, who will not tolerate anything that would upstage him or be more interesting than he is."[33] In early December the film was still stalled, Tourjansky had been dismissed, Milestone had refused to do any more work, and Sam Taylor had become the principal director. The screenplay had been revised a fifth time, and there was near-chaos on the set. "There were days of complete confusion, when the shooting was being directed simultaneously by Tourjansky, Milestone, Schenck's representative Considine, Barrymore, Taylor, and even on the telephone by the director von Stroheim, who was working for another studio."[34]

Considering the confusion, it is remarkable that what ultimately emerged is so engaging and well crafted. It is impossible to say what portion of the screenplay of *Tempest* belongs to Nemirovich, but the film possesses an atmosphere of authenticity that may reflect his own first-hand experience in World War I Russia and in the two revolutions of 1917. The film opens in

1914, in a garrison town near the border with Austria, with the following title: "This is the storm-swept romance of a poor dragoon and a proud princess—of Imperial Russia—in the last long calm before the red tempest of terror." Barrymore plays Ivan Markov, a peasant who rises in rank thanks in part to the efforts of a kindly general. But Markov unwisely falls in love with the general's haughty daughter Tamara (played by German actress Camilla Horn). She denounces him after he compromises her honor by appearing unexpectedly in her bedroom, finding her partially undressed. Thrown in prison, he must sit out the combat of World War I, and is released only when the Tsar is deposed.

Appointed as a high-ranking official in the new revolutionary government, Markov tries unsuccessfully to save the kindly general (now reviled as a counterrevolutionary aristocrat) from execution. At last happily reunited with the repentant and chastened Tamara, he decides to escape with her rather than to fulfill his duties to his revolutionary comrades.

Barrymore turns in a gutsy and subtle performance, transforming very credibly from a callow and cocky young officer to an unjustly accused prisoner. Afflicted by nightmares and visions of the combat he so desperately wants to join, he scales the walls of his cell to peek out at the world. In one scene, the adventurous cinematography shows us the high wall of Markov's cell dissolving into a battlefield toward which he rushes, only to crash into cold stone. The early scenes of the officers' ball are glittering and dynamic. Even in its repeatedly revised form, the screenplay investigates some of the significant moral issues raised by the Russian Revolution, framed in a classic love-versus-duty and rags-to-riches format. As he lies dying, the noble general tells Markov: "My Russia is dead—I am glad that I, too, am dying."

★ Neither *The Last Command* nor *Tempest* shows us what actually happened in Petrograd during the Bolshevik Revolution—they deal with the aftermath. Even for Soviet filmmakers, it was challenging to bring the Revolution to screen, for both ideological and logistical reasons. In 1927, the tenth anniversary of the October Revolution, prominent Soviet filmmakers were encouraged to commemorate the event. From Sergei Eisenstein came *October,* released in America under the title *Ten Days That Shook the World.* This film, widely seen in Hollywood, especially when Eisenstein himself came to town in 1930, deeply influenced the subsequent portrayal of the Bolshevik Revolution by Hollywood directors and producers for many years afterward.

When fifty years later Warren Beatty came to direct his own epic, *Reds* (1981), about the life of American journalist and Communist Party organizer John Reed (author of what is still regarded as one of the most important eye-witness accounts of the Bolshevik Revolution, *Ten Days That Shook the World*, a major source for *October*), he drew heavily upon Eisenstein's visual style. The scenes portraying the rise of Lenin and the Bolsheviks in Petrograd in autumn 1917 are particularly indebted to Eisenstein. When Reed (Beatty) and his girlfriend and companion the American journalist Louise Bryant (Diane Keaton) attend the smoky, raucous rallies of the Bolshevik Party and listen to speeches by Lenin (Roger Sloman) to the workers, the *mise-en-scène*, pacing, and editing are directly imitative of similar scenes in *October*. One has to admit, however, that Eisenstein probably would have disliked the way Beatty (who also wrote the screenplay for *Reds*, along with Trevor Griffiths) focuses his long (196 minutes) film on the romance between Reed and Bryant. For Eisenstein, especially in the 1920s when he made *Strike, Battleship Potemkin*, and *October*, the political struggle itself was always the center of the action. Love stories Eisenstein found sentimental, clichéd, and unnecessary.

Also imitative of Eisenstein is the unusual documentary/feature genre of *Reds*, which incorporates interviews with thirty-two prominent figures ("witnesses") who knew John Reed and Louise Bryant as running commentary on the semi-fictionalized action portrayed by actors. For many reviewers and viewers, this feature of the film provoked the most comment and debate. Beatty also chose not to identify the "witnesses," an artistic choice heavily criticized by many reviewers. In leaving them anonymous, Beatty was expressing his belief that the story/history he was presenting was not only about individuals, but about a movement of which many people were a part. Given the fact that John Reed died at the age of 32 in 1920, there were very few people alive around 1980 (when Beatty was completing the film) who had known him or could remember him. Some of those who were interviewed (former New York congressman Hamilton Fish, author Adela Rogers St. John, novelist Henry Miller, entertainer George Jessel) provided conflicting stories and some even admitted they could not remember very much. The inclusion of their reminiscences, however, lifts *Reds* to another more ambitious level of inquiry

FIGURE 5.

Reds. Paramount 1981. Director Warren Beatty and cinematographer Vittorio
Storaro on the set of *Reds.* Courtesy of the Margaret Herrick Library,
Academy of Motion Picture Arts and Sciences.

highly unusual among big-budget Hollywood features. "Peering dimly into the past as they are interviewed, magnificent under cameraman Vittorio Storaro's compassionate lens, they create a living framework for the period." [35]As its title indicates, *Reds* is not just about John Reed or Louise Bryant or even the Bolsheviks in Russia, but about the reverberations Communism and the Bolshevik Revolution had in the United States. It is the story of a movement as embodied in the tragic (and, yes, romantic) life of one person. And there is not a single Romanov or princess to be seen or regretted.

To maintain the semi-documentary feeling of *Reds*, Beatty chose not to use a big symphonic score of the sort created by Maurice Jarre for *Doctor Zhivago*. Instead, he employed Broadway composer Stephen Sondheim as a musical consultant and arranger, and used primarily diegetic or source music of various kinds, thereby heightening the film's sense of realism and authenticity. The most important single tune in *Reds* is the anthem of the Bolshevik Revolution, the *Internationale* (its lyrics and music were composed by two Frenchmen). This stirring hymn, the official anthem of the USSR until 1943, is the most important single tune in *Reds*. Not only does it rouse Reed and Bryant to ideological engagement and excitement—it also serves as an aphrodisiac and love theme for their relationship, finally consummated sexually at the end of Part I when Bryant yields to Reed's seduction, the *Internationale*'s heroic strains filtering in from the streets.

For Beatty, *Reds* was an intensely personal project, and one into which he poured remarkable energy, stamina, and imagination. Even more notable, the film was conceived and made at a time when anti-Soviet and anti-Communist feeling was running high in the United States. *Reds* was released at the end of 1981. Ronald Reagan, whose antipathy for the USSR was one of the factors that had won him the presidency, sat in the White House. As we shall see, the prevailing image of Russia in other films produced in Hollywood at the time was extremely violent and negative (*Red Dawn, Gulag, Firefox*), imbued with a spirit of what historians Michael Strada and Harold Troper have called "Cold War vigilantism."[36]

Made at a cost of more than $33 million, *Reds* is the only mainstream commercial American feature film that attempts to treat with serious intellectual intentions the history of the early development of Communism as a movement both in Russia and in the United States. Although *Doctor Zhivago* does an excellent job of tracing the impact of the Russian Revolution on the lives of several individuals, it does not focus on the actual events and primary political players. *Reds* broke new ground. As Kurt Vonnegut, Jr., wrote in *Vogue* a few months after the release of *Reds*, "It is my hope now that Warren Beatty's rash and nearly inconceivable movie *Reds* will give Americans a sense of calm and proportion about the Russian Revolution, and especially about their fellow countrymen who found it promising and just. Up to now, discussions of Marxist idealism, as idealism rather than insanity or criminality or worse, have been even harder to come by than unhorrified opinions of masturbation used to be."[37]

Beatty does not spare Lenin and his associates, portraying them as ruthless and rigid ideologues who value policy over people and have no use for freedom of speech when it upsets their plans. As Grigori Zinoviev, head of the Cominterm, whose purpose was to support Communist movements worldwide, novelist Jerzy Kosinski was a brilliant casting choice. Zinoviev's increasing coldness toward Reed after he had returned to the USSR in the aftermath of the Revolution, and his refusal to grant his faction of the American Communist Party recognition, leave Reed isolated and disillusioned, nearly desperate. Although in order to get *Reds* made for Paramount Beatty banked heavily on his enormous personal popularity and clout in the wake of his success in comic films like *Shampoo* and *Heaven Can Wait,* he works hard as director to tell the serious story of an era and of an ideal—Communism. He brings us back to the 1920s, when the USSR was a brand new country that represented to many people—including many people in Hollywood—a viable alternative to cut-throat capitalism, and a shining utopian possibility.

As Carolyn Porter wrote in *Film Quarterly,* "*Reds* has provided us with a memory of a period in our history which adults as well as school children have not so much forgotten as never really known about. It is a historical moment worth remembering, primarily because it was probably the last moment in our history before the ideologies by which twentieth-century America has lived became hardened and fixed. *Reds* gives that moment a resonance which makes it unforgettable, and it goes on to portray its passing with poignance and dismay."[38]

That "moment" before ideologies became "hardened and fixed" extended in Hollywood into the early 1930s. Prominent Soviet cultural figures continued to visit and to discuss possible collaborations. Composer Sergei Prokofiev, now based in Paris but traveling home to Russia with increasing frequency, returned to Los Angeles in early 1930 for the first time since 1921, for performances with the Los Angeles Philharmonic, then conducted by Artur Rodzinski. During his stay, Prokofiev, already celebrated as a pianist and a composer of ballets and operas, was approached by Gloria Swanson's representative, architect-designer Paul Nelson, about writing the score for her upcoming film. In his diary, Prokofiev confided, "This is terrific, and smells of money." After a rehearsal, the composer and his wife Lina were picked up in a Rolls and taken to Swanson's home for lunch.

> Swanson is so beautiful and so famous that you don't know how to approach her. I stood off to the side, leaving it to Lina to converse with her. After lunch I was taken to a screening room, for I was so naïve that I had not yet ever heard a film with music and dialogue, although this kind of cinema had been solidly established for a year or two already. But the complication is that the music has to be ready by April 1, which means I would have to write it in America, between concerts. That is a lot of pressure—wouldn't it be better to return to this possibility for the next production? I left soon after, to rest before my concert, but instead of sleeping I kept on thinking: could I write simple music that would be accessible to the masses, and yet music that I still would want to put my name on?

The following day, Prokofiev read the synopsis of the film, "but there were so many technical terms I couldn't understand a thing, so I had Lina read it and as she read, she explained it to me. The drama is rubbish, but Nelson's designs are most intriguing. I started thinking again what sort of music I could write; one very good theme came to me. If the commission doesn't work out, then in any case I'll still have this theme." The commission didn't work out, mainly because Prokofiev demanded a fee of $5000 to write 90 seconds of music to be heard during the opening credits. Swanson's financial backer and lover Joseph Kennedy ("a very pleasant, calm, and still very young man"), father of JFK, did not believe that Prokofiev's name was "sufficiently popular among the American masses to spend that much on him." To Prokofiev, this indicated their lack of understanding of the importance of the music for the artistic success of the project. "Gloria is a wonderful actress, the scenery is good, but the music will come in off the street, and they don't even notice. It's as if Kennedy were to be dressed in a beautiful tailored suit but wore dirty cuffs. If it were suggested to him to wash them, he would hide them under the sleeves of his jacket and say, 'It doesn't matter, the masses won't notice.' So, I was right this morning: there's no contract, but I still have a good theme."[39]

This was far from the last time that a "serious" composer failed to find a common artistic language with Hollywood producers and stars. Not long after, however, Prokofiev did launch his distinguished career as a composer for Soviet films, with the comically ironic music for *Lieutenant Kije*, made in 1933. No doubt his interaction with Gloria Swanson and her people in Hollywood gave him a better understanding of the medium of film and the role of music in cinema.

★   Only a few months after Prokofiev visited Hollywood, the leading Soviet director Sergei Eisenstein arrived. (Not incidentally, Eisenstein and Prokofiev would later work together on two films, *Alexander Nevsky* and *Ivan the Terrible*.) Eisenstein came to Hollywood in 1930 amid an atmosphere of curiosity and even admiration felt by many prominent Hollywood figures toward the USSR and the emerging Soviet film industry, the first in the world to be developed upon ideological rather than commercial principles. The leading intellectual and creative force in Soviet film of the 1920s, Eisenstein was first invited to visit Hollywood by Douglas Fairbanks and Mary Pickford during their trip to the USSR in 1926. In August 1928, producer Joseph Schenck also visited Moscow and again expressed interest in bringing Eisenstein to America. But it was the concrete proposal extended to Eisenstein by the vice-president of Paramount, Jesse L. Lasky, in April 1930 in Paris that finally provided the means for the director to make the trip.

Initially Lasky's idea was that Eisenstein "would spend six months in the USA making a film for Paramount, after which it would be open for him to return to Moscow to direct a Sovkino production."[40] There was also hope that the relationship could continue beyond that, with Eisenstein dividing his time between Moscow and Hollywood. This arrangement gave Eisenstein, always eager to acquire greater knowledge of film technology, the opportunity to acquaint himself with the latest developments—particularly in sound film—going on in America. Full of excitement and plans, Eisenstein arrived in New York in early May 1930, accompanied by his longtime cameraman and advisor Eduard Tisse. They were joined later by their col-

FIGURE 6.

Sergei Eisenstein and producer Jesse L. Lasky in Paris in 1930, signing a
contract with Paramount Studios. Courtesy of the Margaret Herrick Library,
Academy of Motion Picture Arts and Sciences. Gift of Lasky Family. Wide
World Photos, New York Times.

league Grigory Alexandrov, who would later make some of the most popular Soviet films of the 1930s.

But Eisenstein was not greeted with universal enthusiasm on American soil. Numerous anti-Communist politicians attacked him as part of a "Jewish-Bolshevik conspiracy to turn the American cinema into a Communist cesspool." In his highly entertaining autobiography, *Beyond the Stars,* Eisenstein recalls that "America in 1930 was the America of anti-Semitism, of Prohibition; the imperialist America of Hoover, before, two years later, becoming the America of Roosevelt: the America of the New Era and democratic tendencies, which flourished during his second term, and the military alliance with the Soviet Union."[41] On the east coast, Eisenstein met with Paramount executives, lectured at Harvard and Yale, met Rin-Tin-Tin at a posh luncheon in Boston, and chatted with D. W. Griffith in the lobby of the Astor Hotel in New York. Douglas Fairbanks took him to a speakeasy.

When they arrived in Hollywood, Eisenstein, Tisse, and Alexandrov moved into a rented Spanish-style villa in Coldwater Canyon, equipped with the necessities of local life: a swimming pool, a car, and a black cook. "We bathed, played tennis, saw the sights, and made more friends," said Eisenstein later.[42] But Eisenstein's experience of working at Paramount was similar to what Nemirovich-Danchenko encountered at United Artists. It soon became obvious that the taste of the Paramount executives diverged radically from Eisenstein's, and they found it difficult to agree upon a mutually agreeable subject for a film. They considered and then rejected three major proposals made by Eisenstein, the last being an ambitious adaptation of Theodore Dreiser's novel *An American Tragedy.* Eisenstein knew Dreiser personally, and admired him for his brave socialist critique of American capitalism. Both men had great hopes for their collaboration.

But David O. Selznick, associate producer at Paramount, found Eisenstein's screenplay completely unacceptable. In a memo written to his boss, B. P. Schulberg, Selznick called it "the most moving script I have ever read. It was so effective that it was positively torturing. When I had finished it, I was so depressed I wanted to reach for the bourbon bottle. As entertainment, I don't think it has one chance in a hundred."[43] With the rejection of *American Tragedy,* Eisenstein's association with Paramount came to an end; his contract was cancelled in October 1930 and he was awarded

FIGURE 7.

Sergei Prokofiev (right), Sergei Eisenstein (center), and Edward Tisse (left)
dressed in Russian costumes of the thirteenth century for a humorous photo
taken during the making of *Alexander Nevsky*.

$30,000 in compensation. Disappointed over his failure to make a single film during his time in Hollywood (and aware that returning to Moscow empty-handed would create serious problems for him at home), Eisenstein tried to interest MGM and Universal in the unlikely project of a film based on Edgar Lee Masters's *Spoon River Anthology*. This, too, came to nothing.

In his memoirs, written sixteen years later in Stalinist Moscow, Eisenstein looks back at his inability to work successfully in Hollywood in highly ideological terms. For Eisenstein, the essence of American life in 1930 was gambling. The Paramount studio executives took a gamble when they decided to engage his services:

> I was the protégé of the "risk-takers," the seekers after novelty and excitement, which I represented in Jesse Lasky's company.
>
> They faced the bankers, who represented financial interests and especially B.P. [Schulberg]; they gambled only on certainties, in a cautious and calculating way and, more often than not, were all for repeating winning formulae.
>
> At Paramount, the financial side came out on top; they exaggerated the difficulties of coming to an agreement with us, and on the rebound, said that it was a "romantic" tendency that had brought us into the country. . . .
>
> The feudal discord within the group aggravated the naturally difficult agreement we had regarding screenplays.
>
> According to the contract, I had the right of veto over their proposals, and they avoided agreeing to mine.
>
> After six months we had not made a single film.
>
> We parted.[44]

Even during his time in Hollywood, Eisenstein was well aware of his novelty value, that he and his colleagues were "practically the first Soviets in California."[45] His identity as a prominent director of the USSR colored every creative interaction, creating obstacles for him not faced by other European directors working in Hollywood, such as the German Josef von Sternberg, whose version of *An American Tragedy* was released by Paramount in 1931. At a dinner held in Eisenstein's honor on August 21, 1930, at the Roosevelt Hotel, Frank Lloyd, of the Directors' Branch of the Academy of Motion Pictures Arts and Sciences, directly addressed the difference between the Soviet and American systems of filmmaking before a screening of *Potemkin*. Lloyd focused on the censorship enforced by the Soviet government over the film industry, even over such established artists as Eisenstein: ". . . you may think you are handicapped in your trying to make pictures, but it is nothing compared to what he has to go through to try to give entertainment in Russia." During the question-and-answer session, however, Eisenstein defended the Soviet system in his very fluent if imperfect English, and denied that he was "handicapped" in making movies in Moscow.

> I wouldn't say handicap. It is quite different. The difficulties we have are that we have to treat subjects that have never been touched. . . . We had to make ecstasy, temperament, excitement over things that in ordinary life have no excitement. A cream separator has to be presented with ecstasy and excitement. . . . I think if our technique is something new in Russia, that is because we have to deal with problems with quite new setting, new ways of expression, and combining our subjects because the material is unusual, as you say in California.[46]

Eisenstein also stressed, with his customary irony, that the Soviet and American ways of filmmaking differed fundamentally in the way they engaged the audience. "That is one of the points why our pictures are not such box office material as the American films because we have another purpose and not the purpose of making money and be entertainment—*our one purpose is always educational.* Here the people are all so educated they don't need that."[47]

The unsuccessful collaboration between Eisenstein and Paramount revealed many truths about Hollywood's (and America's) attitudes toward the USSR in 1930. Americans were very curious about Russia, particularly in the wake of the stock market crash of October 1929. There was doubt in some quarters about the viability of capitalism. The great social and economic experiment going on in the USSR had attracted many admirers, including many in the film industry. In the USSR, the limited capitalism and cultural pluralism of the New Economic Policy period had only recently ended, and Josef Stalin had not yet consolidated his totalitarian control over the Soviet government; from the United States the situation in the USSR appeared fluid and somewhat hopeful.

But as Eisenstein pointed out, the attraction of certain Hollywood producers to Soviet talent was inspired by romantic ideals, not reality. That Schenck and Lasky believed they could simply insert a Soviet director into a Hollywood studio and expect quick results showed how naïve they were about the realities of the Soviet system, which had broken radically with the idea of culture (including film) as entertainment and commerce. For his part, Eisenstein, whose film career had unfolded entirely since (and largely thanks to) the Bolshevik Revolution, refused to compromise. He could not write a screenplay pleasing to the executives at Paramount. The standoff was a harbinger of things to come in the wider American-Soviet relationship. And only a few years later, when Stalin regimented artists into unions, proclaimed Socialist Realism the only acceptable approach to artistic work, and made foreign travel virtually impossible, a trip such as the one taken by Eisenstein would have been unthinkable.

Eisenstein's American adventure only grew stranger after he left Hollywood for Mexico, having signed a contract to make a film there with Upton Sinclair. As has been well-documented, this venture ended in failure and scandal. Eisenstein was forced to return to the USSR (after extensive problems with his visa and travel through the United States) in April 1932 without having managed to complete a single film in the nearly three years he had spent away from Russia.

Even if Eisenstein failed to leave a film behind in Hollywood, he did make friends with numerous members of the film community, upon many of whom he left a lasting impression. In her indispensable memoir *The Kindness of Strangers,* screenwriter Salka Viertel, herself a Polish-speaking émigré from Galicia, recalls how she came to know and appreciate Eisenstein, and how poorly the Hollywood establishment understood either him or his work. At a party given in Eisenstein's honor at the ranch of a prominent industrialist, one of those in attendance, a former film star named Mary Miles-Minter, "made a lengthy, confused speech about communism and the Soviets and asked the Russians why they had permitted the execution of the Tsar and his family. It was quite embarrassing."[48]

When she heard of Paramount's rejection of Eisenstein's screenplays, Viertel saw "that Hollywood had no use for him, and we only wondered why he had been called. . . . The world success of his films did not prevent Eisenstein from suffering the fate of most European directors in Hollywood." Viertel was shocked, but not so surprised, when she discovered that most of those who agreed to invest in Eisenstein's Mexican project "had no idea who Eisenstein was. I am sure they would have been horrified had they ever seen one of his films."[49]

Director Josef von Sternberg had already met Eisenstein in Berlin while he was working on his masterpiece *The Blue Angel,* and was happy to see him again in the very different environment of Hollywood. In his garrulous memoirs, *Fun in a Chinese Laundry,* Sternberg makes special note of their reunion and his respect for Eisenstein as an artist.

> The Russians have always, though subservient to political ideologies, managed to invest their work with notable values. Eisenstein was a fluidly expressive commentator, and we frequently discussed all our common interests. He barred none, not even one of such potential danger to him as the subject of government control of the arts. When I asked him how his country rewarded a good film, he told me jokingly, though he might well have been serious, that when a director made a good film in Russia he was rewarded by having a window added to his room, and if his film was bad he was shot for treason. I inquired as to the number of windows in his room and he answered, "One."[50]

Eisenstein also met Walt Disney (he particularly admired Disney's use of sound); Viertel's friend Greta Garbo ("For Garbo, acting was a hard way of making a living") not long before she played the Russian ballerina Grushinskaya in *Grand Hotel;* and Charlie Chaplin—"the most interesting person in Hollywood."[51] Chaplin and Eisenstein met very theatrically, in a cloud of steam in the dressing room of Douglas Fairbanks's personal Turkish bath. The "very dear friendship" between them, Eisenstein later wrote, "lasted all of six months while our negotiations with Paramount tried to reconcile the irreconcilable: the subject of a film that satisfied in equal measure my interests as director and Paramount's interests as boss."[52]

★   In June 1931, only six months after Eisenstein had returned in disgrace to Moscow, another luminary of Soviet culture arrived in the United States on his way to Hollywood—Boris Pilnyak (1894–1937?). MGM had invited him at the urging of boy-wonder producer Irving Thalberg (1899–1936), then at the height of his power and influence. Considerably less famous in America than either Eisenstein or Nemirovich-Danchenko, Pilnyak was the dominant figure in Soviet literature in the early 1920s, after the publication of his novel *The Naked Year.* He fraternized with high-ranking members of the Soviet government, which helps to explain why he was allowed to travel abroad frequently. Pilnyak was hired for a ten-week contract. But he stayed only a few weeks in Hollywood during a five-month stay in America.

Like Eisenstein and Nemirovich-Danchenko, Pilnyak discovered soon after arriving that he had completely different artistic ideas from those who had hired him. Nurtured in the intensely politicized atmosphere of Soviet culture of the 1920s, Pilnyak, fond of highly unconventional form and avant-garde behavior, found the commercial demands placed upon Hollywood screenwriters confining and alien. In his entertaining collage-like book (surprisingly, still not published in an English translation) about his experiences in America, *Okay: An American Novel,* written soon after his return to the USSR, Pilnyak says he was invited to Hollywood "in the capacity of a Bolshevik . . . in order to Sovietize American film." But what he quickly came to realize was that in Hollywood, the "real master was Mr. Capitalism."

Thalberg, like other leading Hollywood producers in the early 1930s, wanted to develop a screenplay for a film dealing with the heroic construction of the new Soviet life. It was to be directed by Frank Capra, with a "dream" cast including Wallace Beery, Marie Dressler, Joan Crawford, and Clark Gable.[53] The news of the monumental goals of the first Five-Year Plan to create huge industrial plants and dams had intrigued the American media, and an estimated three thousand American engineers were being brought to Russia to contribute their technical expertise. To many Americans in 1931, when unemployment was still high, the idea of the guaranteed full employment provided by the Soviet system looked very attractive. The USSR was a new frontier, praised by many prominent left-wing writers (among them, Theodore Dreiser and John Dos Passos). To them and to other groups (blacks, industrial workers) that felt marginalized in the United States, Soviet Communism offered an exciting alternative.

Thalberg had brought Pilnyak to MGM to act as a consultant for a screenplay originally drafted by MGM's scenarist Frances Marion.[54] "The hero was an American engineer named Morgan," writes Pilnyak in *Okay.* "The heroine was the enchanting Tanya. The villain was the GPU." (The GPU was the predecessor of the KGB, the Soviet secret police.) "The good-hearted comedian was the construction manager Nikolai, a worker, a hero of the five-year plan, a Communist. The action takes place in the USSR." In his detailed description of the endless discussions he had with studio representatives as they attempted to shape the material into a workable screenplay, Pilnyak provides an invaluable analysis of the way pro-capitalist (and anti-Communist) messages were inserted into the Hollywood product.

Morgan is traveling to the USSR to work, to "study the great principles of a planned economy, so he can then use this knowledge back home." Meanwhile, Tanya (an enchanting brunette) is being sent away from America—deported, as they say there—because she is a Communist and has led a strike in America. Although class enmity exists between Tanya and the bourgeois Morgan, "they have come to agree in their views, and they love each other, without realizing it themselves." They are sailing on the same ship, although of course in different classes. They sail past the Statue of Liberty. From the lower deck, Tanya curses the symbol of American freedom. On the upper deck, Morgan is whistling an American anthem. Once again, their eyes meet. And so on.

Once they cross the Soviet border real wonders begin to happen. A spy is assigned to trail Morgan (the spy turns out later to be the husband of Tanya's sister, who is dying of consumption and grief over the spy's infidelity). The spy and unfaithful husband immediately falls in love with Tanya. He, of course, is a secret Chekist, a member of the secret police. Besides this hidden Chekist, other more obvious Chekists are also roaming around the USSR—they have black beards, are equipped with bombs, and wear felt boots (*valenki*), their eyes are blazing "like coals." The obvious Chekists arrest professors in front of everyone, tearing them away from their wives, who die right on the spot.

Moscow contains no fewer miracles. Skyscrapers "higher than in New York" are being built. Morgan is working on the construction of a factory called "Steel," "which will be the biggest in the world." The factory's director is Nikolai (some comedian will play this role), a Communist, a hero of the five-year plan, a former American worker who once worked with Morgan (although Morgan is only 22 years old). Tanya, in search of fresh air, travels with her sister—who is dying of consumption—to her hometown in the country, which happens to be located near the "Steel" factory. In this village there is fresh air, and big, new, houses decorated with Ukrainian towels (although the setting is in the Urals), and piles of butter and eggs, which the prosperous villagers are consuming. One revolutionary morning, tanks roll through the village, razing it to the ground to build a collective farm on the bare earth. They shave off the beard of the old man of the village. The Communist Tanya is upset. But the spy is in love with Tanya—he is her sister's husband, a secret Chekist and villain. He insists that bigamy is not a vice, and that under Communism it's possible to have even twenty wives, and Tanya, as a Communist, must yield to his wishes.

Now the spy figures out that Tanya loves Morgan. So he takes revenge on Morgan, accusing him of a criminal act. Meanwhile, Tanya is heading up a band of insurgent peasants protesting the shaving of the old man's beard. Both Tanya and Morgan are threatened with reprisals from the GPU. Neither Tanya nor Morgan suspect this fact, but Nikolai—the Red manager and Communist—finds out. He summons Tanya and Morgan and advises them to flee the USSR. They flee. The GPU pursues them. The audience should now be choking on its excitement—will they catch them? Will they escape? Just like films with cowboys and Indians. But of course they manage to escape. When their ship passes the Statue of Liberty, the enchanting Tanya stretches out her happy hands to it, and Morgan sings the American national anthem. . . . At this point Tanya, now of course thoroughly Americanized, gives to Morgan her hand and her heart and everything else—all that's missing is the national flag!

When at the story conference I was asked—after the synopsis had been read aloud—what I thought of it, I said in all honesty that this synopsis seemed to me utter nonsense. To my amazement, no one was in the least surprised by my evaluation. No one was even offended. We didn't touch on politics, God forbid—this is about pure art!—but I then gave some lessons in the fundamentals of political thinking for a few hours. They all agreed with me readily. I said that if there has to be a villain, then the villain should be a Russian counter-revolutionary. Thalberg asked me to explain to him once again what sabotage was. He listened to me and then said:

"Okay, then instead of the GPU, the villain will be sabotage!"

I told him what the collective farm movement was. Thalberg listened to me and said:

"Well, we don't need a peasant uprising. Think up some other picture that will be exciting, some kind of rebellion. *Shchur* [Sure]!"

I said that an American cannot flee the USSR, because if he were to flee, it would mean he was an idiot, and we can't have an idiot as the hero, and if he is a hero and not an idiot, then he wouldn't try to flee, since not a single American engineer had yet fled from the USSR. *Well* means: so, maybe; *sure* means: of course. Americans begin their sentences with these words when they want to appear to be deep thinkers.

"Well," said Thalberg. "But we have to have a chase in the film, for a stunt. So figure out how a chase could be plausible for the hero, because the American audience really likes chase scenes."

I said that maybe we could come up with something like that if lemons start growing in Greenland, only then Greenland would not be Greenland, but Hollywood. After all, I had been invited to be the author and advisor on what was supposed to be a pro-Soviet film.

"Well," said Thalberg, "we are making a film that is pro-Soviet, and we asked you to participate as a Bolshevik. But you still have to think up a chase! *Shchur!*"

I must say that I wanted to work on the picture because I understood what an enormous significance film had in America, and I wanted to make a film that would be at least 75 percent accurate. This seemed important. When I arrived in Hollywood, I had laid out my agenda to the management. It was simple. I said that the work conditions would be acceptable to me only if I were given the opportunity to maintain a historical perspective—the USSR is building socialism, the USSR is led by the Communist Party. These were the historical facts, and from these facts comes the proper perspective. So they said to me: Okay, *U-ell* [Well]! By then I did have a general idea of what Hollywood was about, and after hearing the synopsis, I was inclined to think of it more as the result of stupidity than of politics. . . .

For two Hollywood nights Joe and I didn't sleep, trying every which way to come up with a chase sequence. We couldn't figure anything out for the character of Morgan. Then we decided that it would be Tanya who would flee, and Morgan would run after her out of love. We kicked Tanya out of the Party. Then we fixed it up so that Tanya had never been in America at all, but that she was a Russian *bourgeoise*, a translator, and so forth. Then we reinstated her first stay in America. But nothing would come out right! And nothing would come out with Nikolai, since it was impossible to think up a combination in which a Communist would help someone to flee and still remain a Communist!—Really, sitting in Hollywood, we had to make oranges grow in Greenland.

We finally came up with only one thing: the speech that I would deliver at the next story conference.

It was Descartes who proclaimed the maxim "I think, therefore I am." And European philosophy struggled with this formula for a century and a half, becoming increasingly confused. Because according to this formula it is exceedingly difficult to reconcile man with the cosmos and very easy to assert that the world is not something real, but only a concept. Philosophers struggled with this dilemma until someone came along and said that the root of evil lies not in the application of this formula to reality, but in the formula itself—the formula needs to be redone. "I exist—that means I am a part of nature." "I think—that means I exist." This is what our search for a chase sequence had turned into. It isn't worth the effort to go searching for answers in Greenland. It's a bad idea to concoct a screenplay in Hollywood and then change Soviet reality to make it fit. Instead, the screenplay should be driven by Soviet reality—omitting the Greenland lemons of chase scenes. So that's what I said.

"U-ell," they replied, "but we want to make a pro-Soviet film."

"And that's exactly why I didn't sleep for the last few nights," I answered.

"But a pro-Soviet film," they said, "means this: let the Bolsheviks do at home what they want, even socialism. We acknowledge the five-year plan and your building program. We approve the official recognition of the USSR and the restoration of diplomatic relations, because then it would be profitable for us to trade with the Bolsheviks. But what is suitable for the Bolsheviks is in no way appropriate for Americans. We have to show in the film that even American Communists cannot live among the Bolsheviks. All of this has to be shown in the film we are intending to shoot."

I heard them out, and understood that this was not about stupidity, but politics, even very stupid politics, and I took out my contract, which stated that I had the right to break this contract with 24 hours notice, and said: "*Gud-bai* [goodbye], *do svidaniya!*" and erased my name from the annals of Hollywood business.

And they said that I could copy whatever I wanted out of books, and think up whatever I wanted to come up with, as long as it worked on film and was pure art. They reminded me that I was privileged. And they asked me with amazement: You mean you really don't want to work with us? You really don't want to veer from history even by half a per-cent, from that "perspective" which you stipulated as a condition of your collaboration?

"No," I said, "I am not a traitor."

"Well, here in America we consider it good business to betray his-tory, and even more so, to deceive the government!" Al Luen said to me, and I think he was being serious. . . .[55]

Pilnyak's abortive sojourn in Hollywood brought to an end an era. The naïve attempt at dialogue with Soviet culture represented by the invita-tions to Nemirovich-Danchenko, Eisenstein, and Pilnyak had produced no concrete results, and revealed how incompatible the American and Soviet systems had become in virtually every aspect, including film-making. With the rise of Stalin, the USSR would become increasingly iso-lated from the rest of the world. Soviet film people were rarely allowed to travel abroad, and Hollywood came to be viewed as ideologically decadent and dangerous. The Russian émigrés who had come to Hollywood in the 1920s had no intention of returning home, and many developed anti-Communist sentiments (if they didn't have them already). The atmosphere became increasingly polarized.

As for Pilnyak, he suffered a fate all too typical for Soviet gadfly intel-lectuals of his generation. Although in Hollywood he defended the honor of the USSR in a story conference with Irving Thalberg, back in Moscow he was perceived in the increasingly regimented Stalinist atmosphere as a suspicious character, too independent and with too many foreign connec-tions and too many unconventional ideas. It didn't help matters that Pilnyak was a friend of the discredited and exiled Leon Trotsky, or that he returned to Moscow with a new Ford he had purchased in the United States; such os-tentation was highly inappropriate in Spartan Moscow of the mid-1930s. Like so many other members of the Soviet cultural avant-garde who flour-ished in the wild and crazy 1920s, Pilnyak fell victim to Stalin's purges of individuals proclaimed to be ideologically pernicious. In October 1937, Pilnyak was arrested. What happened next is still a matter of controversy, although the ultimate outcome is not: Pilnyak was shot as an enemy of the people, either immediately after his arrest or some time later.

That kind of reality Hollywood had no use for.

★*★ 2 ★*★
"Isn't There Some Russian in Your Background?"

"You can't have a revolution with people who believe in hot dogs and boogie woogie."
Clark Gable as Mac Thompson in *Comrade X*

On November 17, 1933, almost exactly sixteen years after the establishment of Lenin's Communist regime in Russia, the governments of the United States and the USSR finally established official diplomatic relations. Whether to grant official recognition to the Soviet Communist regime had long been a contentious issue in American politics. One of the first countries to recognize the Provisional Government that overthrew the Tsarist regime in the February Revolution, the United States was one of the last to recognize the Communist regime set up after the October Revolution.

During the 1920s, most of the major European powers had established embassies in Moscow, but the United States held back—although by the early 1930s there was significant American trade with the USSR and thousands of American engineers and technicians were working there. (In 1929, the Soviet government even signed a contract with Henry Ford for the purchase of large quantities of cars and trucks; Stalin ended this so-called "Fordization" of the Soviet economy in 1934.) Many of these workers, as well as numerous other visitors to Russia, including intellectuals and writers, were very sympathetic to Communism and the great Soviet "experiment," especially after the stock market crash and Depression profoundly shook American national confidence in the strength and future of capitalism. Along with Democrats, progressive Republicans were urging recognition of the USSR for trade and economic reasons, but Republican President Herbert Hoover, a staunch anti-Communist, was opposed. Normalizing relations with the USSR was a significant issue in the 1932 presidential campaign between Hoover and Franklin Delano Roosevelt, who supported recognition. After FDR took office, he moved quickly, signing an agreement with Soviet Foreign Minister Maxim Litvinov that established diplomatic relations. William Bullitt, Special Assistant Secretary of State for Soviet affairs, was instrumental in the negotiations, and he was appointed as the first American ambassador to Moscow in 1934. (Bullitt's wife was none other than Louise Bryant, John Reed's former girlfriend.) A new era in Soviet-American relations had begun.

One of the factors that made the establishment of stronger relations with the Soviet government look more attractive to American politicians was the rise of Hitler in Germany. In January 1933, Hitler became the German chancellor. To many American intellectuals, Communism came to be seen as an important bulwark against the growth of fascism in Europe. In Asia, the USSR was also regarded as an important obstacle to the expansionist ambitions of Japan, particularly in Manchuria. For these reasons, there was a tendency among American political and industrial leaders to overlook or minimize the undemocratic and repressive aspects of Stalin's regime, the flagrant disregard for freedoms (of speech, movement, religion) basic to American democracy. Particularly in the early 1930s, Stalin was seen in a more positive light than Lenin, and was admired for his bold economic policies that were rapidly transforming a backward nation of peasants into a major industrial power. At least temporarily, pragmatism took precedence over ideology in the always emotional American attitude toward the USSR, although as news of Stalin's purges of political and cultural dissidents began to reach the West, doubt and wariness grew.

The contradictory and ambivalent feelings most Americans had about the USSR in the 1930s were shared by Hollywood producers and directors and reflected in the "Russia projects" they undertook. In the early 1930s, and particularly after the election of FDR ensured closer official relations with the USSR, several prominent studios tried to develop screenplays dealing with the human dimensions behind the dynamic story of the country's accelerated industrialization campaign. There was something in this story that had potential appeal for the American audience, itself dazzled by the marvels of mass production. At MGM, where Thalberg had reigned supreme until a heart attack slowed him down in 1932, others stepped in to continue the work he had begun with Boris Pilnyak. Frank Capra, then a rising young director, prepared another treatment of what was called "Soviet" for MGM that was submitted on December 13, 1932, not long after the election of FDR. The hero's name—Morgan—is the same as in the treatment proposed to Pilnyak in 1931, but the details are quite different.[1]

The action of "Soviet" takes place at a dam project under construction somewhere in the Soviet heartland. Morgan, an American engineer, has been brought in to provide technical assistance. Soon he becomes romantically involved with Anna, one of the laborers, for whom he is in competition with a co-worker named Grinko. Grinko warns Anna that "the American is here today—gone tomorrow. . . . He is not their kind. There is a great gulf between them—and no good can come out of any attachment to him."[2] In a scene in a Russian steambath, Grinko and Morgan tease each other about Anna, slapping each other with birch switches in traditional fashion. Blinded by the steam, Morgan is pushed outdoors unclothed, to the great delight of the workers, in a piece of slapstick comedy. Anna attempts to convert Morgan to Communism, urging him to understand the "holiness of labor," but he only wants to "see her in fine clothes with some jewels." "Don't you see—what you are describing to me is what I hate!" she replies. "Thousands of my people have been killed in fighting just that!"[3] After Grinko divorces his wife, he marries Anna, although she is actually in love with Morgan. The dramatic climax comes when a train crashes at the construction site, blocking the water escape tunnel and threatening a devastating flood. Overcoming his jealousy, Morgan at the last moment comes to Grinko's assistance, helping to save the dam and thereby maintaining the crazy schedule of the Five-Year Plan. Their love of labor has overcome their personal enmity.

Capra's treatment was expanded into a complete script by Jules Furthman and drastically revised several times in early 1933. (Twenty years later, Furthman was the screenwriter for another Russia picture, Josef von Sternberg's *Jet Pilot*.) In the first revision, Morgan and Anna "meet cute" on the train from Berlin to Moscow, and then turn up together at the office of Electrostroy, the agency in charge of dam construction. At first, Anna ridicules Morgan as a pathetic, decadent capitalist with too much baggage: "this silly fashion plate who was going to conquer Electrostroy with a suitcase full of women's silk stockings and a dozen bottles of French perfume." Morgan makes it known that he has no use for Communism and has come only to do a job for which he is being paid, although he refuses to live in the luxurious bungalow offered to him and instead chooses to stay in the dormitory, where his room adjoins Anna's. In a later script revision, Anna accepts silk stockings from Morgan: "The temptation is too great. She puts them on, and examines her legs. They look much prettier. It's the first time she's worn silk. She picks up the bottle of perfume, and smells it. These Americans certainly have good things."[4]

The seduction/ideological conversion of a Soviet woman through American/capitalist fashion and luxury soon became a standard feature of Hollywood screenplays about the USSR—most obviously in *Ninotchka* (more about that shortly) and its various spin-offs (the best one is even called *Silk Stockings*). But here, Anna converts from her Communist principles at the end, after Grinko has perished in the flood (instead of surviving as in the original Capra treatment). "Take me with you, Morgan, I'll go anywhere—I don't care, but don't leave me here, it's too terrible, too cruel, you were right, we're crazy, we're animals, lower than animals." She then breaks down and buries her head in his chest. Morgan replies heroically: "Sure you're going with me, but we got to stick around a while, I'm going to finish this job, not for these heels, but for Grinko." Final fade-out. In yet another version, Morgan leaves Anna behind in Moscow: "The last year of my stay in Russia has been the happiest of my life. I will never forget you." A shot of Anna's "sad yearning face" ends the film.[5]

The rewrites of the "Soviet" script provide a graphic illustration of Hollywood's uncertainty over how to treat life in the USSR at this transitional moment in Soviet-American relations. As always in a Hollywood screenplay, a romance had to be at the center of the story. In this and subsequent screenplays about the USSR, an American man becomes involved with a Soviet woman, and the course of their relationship symbolizes the ideological relationship between masculine good-guy America and vulnerable, romantic "mother" Russia. He "rescues" her from the fate of living under Communism, overcoming her initial resistance. As time went on, this paradigm became more stable, but in the early 1930s, there was sufficient doubt about the respective virtues of Communism and capitalism to make screenwriters hesitate.

In the end, Mayer at MGM apparently considered that "Soviet" was insufficiently commercial, or perhaps too politically sensitive. Personal rivalry with Thalberg, who had promoted the project, may also have played a role. In any case, the film was never made, although there was considerable discussion of the project in the industry. This is obvious from an unsigned letter sent to Will H. Hays of the Production Code Administration, dated

February 3, 1933, apparently from one of his staff members, reporting on new scripts received for evaluation.

> This is the modern Russian story on which the studio has been working for a great many months. The complete script is not yet in, but from what we have read it appears to present no particular difficulties as the story is the old formula about building the dam, which has been used in action pictures from time immemorial. The treatment is pretty well devoid of propaganda for or against the Soviets, confining itself to the triangular relationship of a rough Soviet commissar (probably to be played by Wallace Beery) who is determined that the dam shall be built on time, a young American engineer who has come over for the purpose of supervising the building, and the commissar's Russian girl-secretary, with whom both are in love. The problems so far glimpsed seem to be purely details of censorship, with no concern from the standpoint of policy so far.[6]

Lewis Milestone also tried unsuccessfully to develop a project for Columbia with a contemporary Soviet setting in the early 1930s. With screenwriter Laurence Stallings, he adapted a novel by the Soviet writer Ilya Erenburg, *The Rise and Fall of Nikolai Kurbov,* retitled as *Red Square.* The hero is a former revolutionary who becomes disillusioned with the introduction of limited capitalism during the 1920s, with a final scene at a vast construction site in the early 1930s. But Harry Cohn, president of Columbia, reportedly rejected the script, telling Milestone: "Too much social stuff and not enough sex. This is no time for throwing money down the drain."[7]

Even Leon Trotsky, one of the creators of the Soviet Communist state, could not persuade the Hollywood bosses to make a film on a Soviet subject. Having lost out to Stalin in the bitter power struggle that followed the death of Vladimir Lenin in 1924, Trotsky, a brilliant political and cultural thinker and writer, had been expelled from the USSR as an undesirable character in 1929, and had been living in Turkey, France, and Norway. His last stop was Mexico, where he lived from 1937 until his assassination by a Stalinist agent in 1940. In 1936, while he was in Norway, Trotsky wrote a letter to a friend with Hollywood connections asking if there would be interest in a film about the Russian Revolution. This letter was forwarded to Hollywood agent Paul Kohner, who represented numerous Russian émigré actors. Kohner sent it to Edwin Knopf of MGM on September 21, 1936, with a note:

> Attached please find copy of Mr. Trotzki's letter. The gentleman to whom it is addressed, Mr. Marx, asks if we would be interested in having Mr. Trotzki write a story.
>
> The letter seems to indicate the recent reports that Trotzki is planning a counter revolution seem to be rather exaggerated and that he is more interested in earning some American Dollars.[8]

In his letter to Mr. Marx, dated July 18, 1936, Trotsky expresses enthusiasm for the idea of a big-budget Hollywood extravaganza:

> Years ago I had told various representatives from Hollywood how surprised I was that no intelligent film producer could be found with foresight enough to reproduce and preserve the drama of the Russian Revolution, not only for its contemporary value but also for future generations. Of what great value to our culture today would a film be that shows the French Revolution as nearly historically true as possible! Already much time has been lost—the participants and eyewitnesses are dying out, the cities and villages are changing, etc. But as during the years of great prosperity no great producer could be found to do this, it seems rather hopeless to me to find someone for this idea now, during these years of depression. Just because the film should not be propaganda—but a historical film in the real sense of the word—it would demand great expenditures.[9]

★   Trotsky never made it to Hollywood, or even to the United States (he was denied a visa), but other Russian émigrés with experience in theater and film rather than politics continued to stream into Los Angeles in the 1930s. Especially in the aftermath of the Depression, Hollywood seemed to offer the most promise for steady employment and future security. Most of these new arrivals never became famous, or even developed significant careers, but there were some notable exceptions: Akim Tamiroff, Vladimir Sokoloff, Maria Ouspenskaya, Mischa Auer (he arrived a bit earlier, in 1928), Gregory Ratoff, and Leonid Kinskey, to name a few.

Another Russian newcomer to Hollywood was Anna Sten, who starred in a major 1934 screen adaptation of Leo Tolstoy's novel *Resurrection*, entitled more simply *We Live Again*.

Tolstoy's novels *Anna Karenina* and *Resurrection* were particular favorites with Hollywood producers and directors. A 1918 version of *Resurrection* starred Pauline Frederick as Katyusha, the serf girl who is seduced and impregnated by a selfish young nobleman who only later discovers the results of his actions and repents. Dolores del Rio took the same role in a 1927 feature.

But the most extravagant version of *Resurrection* was Goldwyn's *We Live Again.* It was intended to be launching pad for the career of Anna Sten, born in Kiev with the much less euphonious real name of Annel Stenskaya Sudakevich. Like so many of the Russian actors who ended up in Hollywood, she had acted in Russia with the Moscow Art Theater, then worked in the film industry in the USSR and Germany. (In the 1920s, Berlin was a regular stop for Russians bound for America; they waited here to receive visas.) In 1933, Goldwyn brought Sten to the United States in the hope that he could turn her into another star with the same mysterious foreign appeal of the Swedish Greta Garbo or the German Marlene Dietrich. *We Live Again* was Sten's second film. Eventually her repeated failures at the box office discouraged even Goldwyn, and Sten became known in the business as "Goldwyn's folly."

Playing opposite Sten as Dmitri was the Wisconsin-born Fredric March (who would play another Russian aristocrat, Count Vronsky, in *Anna Karenina* on screen the following year). Dmitri delivers some updated lines that are definitely not in the Tolstoy original, such as "Russia's in a pretty rotten condition—we're going to have a Revolution if we don't watch out." Here, Dmitri comes across as a nice boy with democratic and capitalistic sentiments, attempting to enlighten the rather dim peasants, including Katyusha, to whom he remarks with unnecessary candor: "You're only beautiful, you're not bright."

Frederic March had already worked on another film (the classic *Dr. Jekyll and Mr. Hyde*) with the director of *We Live Again,* the Armenian/Russian émigré Rouben Mamoulian (1897–1987), a distinguished Broadway stage and musical director before he got to Hollywood. Born into an Armenian family in the Georgian capital of Tiflis (Tbilisi), and trained briefly by the Russian master stage director Evgeny Vakhtangov back in Moscow, Mamoulian had directed *Queen Christina* (starring Greta Garbo) the previous year. For *We Live Again,* Mamoulian had assembled a crew that was something of a family affair for the Russian émigrés. (Although Mamoulian was ethnically Armenian, his cultural identity was to a large degree Rus-

sian and he spoke fluent Russian.) The sets were co-designed by Sergei
Soudeikin, third husband of the woman who later married composer Igor
Stravinsky. Soudeikin also worked with Mamoulian on stage projects, and
eventually became the principal set designer for the Metropolitan Opera.
Nina Koshetz (1891–1965), a well-known Russian operatic soprano who
had conducted an affair with the composer Sergei Rachmaninoff before
emigrating from Russia to the United States, led the chorus in the Russian
Easter midnight mass scene. (Koshetz later settled in Hollywood, and appeared in several films, including *Algiers,* with Charles Boyer, becoming
famous for her enormous size and culinary talents.)

Like most Hollywood depictions of nineteenth-century Russian life (and
of twentieth-century Russian life for that matter), *We Live Again* features lots
of singing and dancing. The film opens with a scene of peasants working the
fields as they sing contentedly, in the romanticized style of the opening
scene of Tchaikovsky's opera *Eugene Onegin.* This was a work that Mamoulian
knew well and had even directed on stage during his tenure at the American
Opera Company at the Eastman School of Music in Rochester, New York,
immediately after his arrival in America in 1923. The musical direction is by
Alfred Newman, just beginning his prolific career as a film composer, and
incorporates generous quotations from Nikolai Rimsky-Korsakov's *Russian
Easter Overture.* It is during the elaborate Orthodox Easter liturgy that Dmitri
first feels his overwhelming sexual attraction for Katyusha. Years later,
Dmitri's spiritual awakening occurs when he recalls that music, playing the
chords on the piano, and resolving to make right the terrible wrong he did to
Katyusha in his careless youth. There is also an extended sequence showing a gypsy ensemble serenading the self-satisfied young officers. At
times, in fact, the film threatens to become a sort of symphonic poem or
musical, without the moral grit and urgency crucial to the Tolstoy novel.

The scenes celebrating the joys of the simple rural life (an important
theme in the late works of Tolstoy) seem to show the influence of the films
of Soviet directors, especially the Ukrainian Alexander Dovzhenko, whose
masterpiece *Earth* (1930), about life in a farming village on the eve of
Soviet mechanization, uses strikingly similar symbolic imagery of rain,
ripening fruit (a symbol of Katyusha's pregnancy), and farm animals.
Given Mamoulian's erudition and intellectual curiosity, it is likely that he
had seen the Soviet films of Eisenstein and Dovzhenko, which were well
known in Hollywood.

In the new spirit of diplomatic relations, *We Live Again* conveys a certain sympathy and good-natured curiosity about this alien culture. There are no evil Russians here, and no obvious stereotypes. The film's message could even be construed as sympathetic toward Communism, which swept away the inequalities of the Russian class system, since the appealing character of the powerless peasant Katyusha is shown as a victim of a cruel and selfish ruling aristocracy. Later, however, after his conversion and decision to save Katyusha, Dmitri could be seen as a predecessor of Bolshevik revolutionaries, many of whom were also members of the upper classes who had experienced a crisis of conscience over the unfair Russian social and economic system. In the last shot, Dmitri and Katyusha are marching off happily together in the sunset to Siberia (to which Katyusha has been sentenced for prostitution and theft) as a choir sings off-camera the chant of the Easter liturgy: "*Khristos voskres iz mertvykh, smertiyu smert' poprav . . .*" ("Christ has risen from the dead, having conquered death through death").

Mamoulian's biographer Mark Spergel has called *We Live Again* "mannered and lifeless," and the film did not succeed with either critics or audiences.[10] Goldwyn was so dissatisfied that he severed his creative relationship with Mamoulian. The problem, as with a number of Mamoulian's films, is that any sense of reality is sacrificed in the pursuit of a perfect visual or theatrical image, robbing the story of its psychological power. The Russia of *We Live Again* is the Russia painted on the top of a lacquer box, shiny and inert.

But for Joseph H. Breen, head of the Production Code Administration, the censoring body set up by the Hollywood establishment to avoid moral scandals, *We Live Again* dealt in exemplary fashion with delicate content, as he wrote in a letter to his boss Will Hays: "We are happy to report that Mr. Goldwyn has, we believe, a splendid picture in this remake of the old classic. Though dealing with a sex affair and its attendant consequences, the story has been handled with such fine emphasis on the moral values of repentance and retribution, as to emerge with a definite spiritual quality. We feel that this picture could, in fact, *serve as a model* for the proper treatment of the element of illicit sex in pictures."[11]

★ *We Live Again* was not the only ambitious film depicting life in nineteenth-century Russia that was produced in the aftermath of the establishment of diplomatic relations between the United States and the USSR in 1933. Two were released in 1935: MGM's *Anna Karenina* and Columbia's *Crime and Punishment* (described in chapter 1).

A passionate tale of adultery set amid the glittering world of the late-nineteenth-century Russian aristocracy, *Anna Karenina* was transferred to the screen numerous times, beginning as early as 1915, when Betty Nansen took the title role. In 1927, in an MGM version entitled *Love,* Greta Garbo, just beginning her American career, was cast as Anna, opposite her real-life lover John Gilbert as Vronsky. The 1935 MGM *Anna* again featured Garbo, but this time talking, opposite Fredric March as Vronsky and with Basil Rathbone as a diabolical Karenin, Anna's chilly and aloof spouse. David Selznick produced, Clarence Brown directed, and Count Andrey Tolstoy is listed as a consultant.

Playing the roles of Russian characters became something of a specialty for the Swedish Garbo. She also appeared as the temperamental ballerina Grushinskaya in the 1932 *Grand Hotel* (the film in which she uttered her trademark line, with a sad, tired sigh, "I want to be alone"), and would create one of her greatest performances in the title role of *Ninotchka* in 1939. For Hollywood casting directors, accents were fairly interchangeable, as long as the English sounded nonnative, which helps to explain why Garbo and the Egyptian Omar Shariff played Russians and why Russian émigré actors like Akim Tamiroff and Vladimir Sokoloff often played Spaniards.

The prudish censorship imposed upon the content of all Hollywood features by the Production Code Administration made it very difficult for the director Clarence Brown and his screenwriters to adapt the story of an adulteress who abandons her child for her lover. (Censorship problems also plagued the filming of *We Live Again.*) Selznick wrote to Joseph Breen of the Production Code that, "As to the physical contact between Anna and Vronsky, I don't know how love scenes can be played, particularly in a story of this kind, without physical contact."[12] Selznick complained that, "We had to eliminate everything that could even remotely be classified as a passionate love scene." The battle with the censors cast a pall over the filming, and was all too evident in the finished product, which is sorely lacking in the grand and heated passion that drives Tolstoy's novel. In their scenes together, Anna and Vronsky hardly seem to know each other, and the big seduction scene is so proper and buttoned-up that it is difficult to understand why Anna is leaving her husband. In many ways, the urbane Basil

Rathbone seems more appealing. Hollywood producers, directors, and designers often believed that the way to convey a sense of Russian aristocratic life to an American audience was to imitate Britishness, both in language (upper-class British accents proliferate in Hollywood films about the Russian aristocracy) and in behavior. This approach drains the passion out of the 1935 *Anna Karenina,* which lacks scope and drama, confined as it is to drawing rooms and vestibules populated by heavily clothed snobs.

One of the most "Russian" aspects of Brown's film is the borrowing by composer Herbert Stothart of a melody composed by Tchaikovsky (for the song "None but the Lonely Heart," words by the German poet Goethe). This melody is the foundation of the film's score, and is associated primarily with the love between Anna and her son, whom she must abandon when she runs off with Vronsky.

Indeed, Hollywood producers and directors found Tchaikovsky's popular music congenial from the earliest years of the movie industry, and not only for films depicting nineteenth-century Russia. In the silent era, his music was used directly as a source for movie hall pianists, who played excerpts to convey particular recognizable emotions as accompaniment or counterpoint to the action on screen. (In the 2005 film *Aviator,* about movie pioneer Howard Hughes, we hear an excerpt from Tchaikovsky's Sixth Symphony as Hughes is screening one of his early films.) Later, Tchaikovsky's music was heavily imitated by many of the masters of film music, from Max Steiner to Dmitri Tiomkin (himself a Russian émigré) to John Williams. In the silent era, classical music was used because for the most part it was in the public domain and could be used free of charge. The score for D. W. Griffith's *Birth of a Nation* (1915), put together by Joseph Carl Breil, includes excerpts from a number of familiar classical pieces, including Tchaikovsky's dramatic and highly visual *1812 Overture.* Themes from Tchaikovsky's orchestral works also figured prominently in early anthologies prepared for silent movie hall pianists, such as Erno Rappe's 1924 collection *Encyclopedia of Music for Pictures and Motion Picture Moods.*

The makers of a much more recent version of *Anna Karenina,* directed by Bernard Rose for Warner Brothers and released in 1997, also turned to Tchaikovsky to provide the necessary atmosphere and emotional heat. The distinguished conductor Sir Georg Solti was asked to compile a score from the works of Tchaikovsky and another favorite of Hollywood filmmakers,

Sergei Rachmaninoff. The crucial scene of Anna's seduction by Vronsky begins over the Rachmaninoff Elegie Op. 3, No. 1, for piano, and ends over an
excerpt from the last movement of the Sixth Symphony (*Pathetique*). We see
the winter ice breaking up on the river Neva that flows through St. Petersburg, an obvious symbol of the long-awaited "thawing" of Anna's heart by
Vronsky. Here, the Tchaikovsky sound is also historically appropriate,
since *Anna Karenina* was published in 1877, during the height of Tchaikovsky's career and popularity in Russia. At times, in fact, this version feels
like an extended music video. In its graphic treatment of the story's sexu-
ality this *Anna* is worlds away from the overly polite tone of the 1935 version; Sophie Marceau as Anna and Sean Bean as Vronsky take (rather, rip)
their clothes off and revel in the biological aspects of the story so important
to Tolstoy. Anna's miscarriage and resulting illness is displayed in bloody
detail, and the film possesses a compelling physicality.

Director Rose also makes a very interesting artistic choice concerning
the problems of the Russian language itself. While in most Hollywood representations of nineteenth-century Russia, Russians speak in aristocratic
British English, here, Rose has the aristocratic characters speak to each
other in English, but to the servants and to pets in Russian—the servants
also respond in Russian to the aristocrats. Along with the on-location filming in St. Petersburg and Moscow, this makes for a very vivid, imaginative
and more authentic result. The action bursts out of the drawing room onto
the streets and parks and fields.

★   By the 1930s, a significant number of Russian émigré actors were
working in Hollywood. Because of the Russian Revolution, all had experienced difficulties and dislocation in their lives. Akim Tamiroff (1899–1972)
is a good example.

Like most Russian émigré actors who appeared regularly in Hollywood
feature films, Tamiroff never became a household name. He never got the
girl. Always the sidekick but never (well, almost never) the leading man,
Tamiroff (like Vladimir Sokoloff and Gregory Ratoff) excelled in roles requiring strong ethnic identity. In the course of a prolific and steady Hollywood career that lasted for nearly forty years, Tamiroff was a one-man
United Nations, playing characters of a bewildering variety of nationalities: Indian (*Lives of a Bengal Lancer*), Mexican (*Tortilla Flat, Touch of Evil*),
Hungarian (*The Way of All Flesh*, one of his only leading-man roles), Span-

FIGURE 8.

Akim Tamiroff. 1938. Paramount Pictures publicity photo.

ish (*For Whom the Bell Tolls, Bridge of San Luis Rey, Queen Christina*), Chinese (*The General Died at Dawn*), Greek (*Ocean's Eleven, High, Wide and Handsome*), Italian (*Hotel Paradiso*), Balinese (*Honeymoon in Bali*), French (*After the Fox*), Polish (*Me and the Colonel, New York Town, Mr. Arkadin*), and, yes, even Russian (*Anastasia, Romanoff and Juliet, Great Catherine*).

Some of Tamiroff's most memorable characters were those of unfixed nationality, who speak in an ever-changing and free-floating melange of languages. As the drunken and demented cook in *Topkapi*, a jewel heist caper, Tamiroff pursues an English expatriate (Peter Ustinov) from Greece to Istanbul, spouting a hilarious and largely incomprehensible mixture of Greek, Turkish, Russian, German, and English, ever on the outlook for "*russiche spies*" and for opportunities to plant a kiss on a reluctant Ustinov. This same linguistic uncertainty is used to more serious and existential effect in Jean-Luc Godard's dystopian 1965 fantasy *Alphaville*, where Tamiroff plays the dying philosopher Henry Dickson, who speaks in turn in French, English, and Russian, as if searching for an identity after having wandered mistakenly into this gray post-nationalist totalitarian world from the "outlands."

And yet of all the Russian émigré actors active in Hollywood, the "jolly but menacing-looking" Tamiroff had one of the most enduring and varied careers. Cecil B. DeMille said that Tamiroff had "a telepathic sixth sense for knowing what a director wants of him, and how to interpret a part to obtain the utmost comedy and pathos." That his performances also resonated in the wider intellectual arena seems clear from evidence in two classics of American post–World War II literature: J. D. Salinger's story "Uncle Wiggily in Connecticut" (included in his 1953 collection *Nine Stories*) and Walker Percy's novel *The Moviegoer*, published in 1961. In "Uncle Wiggily in Connecticut," a caustic tale of a drunken reunion of two female WASPy college roommates, Eloise, unhappily married and still mourning the death of her one true love, repeatedly refers to her fondness for Akim Tamiroff as she becomes increasingly intoxicated and chats with her girlfriend Mary Jane, both of them college dropouts.

"Akim Tamiroff. He's in the movies. He always says, 'You make beeg joke—hah?' I love him . . . ," Eloise says.[13]

Here, the reference to Tamiroff and his un-American accent seems to symbolize Eloise's longing for a more adventurous existence than the outwardly prosperous but inwardly desperate life she leads in the suburbs with a dull husband and a bratty, annoying daughter. This story was published during the Korean War, at a time when anything with Russian associations was considered dangerous, tantalizing, and risqué.

In *The Moviegoer*, the first-person narrator, Jack, a Korean War veteran, almost obsessively compares real life with the movies and finds it wanting. For his disabled half-brother, he also imitates the mannerisms of various Hollywood stars. On one occasion, he "does" Tamiroff, as Spyros, the ex-con mobster mastermind of the scheme to rob Las Vegas casinos in the ratpack film *Ocean's Eleven* (1960). (As it happens, *Ocean's Eleven* was directed by fellow Russian Lewis Milestone, with whom Tamiroff had a long artistic and personal relationship. When *Ocean's Eleven* was remade in 2001, the role of the Tamiroff character was significantly reduced.) "During my last year in college I discovered that I was picking up the mannerisms of Akim Tamiroff, the only useful thing, in fact, that I learned in the entire four years," Jack observes.[14]

Yes, Tamiroff was the eternal sidekick, the usually amusing groomsman rather than the groom. His breakthrough role (for which he was nominated for an Oscar for best supporting actor) was playing second fiddle to Gary Cooper in *The General Died at Dawn*—directed by Milestone—in 1936. Cooper had met Tamiroff several years before, and became so impressed with Tamiroff's craft, dedication, and versatility that he helped him get a seven-year contract at Paramount Pictures in 1933. They appeared again together in *For Whom the Bell Tolls,* a rather wooden 1943 adaptation of Hemingway's Spanish Civil War novel in which Tamiroff (as the partisan Pablo) loses the girl (Ingrid Bergman) and the moral high ground to Cooper, and engages in the sort of drunken hell-raising behavior that increasingly became his trademark. It was for his role in *For Whom the Bell Tolls* that Tamiroff received his second Oscar nomination. Other sidekick roles included attendant to John Gilbert's dashing suitor in *Queen Christina* (directed by Rouben Mamoulian), hanger-on to a miscast Spencer Tracy in *Tortilla Flat,* financial advisor to Yul Brynner in *Anastasia,* and corrupt crony to Orson Welles in *Touch of Evil.* Welles also cast Tamiroff as Sancho Panza, the ultimate sidekick, in his unfinished film *Don Quixote.*

So, yes, Tamiroff was a sidekick—but a thinking man's sidekick, and one with a wicked way with accents that set him apart from the crowd.

In an obituary for Tamiroff, *Newsweek* said he had "the thickest Russian accent this side of Minsk."[15] The *Los Angeles Examiner* reflected the confusion over the ever-changing national identity of the characters he played when it stated that he was a "Russian mountaineer" in *For Whom the Bell Tolls*—but that would have been Pavel rather than Pablo.[16] As for Tamiroff, he also knew that it was his accent (or rather, accents) that was his "golden goose": "Everybody says my accent is worth a million dollars. . . . Sure, it's all due to that funny way I talk, and to think I worked so hard and spent so much money trying to get rid of that accent."[17] After he signed his contract with Paramount, executives there actually discouraged him from trying to learn English better: "You do that and you're fixed."

It should come as no surprise to learn that behind the frequently drunk, disorderly, and inarticulate façade of Tamiroff's screen persona lay a much more complex and disciplined reality. Tamiroff was famous for his rigorous, almost fanatical preparation for each role, no matter how small. His wife, the actress and fellow Russian Tamara Shayne, once described how he practiced for hundreds of hours with a bullwhip (he had to flick a cigarette out of someone's mouth) for his role in *Union Pacific*.[18] The extremely demanding and discriminating Orson Welles, with whom Tamiroff became friends, had great admiration for his acting skill and used him in three completed films: *Mr. Arkadin, The Trial,* and *Touch of Evil.*

Tamiroff had the kind of training and credentials that Hollywood directors and producers of the 1930s and '40s found very impressive: nine years of study with Stanislavsky as a member of the Moscow Art Theater troupe. Born in Baku in 1899, the son of an oilman who died when Tamiroff was only four, Tamiroff received his big break when he was admitted to the MAT school in 1918. According to one of several versions of this event, it was the director Richard Boleslawski who came to Baku to audition potential candidates and discovered Tamiroff. "You have interesting eyes," Boleslawski allegedly told him. "You look as if you are suffering. Please read these lines for me."[19] All versions of the story agree that Tamiroff went to Moscow and became a member of the MAT troupe. In the early 1920s he went on tour with the company to Europe, playing the Cat in Maeterlinck's play "The Bluebird."

As a student of Stanislavsky, Tamiroff received a very thorough grounding in all aspects of acting technique, which surely helps to explain his versatility and legendary professionalism. For the many different kinds of characters he portrayed, Tamiroff relied heavily upon observation: "An actor must first be a shrewd observer of humanity," he said. "Then he must be able to project his observation when he is called upon."[20] Even so, he was never too solemn about his MAT training and the idea of psychological immersion in a dramatic role. In *Anastasia,* he says off-handedly (as the banker Chernov): "As the great Stanislavsky used to say, when an actor believes he is the character he is playing, fire him." And of course not all classically trained actors were able to make the transition from stage to film, as Tamiroff was well aware. "I call a camera 'The Box' and it can be a friend or a foe. If the Box likes you, you're a success in pictures. If it doesn't like you, give up quick."[21]

It was the MAT tour to the United States in 1923 that changed Tamiroff's life. Like several other members of that touring troupe who would later gravitate to movies, he decided to remain in America rather than return to the chaos and privation of the post–Civil War USSR. Tamiroff joined the cast of the popular long-running cabaret-style revue *La Chauve-Souris* (The Bat), his home base for several years. Later, he created the American Academy of Stage Makeup, where he passed on the knowledge of stage makeup that he had learned from Stanislavsky. But whatever money he had accumulated he lost in the 1929 stock market crash. Many years later, in an interview, Tamiroff claimed that he even had to go to work as a streetcar driver (working as a streetcar driver is a standard feature in many show-business immigration narratives) to make ends meet, but that his new wife Tamara Shayne objected. She went to work as a waitress so he could study English, and in the evenings he would sneak into the movies when the ticket attendant went on break—"I became big specialist in movie endings."[22]

Like many other stage actors during the Depression, Tamiroff and Shayne (she appeared in small roles in numerous films, including *Song of Russia* and *Romanoff and Juliet*) decided to head west (allegedly in a vintage Model-T Ford) to the opportunities in Hollywood. Tamiroff later called the first few years there "the toughest period in my life."[23] After a few unbilled bit parts, he made his debut in *Okay, America* in 1932, and came to the attention of Gary Cooper, who helped to get him a Paramount contract. The two appeared together in a series of army pictures, beginning with *Lives of a Bengal Lancer* (1934), about the British in India, in which Tamiroff plays the Emir of Gopal opposite Cooper's stiff-upper-lip Anglo-Saxon hero; *The General Died at Dawn* (1936), with Tamiroff wearing a rubber mask as the evil General Yang, and Cooper as a mercenary out for adventure; and *For Whom the Bell Tolls* (1943). Cooper and Tamiroff made a perfect pair: the strong-silent type from Montana, blond, tall and slim contrasted with the short, stocky, and hopelessly garrulous, darkly ethnic type. Don Quixote and Sancho Panza. This same sort of relationship is obvious in *Anastasia* between the erect, taciturn, and ethereal Yul Brynner and the earthy, verbose, and nervous Tamiroff.

In *Touch of Evil* (1958), a complex and opaque film with considerable intellectual pretensions and an inventive score by Henry Mancini, Tamiroff's persona acquires a more sinister edge. In his greatest role, he again "plays Mexican," as "Uncle Joe" Grande, head of the Grande family clan in a corrupt Mexican border town, opposite Orson Welles as a burnt-out police chief. "Uncle Joe" controls the drug traffic, most often with the chief's cooperation. Charlton Heston also plays Mexican, a narcotics investigator on a honeymoon with his lovely new American wife (Janet Leigh). Marlene Dietrich, in a memorable cameo role, is the madame of the local whorehouse where much of the illegal dealing goes on, to the accompaniment of demented player piano music. With a pencil-thin mustache, Tamiroff exudes the evil of the film's title, sending his nephew Pancho to torment Janet Leigh in a motel (Hitchcock would stage a similar scene in *Psycho* two years later) as Heston tries to investigate a suspicious murder. Tamiroff's relationship to the gigantic Orson Welles is yet another example of the big guy–little guy dynamic, which achieves its climax in the scene of Uncle Joe's grisly murder—by hanging—by one of the chief's men. Welles cast Tamiroff in another film, his highly stylized and mysterious *Mr. Arkadin* (also known as *Confidential Report*), made in Spain and released in 1955, as a Pole living in the ruins of postwar Berlin.

Tamiroff often said that he considered himself a comedian, and his performances on screen do frequently make us laugh. But they also make us uneasy by veering over the line from comedy into pathos and pain. Pablo and Chernov and Uncle Joe Grande are outsiders, and they harbor resentment and bitterness toward those to whom they must cater, those with sexual or economic or physical or perceived ethnic superiority. As a Russian émigré in anti-Soviet America, Akim Tamiroff could understand the role of outsider quite well indeed. Like many Hollywood Russian emigres, Tamiroff chose to leave the United States for a while in the early 1950s, during the period when Senator Joseph McCarthy and the HUAC were investigating Russian and Communist influence in the film industry.

He made films in France, England, Spain, Monte Carlo, Munich, and Italy, but returned to Hollywood and appeared on television in *Naked City, The Defenders, The Man from U.N.C.L.E.*, and *The Rifleman* before retiring to Palm Springs in 1968.

★   No less versatile than Akim Tamiroff, Vladimir Sokoloff (1889–1962) once estimated that he played thirty-five different nationalities during his fifty-year acting career, appearing in more than a hundred films. Like Tamiroff, Sokoloff, the son of a Moscow high school teacher, studied with Stanislavsky and appeared with the Moscow Art Theater in his youth. In 1914, he was a founding member of the Moscow Kamerny Theater, which continued to perform throughout the difficult years of World War I and the Russian Revolution. Small and exceptionally agile, Sokoloff was particularly noted for his portrayal of "clowns, buffoons, cuckold husbands and humorous servants."[24] With the Kamerny Theater, Sokoloff went on tour to Germany, where he was discovered in Berlin in 1923 by Max Reinhardt, the great director and impresario, who brought him on tour to the United States in 1927. In 1926, he made the first of several German films, and later appeared in French films (including the original *Mayerling*) before eventually making his way to Hollywood.

Sokoloff's American film debut as the French painter Cézanne in *The Life of Emile Zola* (1937), directed by Paul Muni, was very well received, and he never lacked for work after that. The *Los Angeles Times* labeled him an actor "certainly set for a large future." Sokoloff also continued to appear occasionally on Broadway, and even directed in a small theater, The Beechwood Players, in Hollywood. In an appreciation published in *Films in Review* just after his death, it was noted that Sokoloff "was a character actor who projected the meek humility of the gentle innocent. He was never craven, but neither was he ever resolute, and the script almost always handed him the short end of the stick."[25] In interviews, Sokoloff downplayed the Stanislavsky influence on his work and claimed that, before he died in 1938, Stanislavsky told him to "adapt and adjust. No longer accept my method letter for letter. The world is changing. Acting is changing and it will change even more."[26] Sokoloff's acting skills and versatility made it possible for him to work extensively not only in film, but also in television—he even appeared in several episodes of *The Twilight Zone*.

Like Akim Tamiroff and other Russian actors in Hollywood, Sokoloff frequently appeared in films where a Spanish accent was required. He, Tamiroff, Mikhail Rasumny, and Fyodor Chaliapin, Jr., all appeared as Spanish Civil War partisans in the 1943 screen version of Ernest Hemingway's novel *For Whom the Bell Tolls;* Sokoloff reprised the role of Anselmo in a television version some years later. In one of his last films, Sokoloff played the wise Old Man of the sleepy Mexican village in *The Magnificent Seven,* in a cast that also included Yul Brynner.

Sokoloff "played Russian" in several films. In *Comrade X* (1940), with Clark Gable and Hedy Lamarr, he was cast in the small role of the evil Soviet Commissar Michael Bastakoff, who throws off some notable English malapropisms in a man-to-man talk with Gable, playing an American journalist: "As you say in your country, I want to play ball on you, to put my cards under the table." During World War II, when pro-Soviet films set in Russia were in fashion, Sokoloff and other Russian émigré actors were much in demand. In *Mission to Moscow,* he plays the ruthless Soviet President Mikhail Kalinin as a kindly, reasonable man, while in *Song of Russia* he is cast as the selfless director of the local music school in the Russian village where the heroine first learned to play the piano. Sokoloff returned to his Russian roots in his very last film, *Taras Bulba,* playing a Cossack. Never one to sacrifice authenticity, Sokoloff did the horse-riding himself, and was thrown from his mount during filming in Argentina, incurring painful injuries that may have contributed to the fatal stroke he suffered just a few months later.

★   Another Russian émigré actor who first found success in the movies in the 1930s was Mischa Auer (1905–1967), whose real-life biography reads like something even a studio public relations office would have trouble inventing. Born as Mischa Ounskowski in St. Petersburg, his father was a Russian naval officer and his mother the daughter of the celebrated violinist Leopold Auer, the father of the brilliant modern school of Russian violin playing. (Auer's students included Jascha Heifetz, Nathan Milstein, and Mischa Elman.) After little Mischa's father died when Mischa was only three, he was taken in by Auer, who renamed him Mischa Auer, and raised on an estate outside the Tsarist capital of St. Petersburg.

After the 1917 Revolution, Leopold Auer emigrated to the United States, and Mischa was separated from his mother and sent to Siberia with a group of children who were eventually forced to roam the countryside in search of food. Finally reunited with his mother, Mischa Auer lived with her for a while during the Civil War under British protection in southern Russia, but his mother contracted typhus and died. By selling a few jewels she had managed to keep, Mischa was able to get to Italy, where he found a family friend who put him in touch with his grandfather, now in New York. The great violinist brought the teenager to America and enrolled him in the School of Ethical Culture. By the mid-1920s, Mischa Auer was already appearing on stage. A touring theater engagement brought him to Los Angeles in 1928, and he quickly found work doing small roles in film. In later years he said, "It took me three years to make a living in Hollywood, but it's a wonderful country. You can live on oranges and credit, and have a car to boot."[27]

Like Tamiroff and Sokoloff, Auer was usually cast as the sidekick, but he brought a unique, zany comic sensibility to the screen. His breakthrough role was as Carlo, the parasitical "protégé" of Angelica Bullock, the scatterbrained mother of the Bullock household in the 1936 screwball comedy *My Man Godfrey,* starring Carole Lombard and William Powell and directed by Gregory La Cava. To this parable about wealth and image, set in the depths of the Depression, Auer brings a strange and slightly threatening presence, stuffing an orange in his mouth and jumping on the furniture to imitate a gorilla as entertainment for the family and their guests, and providing an amazing display of circus-like physical agility and resourcefulness. Apparently of Russian origin (at least he speaks a few words of Russian to Angelica Bullock at his first appearance on screen in the film, and sings in Russian), Carlo spends most of his time eating with great pleasure, and occasionally sits down at the piano to play the same gypsy/Russian popular song over and over: *Ochi chernye* ("Dark Eyes"). But Carlo only repeats mournfully the same words (*ochi chernye*) as the song progresses—whether he doesn't know the rest of the lyrics, or has forgotten them, is unclear, and a source of considerable laughter among the family and their guests.

Angelica's long-suffering husband finds Carlo intolerable, his ornamental uselessness a symbol of the carelessness and fiscal irresponsibility he continually criticizes in his daughters and wife. Carlo embodies all the empty pretensions of wealth and class, and it is no accident that he is finally forcibly expelled from the Bullocks' apartment ("He made a quick exit through the side window," Mr. Bullock explains, returning to the room

FIGURE 9.

My Man Godfrey. Universal 1936. Mischa Auer as Carlo, imitating a
baboon. Courtesy of the Margaret Herrick Library,
Academy of Motion Picture Arts and Sciences.

after the crash of breaking glass is heard off-screen) just before the noble leading man Godfrey makes his Pygmalion-like transformation from butler to masquerading gentleman and restauranteur. Godfrey—William Powell—may be apparently down on his luck, but he is willing to work honestly to pay his way—unlike the *poseur* and fake artist Carlo. In his portrayal of the oblivious Carlo, who likes nothing better than to strike melodramatic poses by the window, Mischa Auer offers an inspired bit of self-parody, sending up the image of the "artistic" Russian, accustomed to the high life but possessing no practical skills.

Before *My Man Godfrey*, Auer had been cast as a heavy. "I was usually a leering villain, killed in the first reel. Fortunately, in 1936 Gregory La Cava decided I might do as a phony artist, something between a gigolo and dilettante. That's when I hit the Hollywood mother lode. That one role made a comic out of me. I haven't been anything else since. It's paid off very well. Do you wonder that I'm flattered when people say I'm mad?"[28] So successful was Auer in *My Man Godfrey* that Universal signed him to a long-term contract. In subsequent films, he performed variations on the character of Carlo as the Russian ballet master in Frank Capra's film version of *You Can't Take It With You* (1938), as a Russian butler in *Elsa Maxwell's Public Deb #1* (1940), and as a Russian singer and Don Juan in *Twin Beds* (1942), starring Joan Bennett, but he never found another role that resonated with the public the way Carlo (he doesn't even have a last name) did. As the years went on, he worked less and less successfully. Like many other Russian émigré Hollywood actors, Auer chose to live in Europe for an extended period in the 1950s and 60s, and died in Rome.

★   The same year that *My Man Godfrey* made Mischa Auer a star, Maria Ouspenskaya (1876–1949) made her Hollywood screen debut (she had also appeared in a few silent films in Russia before emigrating) in *Dodsworth*. She played the role of the German Baroness von Obersdorf (described in the script as "a small, impoverished, but notably distinguished old lady from Vienna"[29]) in this adaptation of a Sinclair Lewis novel that had also been dramatized on Broadway. So successfully did she establish her screen persona as a cultivated European lady of wisdom and culture that she was nominated for an Oscar for supporting actress. Over the years, Ouspenskaya became increasingly wedded to this image, and was almost always referred to in newspaper stories as "Mme. Ouspenskaya." Similar roles followed over the coming years: Madame Marie von Eln in *King's Row* (1942); Frau Gerhardt in the anti-Nazi drama *The Man I Married* (1940); the Russian ballet teacher Madame Basilova in *Dance Girl Dance* (1940); the dance teacher Madame Olga Kirowa ("impressive, a personality," with "a wintry smile," demanding only the best of her students, according to the script[30]) in *Waterloo Bridge* (1940); Polish Countess Walewska in *Conquest* (1937), where she more than keeps up with Charles Boyer and Greta Garbo. Like Sokoloff and Tamiroff, this Moscow Art Theater actress could easily play various nationalities: Russian, German, French, Austrian, Polish, American—even Indian (the Maharani of Ranchipur in *The Rains Came*), gypsy (*The Wolf Man, Frankenstein Meets the Wolf Man*) and yes, even an Amazon (*Tarzan and the Amazons*).

Having devoted most of her career to the stage, Ouspenskaya made relatively few films, all during the last twelve years of her eventful life. But as Homer Dickens wrote: "There are several reasons why an actress like Mme. Ouspenskaya should be long remembered for just a handful of portrayals. In her films, for example, she would usually have but one or two scenes but she accomplished so much within those brief appearances that she endeared herself to thousands of moviegoers everywhere. Her unusual accent, luminous eyes, and bold Tartar features created an image not easily forgotten."[31] With her plastic face and timeless, Buddha-like features, she was often cast in grandmotherly roles, even as a young actress.

Ouspenskaya's original ambition was to become an opera singer, and she studied briefly at the Warsaw Conservatory before moving on to Moscow and starting to work in the theater. In 1911 she was accepted into the Moscow Art Theater, where she rapidly established herself in the company, playing more than one hundred roles, and even became an instructor. One of her trademark roles with the MAT was as Marina, the infinitely patient and wise servant in *Uncle Vanya,* the embodiment of continuity and perseverance. Like all Russians of her age, she had to deal with severe privations during the period of the Russian Revolution and the Civil War. She told one writer that her early life was "a hard, bitter struggle. We lived through revolutions, famines, typhoid plagues. During one period I never saw my bed for twenty-two days while I nursed friends and family. I saw horses trample civilians to death. Trucks piled high with the corpses of innocent children. Hoodlums attacking women on the streets."[32] In a story published in the *Boston Globe,* Ouspenskaya claimed that she cared for her deathly ill sister and hid from her the news of the collapse of the Tsarist empire, fearful that it would kill her. "This was her most trying role—a part that called for the utmost make-believe while the life of her 'audience' depended upon the conviction with which she enacted her characterization."[33] A similar story was made into a film in Germany in 2003—*Goodbye, Lenin*.

But the course of Ouspenskaya's life was changed when she came on tour to New York with the Moscow Art Theater in 1923. In an autobiographical sketch written in Russian about her first impressions of America, Ouspenskaya wrote that she believed the USA would be so technically advanced that it would be possible to hail an airplane like hailing a cab, and prepared for that task in Moscow by taking a plane ride with a stunt pilot.

We approached America early in the morning. A heavy snow was falling. Through the curtain of snow I see the magnificent Statue of Liberty; with emotion I bow to her, with a deep Russian bow. And so, through the snow I see the city and here and there, the massive shapes of skyscrapers. I search hungrily for airplanes, but I don't see anything except a flock of seagulls. But that doesn't bother me, because it's so early in the morning and the snow is so heavy—surely one or the other is preventing the airplanes from appearing. Then we reach the dock, the crowd of well-wishers: the cameras start flashing, the movie camera cranks away. Speeches are given. We meet friends, there are exclamations, embraces, new acquaintances, customs—everything is in order. I don't ask anyone about having an airplane fetch me, because I'm afraid that it would be very expensive and I have only a few dollars in my pocket and so I modestly get into a taxi. The next day was clear. I go out on the street, look at the sky and give an occasional whistle in the hopes of attracting an airplane, but the one big airplane I can see in the sky is flying so high that it couldn't possibly be a taxi. In my passionate search for a plane in the sky I nearly fall under a yellow taxicab.

A few days later I find out that this was all a fantasy of mine, but that perhaps in five years it will come to pass. So, I think, my fantasy is running a bit ahead of life, I will have to be patient.

But once I go to the cinema and they show on the screen a machine that can just as easily speed along the ground like a car, glide across ice like a sleigh, or speed through water like a motorboat—and then at any minute rise up into the air and fly off into the clouds. So it turns out that American reality is even ahead of my fantasies.

But since I am incapable of living without a dream, then I start torturing myself with the thought: what heroic feat could I perform so that I would receive as a reward a machine like that?

It's the same on stage: I always am dreaming of creating a special image, an image of heroism for all the world to see, but so far I have only created characters of ordinary, even laughable and not at all heroic people.[34]

Ouspenskaya returned to the United States with the MAT in 1924, and this time, along with several other members of the troupe, decided to remain in America. Richard Boleslawski, who later directed *Rasputin and the Empress,* had created the American Laboratory Theatre, and gave Ouspenskaya a job. To improve her primitive English, she studied in a special class for foreigners at Columbia University, and even became an expert at dialects and phonetics. As a pedagogue, Ouspenskaya was legendary, and exerted a significant influence on the education of several generations of prominent stage and film actors. In 1929, she founded the Maria Ouspenskaya School of Dramatic Arts in New York, where she promoted the ideas of her mentor Stanislavsky, including exercises in improvisation and "the technique of acting which includes the control of feelings and emotions, with the development of memory and feeling."[35] Ouspenskaya never claimed that she could create great actors: "The actor's art cannot be taught. He must be born with ability. But the technique through which his talent can find expression . . . that can and must be taught."[36] As Madame Basilova in *Dance Girl Dance* Ouspenskaya makes this same point to a student a bit more succinctly: "You do not learn *oomph*. You are born with it."[37]

In 1940, largely to accommodate her growing Hollywood film career, Ouspenskaya moved her school from New York to Hollywood, where she continued to train eager young actors in what she considered to be a more conducive—and less expensive—environment. ("In Hollywood in our new studios we have a very large private swimming pool as well as plenty of space out of doors where the students can rehearse and relax in the open air."[38]) By now, as John Franchey wrote, Ouspenskaya had acquired cult status: "To Hollywood at large she is the magnificent matriarch, the living theatrical legend, the oracle of art whence issue eternal truths concerning acting and the stage."[39] To her friends, who included the young actor Eddie Albert, she was "Ooksie," beloved for her bizarre hats and for keeping a pet monkey in her house near the Hollywood Bowl. Others, however, including many of her students, were afraid of her eccentric, stern demeanor and old-world manners, not to mention her leathery, weather-beaten face. She was rarely without a cigarette.

Ouspenskaya remained remarkably free of the Hollywood obsession with physical appearance, image, and wealth. She never married and never signed a long-term contract with a studio, although she did have offers, having won two Oscar nominations for best supporting actress, one for *Dodsworth* and another for *Love Affair* (1939), a highly regarded romantic comedy/drama, where she plays the grandmother (what else?) of Charles Boyer, whom he visits in Madeira. (The film was later remade as *An Affair to Remember.*) Working on a single-picture basis, she didn't have to make films she didn't like. In *King's Row,* she appeared with Ronald Reagan (Drake), playing the grandmother (Grandmère Marie) of Drake's best friend Parris in a Peyton Place melodrama set in small town America circa 1890. Speaking her first lines in French and German, it is Grandmère who instills in Parris the genteel European values of her Viennese past, encouraging him to play the piano and be a noble person. (The film's lush orchestral score by Viennese émigré Erich Korngold helps to create an atmosphere of old world European yearning.) When Grandmère dies of cancer halfway through the film, Parris goes off to study psychiatry in Vienna, inspired by her example to escape the confinement, limitations, and vulgarity of life in the provinces, although he returns to help Drake after his legs are amputated following a railroad accident. In most of her early films, Ouspenskaya's foreign characters occupy the moral high ground, dispensing sage advice and providing aristocratic *bon ton* to ordinary but receptive Americans. She always plays an outsider, like Mischa Auer.

For many, Ouspenskaya's two appearances as the mysterious gypsy Maleva in *The Wolf Man* (1940) and the sequel *Frankenstein Meets the Wolf Man* (1943) are her most memorable. Playing the mother of Bela Lugosi (his character's name is also Bela), she has some vivid scenes, intoning with her strange alien accent lines like these: "Even the man who is pure in heart / And says his prayers by night / May become a wolf when the wolf bane blooms / And the moon is pure and bright . . ." Bela bites Larry Talbot (Lon Chaney, Jr.), turning him into a nocturnal wolfman. Ouspen-

FIGURE 10.

King's Row. Warner Brothers 1942. Scotty Beckett and Maria Ouspenskaya (as Grandmère Marie). Vitagraph, Inc. Department of Special Collections, Charles E. Young Library, UCLA. Collection 646. Maria Ouspenskaya Papers. Box 4.

FIGURE 11.

The Wolf Man. Universal 1941. Maria Ouspenskaya as Maleva and Lon Chaney, Jr., as Larry Talbot. Department of Special Collections, Charles E. Young Research Library, UCLA. Collection 646. Maria Ouspenskaya Papers. Box 4.

skaya's performance is the spiritual heart of the film, full of pain and enigma, her timeless face and low voice and minimal gestures capable of creating in just a few brief scenes not only a complete character, but a complete atmosphere that infuses the tale with an impending sense of doom and horror. That Ouspenskaya was cast as a gypsy, a wanderer without a home, was fitting considering her own status as an émigré for whom acting was the only real refuge. During the filming of *Frankenstein Meets the Wolf Man*, Ouspenskaya broke her ankle when a wagon overturned in which she and Chaney were riding.

By 1943, judging by a letter she wrote to the secretary of her agent Paul Kohner, Ouspenskaya had achieved a sense of success in the American film business. "After all, I'm the only character actress here in America, as well as overseas, who has had such success and drawing power which surpasses even Marie Dressler," she wrote. "I cannot send you all the fan mail I've gotten lately, but trust me that it's time for you and Paul Kohner to get busy about me."[40] And yet in 1944, Ouspenskaya had not worked for several years, and was writing Kohner pleading letters to find her a job, complaining that she was "desperate" and being overlooked for parts appropriate for her talents.[41] Some indication of the way in which Ouspenskaya and other Russian émigré "character" actors were viewed by the studio producers can be seen in a note sent to her by Kohner's associate Elizabeth Dickinson in January 1943, informing her that she had not gotten a part in a play she was hoping for. The producers had decided that "they may want no accents of any kind in the play, in which case, unfortunately, this will be out."[42]

Apparently Ouspenskaya enjoyed the Hollywood social scene, and an acquaintance encouraged Kohner to get her invited to openings and parties: "The old gal likes to be seen in public, I gather, and these things will keep her happy."[43] In one of Ouspenskaya's last films and her first western, *Wyoming* (1947), she plays the faithful family servant, a role very similar to that of Marina in Chekhov's *Uncle Vanya*, one of the roles on which she had built her early career in Russia. But Harry MacArthur's comment on her performance in *Wyoming* in the *Washington Star* was devastating: "Admirers of Mme. Maria Ouspenskaya will be saddened to find that she has been called upon to take part in this muddled affair. She's fine, of course, but the joys of running her acting school must now be marred by the thought that her star pupils will some day wind up in things like this."

Ouspenskaya's death was a dramatic and terrible one. On November 30,

1949, one of the innumerable cigarettes she liked to smoke set fire to her bed while she was sleeping at home in her small apartment in Hollywood. A friend who was staying with her rescued her, but Ouspenskaya succumbed to severe second and third degree burns a few days later, on December 3. Her funeral on December 6 was conducted by Yogi Paramhansa Yogananda, Ouspenskaya being a longtime member of the Self-Realization Fellowship. Among those attending the service were fellow Russian émigré actors Akim Tamiroff and Leonid Kinskey.

A few weeks after her cremation, newspapers reported that at the time of her death Ouspenskaya was nearly broke, and left behind an estate valued at $358.32.[44]

★   Gregory Ratoff (1897–1960) was one of the few Russian émigré "character actors" who succeeded in diversifying himself—by becoming a director and producer. Perhaps it was his early training in the law in St. Petersburg before World War I that gave him some practical managerial, legal, and financial skills that he could later use in various aspects of the film business. Ratoff also studied theater, and made his stage debut as a butler in *Mad Money*, by the great Russian playwright Alexander Ostrovsky. Around 1920, Ratoff left Russia for Berlin, and helped to create a Russian theater group that went on tour to European capitals. In Paris, he was seen by Broadway producer Lee Shubert, who brought him in 1922 to New York, where he appeared in many of Shubert's productions and then started producing his own plays. In 1923, he married another Russian émigré actor, Eugenie Leontovich, a member of his theater troupe. Not speaking any English, Ratoff learned the language by reading newspapers with the aid of a dictionary. Some years later he described the process for the *New York Times:* "I read. I look. I look, I read. A word in paper; a word in dictionary. I learn."[45] While Ratoff did learn how to read and understand English, he never lost his trademark accent, "as savory as a pastrami sandwich," which transformed "if" to "eeef" and "kill" to "keel" and "this" to "theeees." Like the other émigré Russian actors, he learned to use what could have been viewed as an insurmountable defect to his advantage, and happily made fun of his language abilities: "By making pictures all over world, I combine tremendous pleasure and work. I speak French, German and Russian. I murder Italian. English, I only manslaughter."[46] In the business, Ratoff was famous as a colorful character of intense enthusiasm,

who "pounds into a room with all the heavy zest of a friendly hippopota-
mus" and whose "customary medium of conversation is a roar."[47]

Ratoff was famous among the Russian émigré theatrical community for
his bravado and cunning. During his early days in New York in the 1920s,
he was able to persuade everyone he met that he could help them, as
Leonid Kinskey later recalled:

> And Gregory was going around Broadway and meeting all famous actors
> and telling them: "My name is Gregory Ratoff, I am about to produce a
> play, and you are going to be in that play because you are a wonderful
> actor." And that was going on for quite a while. He had no play, he had
> nothing. But in the meantime, he became very close to Shuberts, and
> one day he learned that there was a play in which there was a wonderful
> part for his wife. And he stole the script. And she learned the thing
> thoroughly, the part, in the best English she possibly could master. And
> Gregory says to Shuberts: "Listen, I got some actress for you, a fantas-
> tic actress that fits the part. Nobody can play it better than she." He said,
> all right then, bring her in, let her read. Everything was prepared, you
> know, she pretended she was reading. "First reading like that? I never
> saw anything like this in my life!" He was absolutely fascinated. Leon-
> tovich got the part. From there on, Leontovich became a very important
> actress. Gregory was a remarkable promoter. Fantastic promoter.[48]

Brought to Hollywood by David O. Selznick, Ratoff was first cast in *Symphony of Six Million* (1932), a tearjerker about Jewish home life, adapted
from a novel by Fannie Hurst. Ratoff's most memorable role, however, was
as the "unconsciously funny" and warm impresario Max Fabian in one of
the greatest Hollywood films about show business, *All About Eve* (1950).
Here, Ratoff uses his trademark heavy accent to hilarious dramatic effect,
playing on stereotypes of poorly educated immigrant producers spouting
malapropisms in the mold of Samuel Goldwyn. At the long party scene at
the chic Manhattan apartment of actress Margo Channing (Bette Davis),
Fabian is one of the eccentric collection of guests who are alternately celebrated and insulted by their sharp-tongued hostess. Fabian has brought to
the party a young actress he is currently promoting—played by Marilyn
Monroe. Even she is hardly dazzled by Fabian, confiding to another guest
her observation on producers : "Why do they always look like unhappy
rabbits?" Throughout the party, Fabian is suffering from heartburn, which

FIGURE 12.

All About Eve. Twentieth Century Fox 1950. Gregory Ratoff (center) as Max Fabian and Bette Davis as Margo Channing. Courtesy of the Margaret Herrick Library, Academy of Motion Picture Arts and Sciences.

becomes a running gag: "I am a dying man," he whines to Margo, who dismisses him as "a sly puss."

Before *All About Eve,* Ratoff had played the role of a producer in numerous plays and films, beginning with the drama *Wonder Boy* in 1931, then in the movies *Once in a Lifetime, What Price Hollywood,* and *Sitting Pretty.* In fact, Ratoff had grown weary of being typecast, and claimed he would not have accepted the role as Max Fabian from anyone else but his old friend the super-producer Darryl Zanuck: "If it wasn't for Mr. Zanuck, they couldn't get me to play this part for ten times the money. It is debt of loyalty to Mr. Zanuck, who made me a director."[49]

As a director, Ratoff worked with many great actors, including Loretta Young, Tyrone Power, Orson Welles, Linda Darnell, and Betty Grable. He also helped to make Ingrid Bergman a star. It was her performance—her first English-language appearance on screen—under Ratoff's direction in *Intermezzo* (1939) that first brought Bergman, at the age of 26, wide critical and public acclaim in Hollywood. Ratoff's mentor Selznick had seen Bergman in the Swedish version of *Intermezzo* (1936) and decided to remake the film, with Leslie Howard co-starring as Holger Brandt, a concert violinist who falls in love with his daughter's piano teacher, Anita Hoffman (Bergman). Set against the background of a lushly romantic musical score (Rachmaninoff, Tchaikovsky, Grieg, Chopin, both real and imitated, all at the top of their voices), *Intermezzo* charms mainly on the strength of Bergman's performance, which projects that special combination of innocence and seduction, of spiritual purity and depth, that she would use to such great effect later in *Casablanca* and *Anastasia.* Despite a very abrupt ending that leaves us in the dark as to Anita's fate after she is finally cast aside by the violinist in favor of marital fidelity, *Intermezzo* is a minor classic, and demonstrates Ratoff's subtlety and flair as a director, particularly with subjects involving the life of stage performers, a world he knew so well. During World War II, Ratoff made another notable film (discussed in the next chapter) about love between musicians, *Song of Russia.* This self-described "wanderer" remained very active as a director and actor right up until his death in 1960—one of his last appearances on screen was in the small role of Lakavitch in *Exodus.*

★ Russian émigré actors were hardly in short supply in Hollywood by the late 1930s, then. And Russian ballet dancers seemed to be everywhere in America, too, performing with the various touring companies that had spun off from the original Ballets Russes after the death of its creator Serge Diaghilev in Europe in 1929. It was the Ballets Russes companies, presented by the shrewd Russian/Ukrainian émigré Sol Hurok, that first brought ballet to many Americans. "Most American audiences had never seen ballet and didn't know anything about it," the ballerina Alexandra Danilova, one of the young stars of these tours, later remembered. "We could sense their astonishment from the stage. I loved dancing for these audiences; I knew I was introducing them to ballet."[50] Traveling more than twenty thousand miles each season in an uncomfortable caravan of eleven Pullman cars, the 125 (nonunionized) performers rarely spent more than several days at a stop, catching what sleep they could on the train as it rumbled through small cities and towns like Albany, Utica, Akron, Youngstown, Terre Haute, Peoria, Davenport, Wichita, and Lincoln.

Eager to imitate New York high society, and impressed by the stylish national magazines that were featuring the glamorous Ballets Russes in many articles and photo spreads ("Ballerinas in Bathing Suits"), the wealthy and influential citizens of the small towns where Danilova and her colleagues performed happily used the company as an excuse to dress up and feel elegant. As a result of these populist cross-country tours by the Ballets Russes troupes, ballet for most Americans became synonymous with Russia and Russians, an association that has endured to the present day. Just how strong was the Russian presence in the world of stage entertainment by the late 1930s is obvious from a line of dialogue in the original *A Star Is Born* (1937). Libby, the hard-bitten press agent, looking for an angle from which to promote the up-and-coming homespun American song-and-dance actress Esther Blodgett (Janet Gaynor), asks hopefully: "Isn't there some Russian in your background?"

The jealous and scheming world of the touring Russian ballet companies was also celebrated in the slick film version of the Richard Rodgers/Lorenz Hart Broadway musical *On Your Toes*, produced in 1939 by Warner. Its dazzling dance sequences were choreographed by George Balanchine, who began his career in Russia before emigrating to Europe to work with the Ballets Russes. In the 1930s, Balanchine came to the United States and, like so many others, gravitated toward Hollywood, where there was work to be had. Between 1938 and 1942, he worked on four films, including *The Goldwyn Follies* and *On Your Toes*, which he had choreographed on

Broadway. But Balanchine was too independent to work comfortably within the studio system, and returned to New York, where he established the New York City Ballet.

Russian ballet composer Sergei Prokofiev (who had collaborated with Balanchine on *Prodigal Son* for the Ballets Russes) also made his last trip to Hollywood in early 1938, having only recently completed *Romeo and Juliet,* which was staged in Czechoslovakia later in the year. As an established film composer in the USSR, where he had set up permanent residence in 1936, Prokofiev was greeted with even greater enthusiasm than on his previous visits. He even met Walt Disney, whose recently released film *Snow White and the Seven Dwarfs* Prokofiev had seen and adored in Denver.

Disney was fascinated with the possibilities of combining music and animation, and was eagerly looking for composers with whom he could collaborate. But Prokofiev had already tied his future to Soviet Russia, where his children had been left behind in Moscow. To them he wrote of the exotic sights of Los Angeles: "It is very warm here—I've forgotten what an overcoat is, and the trees are covered with oranges and pineapples. Most American films are made in Hollywood, and they build whole houses, castles and even cities of cardboard for them. Today I went to a filming session. A big tall warehouse had been turned into the square of an old town and people galloped through it on horses. I have also been to the house of Mickey Mouses's papa, that is, the man who first thought up the idea of sketching him."[51]

Prokofiev was also feted by Rouben Mamoulian, who held a banquet in his honor, with Mary Pickford, Marlene Dietrich, Gloria Swanson, Edward G. Robinson, and Douglas Fairbanks, Jr., in attendance. Another guest was Viennese composer Arnold Schoenberg, who had been living in the United States since 1933. Although Prokofiev was curious to meet Schoenberg—whose music he had been the first to play in Russia in 1911— in the flesh, he remained unmoved by Schoenberg's complex twelve-tone system. The more glamorous film people, who were working in such a modern and exciting medium, made a much greater impression on him.

In spring 1938 Prokofiev, never noted for good timing, headed back to Moscow, just as a growing tide of artistic refugees was coming to the United States from all over Europe, escaping the growing Nazi threat. Among them were many Russians who had already emigrated once to flee the Bolsheviks, and were forced now to do so again. Prokofiev's long-time competitor and sometime nemesis Igor Stravinsky left Europe and settled in Los Angeles in 1940, where he took up permanent residence in West Hollywood, still the heart of the Los Angeles Russian émigré community today. In that same year, Walt Disney brought Stravinsky's music to the screen in the animated feature *Fantasia,* which includes the famous segment illustrating his 1913 ballet *Rite of Spring* as a drama of evolution, complete with rampaging dinosaurs. (It is worth noting that three of the eight segments of *Fantasia* are set to works of Russian music: *Rite of Spring,* Tchaikovsky's *Waltz of the Flowers* from *The Nutcracker,* and Modest Mussorgsky's *Night on Bald Mountain.*)

Fond of the mild climate and sunshine, and far removed from the terrible devastation visited upon Europe and the USSR by World War II, Stravinsky would remain in Los Angeles for most of the rest of his life. Indeed, this great Russian composer resided happily in LA for nearly thirty years, about as long as he lived in Russia.

★   The major Hollywood films representing Russians, Russia, and the USSR that were produced in the late 1930s did not feature real Russians as principals in the cast, however, since these actors possessed insufficient box-office appeal. Instead, producers turned to big-name actors to portray Russian characters: Claudette Colbert, Charles Boyer, Basil Rathbone, Nelson Eddy, Greta Garbo, Hedy Lamarr. Real Russians were relegated to minor roles. Four films of the late 1930s dealing with contemporary (post-Revolutionary) Russian life are of particular artistic and cultural significance: *Tovarich* (1937, Warner), *Balalaika* (1939, MGM), *Ninotchka* (1939, MGM) and *Comrade X* (1940, MGM). Only one of these, *Tovarich,* was directed by a Russian émigré: Anatole Litvak. Two, *Balalaika* and *Ninotchka,* were made by recent émigrés from Germany, Reinhold Schunzel and Ernst Lubitsch, respectively. King Vidor, the Texan who piloted *Comrade X,* was the sole American-born director. Two of the projects (*Tovarich, Balalaika*) were adapted from stage plays, while two (*Ninotchka, Comrade X*) were original screenplays adapted from stories.

Tovarich came to the screen from a highly successful romantic comedy with the same title written in 1933 by French playwright Jacques Deval (1894–1972), which ran successfully in France and England and opened on Broadway in 1936. Several major Hollywood studios and directors were interested in acquiring the movie rights, and in an article on the Broadway

FIGURE 13.

Tovarich. Warner 1937. Publicity poster.

premiere, *Motion Picture Daily* reported that Ernst Lubitsch was in the audience.[52] Warner Brothers reportedly paid the large sum of $150,000 for the film deal. Russian émigré actress Eugenie Leontovich had played the leading role of Tatiana in London and elsewhere, but the film role went to Claudette Colbert, who had proven her ability to do light comedy in such films as *It Happened One Night* and *She Married Her Boss.* She was teamed with another French-born actor, Charles Boyer, as her husband Mikhail. Besides the fact that at the time both Colbert and Boyer were hot box-office properties, their real Frenchness no doubt worked in their favor for a story set in Paris—although both play Russian émigré aristocrats. Since the Russian aristocracy had long been associated (both historically and in the popular imagination) with French manners and even the French language, this casting choice made a certain kind of European sense, especially since the screenplay calls for the characters to be able to pass as French-speaking.

The plot of *Tovarich* (the word for "comrade" in Russian, it came into popular use in the USSR after the Bolshevik Revolution because it was free of the class associations conveyed in other forms of address) turns upon the familiar and topical theme of Russian royalty come down in the world. Tatiana and Mikhail, both of them members of one of Russia's most noble families, have been forced to live in exile in Paris after the Russian Revolution, and are reduced to poverty. In desperation, they answer a newspaper ad for domestic servants and—of course hiding their real identity—are hired into a wealthy household headed by a banker (Dupont) who is by chance involved in financial transactions with the Soviet government. After the cook meets Mikhail, he observes: "He has a funny accent. Probably Swiss." The windows of their room look out on the Russian Orthodox Church, and they are forever comically confusing the ringing of the church bells with the servants' call bell. Dupont knows his new servants are Russian, and finds their customs quite amusing: "You Russians seem to spend your entire life kissing each other." Witty and gentle, Tatiana and Mikhail immediately win over Dupont's son and daughter, and begin to Russify the household. Dupont's wife even buys a borzoi dog and gives it the name of the Russian folksong *"Ochi chernye,"* and the children take Russian lessons.

But when the Soviet Commissar Gorotchenko (the sinister Basil Rathbone) is invited to dinner, Tatiana and Mikhail are recognized. Gorotchenko, it turns out, was Tatiana's torturer in the infamous Lyubanka prison back in Moscow. When Mme. Dupont realizes her new beloved servants are in fact Russian royalty, she can only respond petulantly: "Why did you have to be born a Grand Duchess and a Prince when good servants are so hard to find?"

Now Gorotchenko reveals that he is about to sell off oil prospecting rights on the Caspian Sea to foreign powers in order to pay off massive government debts at home, and asks Mikhail if he would be willing to contribute the 40 billion francs he controls in the former Tsarist treasury to keep the territory under Russian control. (Why Mikhail is unable to access any of these funds for himself remains unexplained.) His Russian patriotism awakened, as we can hear in the excerpts from music of Glinka and Mussorgsky's *Boris Godunov* in the score arranged by Max Steiner, Mikhail agrees to sign over the money to Gorotchenko—even though he tortured Mikhail back in Russia. He and Tatiana stay on in the Dupont household as servants, affirming their spiritual nobility. That life back in the USSR is far from comfortable is made clear in the sadistic character of Gorotchenko, a cynical, unprincipled, power-hungry bureaucrat who says of his own time abroad: "When I returned to Russia I left my idealism behind."

For the most part, however, *Tovarich* avoids political or ideological commentary. Its more universal message—that money and status do not necessarily bring happiness, that nothing is more valuable than true love between loving mates—informs many other Hollywood films in the post-Depression era. The image of fabulously wealthy Russian aristocrats having lost their fortunes resonated well with an American audience that had recently witnessed similar instances among its own monied classes.

★ *Balalaika* attempts to deal more directly with the ideological and political complexities of the Bolshevik Revolution. Adapted from a stage play by Eric Maschwitz, the screenplay turns on a romance between a St. Petersburg cabaret singer and secret revolutionary Lydia Marakova (Ilona Massey), and the dashing Cossack officer Prince Peter Karagin (Nelson Eddy) who also happens to have quite a voice on him. Most of the action takes place in St. Petersburg just before the Bolshevik Revolution, but moves to Paris at the end, after the Revolution has forced both Lydia and Peter to flee. Like Tatiana and Mikhail in *Tovarich*, the former aristocrat Peter and his family have come down hard in the world, and are now running a restaurant staffed by members of the impoverished Russian gentry

FIGURE 14.

Balalaika. MGM 1939. Ilona Massey (center) as Lydia Makarova. From the
collection of Sol Dolgin. Courtesy of the Margaret Herrick Library, Academy of
Motion Picture Arts and Sciences.

catering to tourists hungry for some Tsarist nostalgia—named the Balalaika Café in honor of the cabaret where Lydia sang in St. Petersburg. Drawn together by strong mutual attraction (not to mention their shared singing capabilities), Lydia and Peter are torn apart by their opposing political and social views, only to be reunited at the end, through a rousing rendition of the song of the Volga boatmen (*Ei, ukhnem*).

In a letter to Louis B. Mayer of December 13, 1937, Joseph Breen of the Production Code Administration pointed out a number of potential problems with adapting the play for the screen:

> As a matter of general caution, we suggest you assure yourselves that there will be no objection from the citizens or government of any country to the treatment of the characters or subject matter.
>
> The showing of a prostitute should be eliminated.
>
> All characters and action having to do with the sale of obscene postcards must be dropped.
>
> All the dialogue which is suggestive of a comedy play upon sex situations should be eliminated.

In later correspondence with Mayer, Breen also objected to the characterization of a male secretary as a "pansy," and advised that any "scenes of revolutionary and mob violence" should "be handled with the greatest care, to avoid possible deletion. In addition, there must be not details of brutality or gruesomeness."[53]

Breen needn't have worried. No one could ever accuse *Balalaika* of being realistic, sexually explicit, or (horrors!) gruesome. Instead, this frothy film treats the Russian Revolution as a madcap operetta, something like *The Student Prince* with angst, still allowing plenty of time for singing, dancing, dressing up, and drinking elaborate champagne toasts.

For Ilona Massey (1910–1974), *Balalaika* was her first starring Hollywood role, opposite Nelson Eddy at the height of his considerable popularity. Massey was Hungarian, born poor as Ilona Hajmassy in Budapest, and appeared in opera, on stage, and in Austrian films before ending up in Hollywood, which was luring many other Hungarian film people (including Michael Curtiz) in the 1930s, as Hungary became an increasingly fascist country. Touted as the "next Marlene Dietrich," Massey never lived up to the hype. Her soprano voice is light and lyric, not heavy and sexy, and her acting technique is extremely mannered and limited. A very heavy

Hungarian accent did not make it any easier for her or the rest of the cast. In *Balalaika,* Massey has several scenes where she sings opera (including *Carmen,* of course). After *Balalaika,* Massey did not receive any other major starring roles; like most of the Russian émigré actors in Hollywood, she was relegated to character parts, and was cast as the Baroness Elsa Frankenstein in *Frankenstein Meets the Wolf Man.* This casting had a certain cultural authenticity, since the action of the film takes place in Transylvania, a longtime province of Hungary.

As the Cossack officer and Prince, Nelson Eddy swaggers and smiles a lot, rides horses convincingly, and even pulls off the role of a military commander in a sequence set during World War I. In one of the most emotionally successful scenes, the German soldiers sing "Silent Night" to the Russian troops across the trenches on Russian Orthodox Christmas (several weeks later than Western Christmas). But mostly, Eddy sings. He sings on horseback with his Cossack buddies while drinking (in large quantities), and for and with Lydia. His sheer robust good spirits and energy save most of the scenes in which he appears. Once again, the message seems to be that Russia and its political problems can be understood best through singing and dancing. No personal or ideological issue is so vexing that it cannot be solved by a rousing chorus or a foot-tapping peasant tune. Further, the revolutionary activities of Lydia and her family are confined to the period before the 1917 Bolshevik Revolution, and are directed against the Tsarist regime. We see nothing of life in Russia after the Revolution. The film is a "nostalgic swan song to the Czarist Russia that once was," leaving us with an overwhelming feeling of nostalgia for the "dear dead days when caviar came in buckets and champagne in magnums."[54]

Hollywood's "tourist approach" to Russia is illustrated in *Balalaika* in the appearance of a pair of middle-aged American tourists toward the film's end. Eager to experience the best of Parisian night life, the wife drags her reluctant, portly husband ("my feet hurt") to the Balalaika Café, where they sit voyeuristically at one of the best tables and consume quarts of caviar as they marvel at the entertainment. This insertion of typical American characters was obviously calculated to appeal to the average American moviegoer, who might find a tale of far-away wartorn Russia a bit remote.

The tune-filled musical score of *Balalaika* was composed by Herbert Stothart (1885–1949), an American who worked for many years at MGM

and exhibited a special fondness and aptitude for films with Russian subjects. His first film music, in fact, was written for the classic Soviet silent
film *The End of St. Petersburg*, directed by Vsevolod Pudovkin. His success
on this project led producers to choose him as composer for *Rasputin and
the Empress, Anna Karenina, Balalaika,* and *Song of Russia*. For Stothart,
Russian music meant nineteenth-century Russian music, even if the action was set in the twentieth century—just as it did for most Hollywood
film composers.

Notwithstanding the film's frivolous treatment of the Russian Revolu-
tion, the critical and public reception of *Balalaika* in the United States
was complicated by the changing international political situation. When
Louis B. Mayer first started working on this feature in late 1937, the United
States and the USSR were entering a period of notably friendly relations.
Largely out of fear of the rising power of Nazi Germany on the West and
Japan on the East, the government of the USSR actively sought rapprochement with the Western powers, including the United States. This spirit of
rapprochement reached its peak in early 1939, and was symbolized by the
popularity of the spectacular Soviet Pavilion at the 1939 New York World's
Fair, which opened on May 1, 1939, with the hopeful theme "Building the
World of Tomorrow." Constructed at great expense in a theatrical art deco
style, the Soviet Pavilion was the largest and most popular of all the foreign
pavilions at the Fair, and was adorned with dioramas of different ethnic
groups of the USSR existing in happy cooperation.

But the Soviet-American relationship deteriorated soon afterward. On
August 23, 1939, Stalin stunned the world by approving a wide-ranging
treaty with the Nazis, guaranteeing that Germany would not invade the
USSR (at least in the short term) in return for the promise of Soviet neu-
trality. The signing of the treaty paved the way for the Nazi invasion of
Poland on September 1, which led Britain and France to declare war on
Germany. At the same time, Soviet forces were occupying territories in
Western Belorussia and Ukraine, and launched the Winter War against
Finland in 1939–1940. Public opinion in the United States toward the
USSR was drastically affected by these events. Not surprisingly, the USSR
declined an invitation to participate in the 1940 New York World's Fair.

Critics who reviewed the opening of *Balalaika* in December 1939 noted
that sympathetic screen portrayals of Russians (whether revolutionaries
or princes) were not much in favor at the moment. A preview article in

Variety warned that the movie "may, unfortunately, encounter some popular resistance because of its coincidence with present world affairs through its Russian story material. The treatment itself is politically innocuous, taking no issue, even in the mild musical manner, with internal Russian matters, but political sympathies in this country have been somewhat affected by the Russ-Finn war, started after the picture was well under way. Some selling emphasis to counteract any popular reaction in this connection might therefore seem advisable."[55]

The critic for *Variety* agreed. "*Balalaika* has a number of factors to negate its chances for socko reception. For one thing, the Russe idiom is by no means popular right now, no matter how you serve the caviar. Whether of the czaristic vodka vintage, where this film starts, or into the post-proletarian revolutionary era—showing the former imperialistic aristocrats in humble service in Paris—the historical elements don't rest well."[56]

★ MGM released another major film dealing with the USSR in the confusing autumn of 1939—*Ninotchka*. Because of its mildly anti-Soviet subject matter and tone, however, the growing tension between the United States and the USSR influenced its box-office and critical reception in a positive way. One of the most subtle and entertaining films ever made about the ideological clash between Communism and capitalism, *Ninotchka* evolved from a story idea by Melchior Lengyel originally brought to MGM in 1937 by Gottfried Reinhardt, son of the famous German director Max Reinhardt. From the beginning, Greta Garbo (who had already played Russian in two versions of *Anna Karenina*) was the choice to play the female lead, a Soviet commissar whose life is transformed when she comes to Paris on official business. As Lengyel described her: "Russian girl saturated with Bolshevist ideals goes to fearful, capitalistic, monopolistic Paris. She meets romance and has an uproarious good time. Capitalism not so bad after all."[57] Originally, Cary Grant was to be cast as the male romantic lead opposite Garbo.

In May 1938, a fifteen-page treatment of the story was submitted for approval to the Production Code Administration. Joseph Breen raised strenuous objections over the "illicit sex affair between the two sympathetic leads," pointing out that "the sex affair must definitely and affirmatively be shown to be wrong; it must not be condoned; it must not be justified; it must not be made to appear right and acceptable; and the sinners must be punished."[58] One year later, a revised script was submitted and eventually approved. The shooting of *Ninotchka* went quickly: begun on May 31, 1939, it was completed on July 27, only five weeks before the Nazi armies invaded Poland.

Director Ernst Lubitsch (1892–1947), one of the recognized masters of suave, sophisticated satire in Hollywood (among his many films is a brilliant version of Noel Coward's play *Design for Living*) came to the *Ninotchka* project in late December, after George Cukor withdrew to focus on the filming of *Gone with the Wind.* Lubitsch, who had been making films since 1913, came from Central Europe; he was born in Berlin but his father had been born in Grodno, Russia, and had arrived in Berlin in the mid-1880s. As a young actor in Berlin, Lubitsch worked closely with Max Reinhardt and the Polish actress Pola Negri before coming to the United States in 1921. In 1928 he began a very productive association with Paramount Studios, where he worked until 1938—*Ninotchka,* in fact, was the first film Lubitsch made after leaving Paramount.

Because of his father's Russian origins, and because of growing up in Berlin, a city not far from the Polish border and with a very large population of Russians (especially in the years just after the Bolshevik Revolution, when it was sometimes jokingly referred to as "Moscow on the Spree"), Lubitsch had a particular fondness for Russian subjects. His 1924 film *Forbidden Paradise* (based on a play co-authored by Melchior Lengyel), about Catherine the Great's attempt to seduce the handsome fiancé of one of her ladies-in-waiting, was a big box-office and critical success. In 1928, he directed the silent feature *The Patriot,* dealing with the assassination of Catherine's son, Tsar Paul I. As production chief at Paramount, Lubitsch also signed up Lewis Milestone.

Not long before taking on the *Ninotchka* project, in 1936, Lubitsch had taken an extended honeymoon trip to Moscow with his new American bride. Conversations they had there with an old German friend who had become a committed and dogmatic Communist made a deep (and not very favorable) impression on him, and helped him discover "the matrix for the title character" of the "Lady Comrade" Nina Ivanovna Yakushova.[59] The same year, he became an American citizen, which perhaps helps to explain his affectionate and humorous convert's embrace of capitalism in *Ninotchka.* "The trip to Russia disabused Lubitsch of any romantic feelings he might have had about socialism in any form," writes Lubitsch biographer Scott Eyman.[60]

To the style of *Ninotchka* Lubitsch brought his special combination of sexual innuendo, physical and sight gags, and amusement at the weakness of human character. Lubitsch was particularly fond of films that displayed "conflicts of culture." The screenplay, adapted from Lengyel's story by the impressive team of Charles Brackett, Billy Wilder, and Walter Reisch, gave Lubitsch lots of marvelous material to work with. Like Lubitsch, Wilder had migrated to Hollywood from Central European origins—in his case, Galicia, the southern part of Poland under Austro-Hungarian control until World War I. The three writers and the directors spent weeks refining the script, adding more humor and finding exactly the right props and plot devices.

The story revolves around Nina Ivanovna Yakushova, a severe Soviet commissar who is sent to Paris to expedite the sale of jewels that formerly belonged to the Romanov family. (Ninotchka is the affectionate diminutive nickname derived from Nina, pronounced with the accent on the first syllable in Russian, but consistently mispronounced by non-Russians in the film with the accent on the second syllable.) The sale was originally assigned to three bumbling male commissars, but they have been seduced by the pleasures of capitalist life and need to be brought back into line. In Paris, Nina meets the playboy Count Leon d'Algout (Melvyn Douglas), gigolo of the émigré Russian Duchess Swana (Ina Claire), who claims the jewels belong to her as a surviving member of the royal family. Soon Leon is courting Nina, and despite all her socialist principles and ideals, she eventually yields to his attentions, transforming from a prim disciplinarian into a sweet and fun-loving girl. Sent back to Moscow, where she wilts in the absence of her admirer and the capitalist delights to which she became accustomed, she manages to get to Constantinople, where in the final scene she is reunited with Leon and the three crazy commissars, who are now running a restaurant.

In developing the script, Lubitsch sought to find a visual key to convey the process of Nina's emotional and ideological conversion. The writers gathered at Lubitsch's house, and he suddenly came up with what he had in mind during a visit to the bathroom. "Boys," he said, "I've got it. I've got the answer. It's the hat!"[61]

When she arrives in Paris, Nina finds the extravagant fashionable clothing worn by the local inhabitants useless and silly. Utilitarianism is

FIGURE 15.

Ninotchka. MGM 1939. Greta Garbo as Nina Yakushova, wearing the hat, and
Melvyn Douglas as Count Leon d'Algout. Courtesy of the Margaret Herrick
Library, Academy of Motion Picture Arts and Sciences.

her guiding principle. A fanciful hat she sees in a store window initially strikes her as ridiculous. As she stays longer in Paris and comes closer to Leon, however, her utilitarian ideas begin to weaken. Eventually (right after Leon has made her laugh for the first time when he falls off his chair in a restaurant) she buys the hat and wears it, at first timidly, alone in her room, but with a growing sense of liberation. The moment when she wears the hat (a strange conical creation that is the antithesis of the dreary berets and rainhats she has been wearing up until now) to her romantic rendez-vous with Leon represents her realization that the Communist precepts she has been following so religiously leave no room for individual enjoyment, self-expression, or pleasure. Just like the three commissars sent to Paris before her, she has been seduced by the choices afforded by capitalism.

In *Ninotchka,* as in so many other Hollywood films about the USSR, the female protagonist is "converted" to womanliness and is sexually liberated through exposure to the products available in a market economy: hats, perfume, champagne, steak, jewelry, room service. The film's message, delivered at a time when the international debate over the relative merits of Communism and capitalism was at a crucial stage, is that capitalism is sexier and more fun—almost a natural human instinct, in fact, like eating and making love.

Some years later, Billy Wilder described in an interview with *Cahiers du cinéma* how Lubitsch developed the image of the hat as a symbol of Ninotchka's changing attitudes:

> We worked weeks wondering how we could show that Garbo was becoming bourgeois—that she was starting to become interested in capitalist things. We wrote a bunch of different things, then one day Lubitsch said, "We're going to do a scene with a hat." She would be seen arriving at the start, accompanied by three commissars; she then passes in front of a window in which she sees a rather extravagant hat. She says, "How can a civilization survive when women put such hats on their head! It won't be long now, comrades." Then she passes in front of the window and laughs. Later, finally, she chases the three commissars out, closes the door, opens her package, takes the hat out, puts it on and looks in the mirror. That's pure Lubitsch—total simplicity.[62]

In *Ninotchka,* Lubitsch makes the point that humor is incompatible with Communism. When she arrives in Paris, Ninotchka fails to understand jokes, particularly those involving irony or satire. She is not amused by the antics of the three commissars (named Iranoff, Buljanoff, and Kopalski, like a borsch-belt comedy team) and their endless clowning capers. (A particularly brilliant sequence shows them hosting a wild party with the night club cigarette girls in their hotel room, but only from outside the door, with repeated entrances, exits, ejections, shrieks, and laughter.) Perhaps Lubitsch had noticed on his recent trip to the USSR that satire and irony were virtually forbidden there. For him, laughter is one of the basic necessities of existence.

As Ninotchka learns to smile and laugh, she is humanized, losing the robot-like behavior to which she has been conditioned as a Soviet citizen. In a clever sight gag, the converted Ninotchka even makes the dour photo of Lenin she keeps on her night table break into a smile. Humor, Lubitsch realized, was a leveler, and the most dangerous of weapons, which is why it was so feared by the Soviet censors. The role of Ninotchka also allowed Garbo to take a comic role for the first time in her career. That Garbo was not a native speaker of English proved an asset; the odd Swedish cadence in her speech made her English sound mechanical, flat, and unemotional, just right for the character she was playing.

The script of *Ninotchka* is stuffed with stinging barbs directed at Communism and Soviet domestic policy. When Ninotchka arrives in Paris, she is asked how things are going in Moscow, and she assures the three commissars that, as a result of the ongoing mass trials (about which much had been written in American newspapers), "There are going to be fewer but better Russians." Garbo's deadpan delivery only heightens the humor. Melvyn Douglas tells Ninotchka naughtily, "I've been fascinated by your five-year plan for the last fifteen years," but his sarcasm is lost on her. After her conversion, throwing open the window of her hotel room to enjoy the fresh spring air, Ninotchka observes that there is still snow on the ground back in Moscow: "We have the high ideals, but they have the climate."

Of particular interest is the sequence late in the film set in present-day Moscow—one of the first attempts in a Hollywood film to portray contemporary life in the USSR. After striking a deal with Swana, who demands that she return to Moscow and remove herself as a rival for Leon's affections in exchange for allowing the sale of the jewels, Ninotchka returns home.

The opening scene in Moscow is the May Day parade, with ubiquitous banners bearing Stalin's portrait, and Ninotchka dressed in a plain white uniform and kerchief, marching with a frown in a regimented corps of identically dressed women. From inhabiting an entire suite in a fancy Paris hotel she is reduced to living in one corner of a crowded communal apartment with two roommates: a cellist and a snoring streetcar conductor. Nosy neighbors enter to use the bathroom. The cellist, Anna, warns her not to hang her fancy Paris underwear on the clothesline—"All you have to do is wear a pair of silk stockings and you're accused of counterrevolution." When Ninotchka describes the hat she bought in Paris, she confesses that "I'd be ashamed to wear it here." "It was as beautiful as that?" asks Anna mischievously. When Ninotchka turns on the radio, she can find nothing but anti-capitalist propaganda—"No music," she sighs. The three commissars, who returned with her from Paris, arrive, and they reminisce and joke as they pool their precious single eggs to make a communal omelette. Nina receives a letter from Leon, but the entire text is crossed out and stamped "Censored."

In the next scene, set in a room inside the Kremlin with snow falling on the churches outside, Ninotchka is called to a meeting with the high-ranking Party official Razinin, played by Bela Lugosi. (By then, Lugosi, a Hungarian émigré, was already famous for his numerous screen portrayals of Dracula and mad doctors.) Here, Lugosi is sinister but not grotesque, a no-nonsense Bolshevik who orders Ninotchka to travel to Constantinople to bring to heel the three wayward commissars who have strayed from their fur-selling mission there and have opened a restaurant serving Russian food. She resists—"The foreign atmosphere puts you out of gear"—but he insists.

She is greeted in Constantinople by her three comrades, dressed elegantly, and taken to a lavish hotel suite where they present her with Leon, who has somehow engineered her exit from Russia. To the end, the patriotic Ninotchka has divided feelings about leaving Russia, but love and freedom prevail, and she yields to Leon's love. Just like Prince Karagin in *Balalaika*, Iranoff, Buljanoff, and Kopalski (played by Russian émigré Alexander Granach) have opened a Russian restaurant abroad, serving traditional Russian delicacies (no longer available in the USSR) and creating an island of Russian nostalgia with the help of the market economy.

And yet Lubitsch does not spare capitalism or Tsarist Russia in *Ninotchka*. The Duchess Swana, a White Russian émigré, is egotistical, vain, and greedy. And in the film's very last scene, we see Kopalski picketing the restaurant he has created with Iranoff and Buljanoff, wearing a sign that reads: "Iranoff and Buljanoff unfair to Kopalski." Life may not be fair under capitalism, *Ninotchka* tells us, but it is much more human and entertaining. And Ninotchka is not the only one who is transformed: the irresponsible playboy Leon has been converted into a caring and attentive partner by his relationship with her.

Because of the rapidly changing international situation in summer and fall of 1939, MGM requested permission from the Production Code Administration to add a title at the beginning of the film, a kind of disclaimer "to show that it represents the gay Paris of pre-war days."[63] As we see the first shot of a Paris street, these words appear on the screen: "This picture takes place in Paris in those wonderful days when a siren was a brunette and not an alarm and, if a Frenchman turned out the light, it was not for an air raid."

As it turned out, the satirical anti-Communism of *Ninotchka* resonated strongly with the public and critics at this threatening moment. In the *New York Times*, Frank S. Nugent raved, calling it "one of the sprightliest comedies of the year, a gay and impertinent and malicious show which never pulls its punch lines (no matter how far below the belt they may land) and finds the screen's austere first lady of drama playing a dead-pan comedy role with the assurance of a Buster Keaton. . . . Stalin, we repeat, won't like it; but, unless your tastes hew too closely to the party line, we think you will, immensely."[64] At Radio City Music Hall in New York, *Ninotchka* was particularly successful, with a total gross of $306,441 in a three-week run. "We could easily have run the picture another week or two, maybe three," said the hall's managing director. "There did not seem to be any let-up."[65]

Not surprisingly, the film was banned in a number of countries (including Estonia and Lithuania, occupied by Soviet forces in early 1940) because of its negative portrayal of socialism. In Mexico, the film was passed by the censor, "but opposed by the Labor Unions with the result that no theater in Mexico could show this presentation."[66] Louis B. Mayer was not overly impressed with the financial success of *Ninotchka:* it earned $2.2 million worldwide and had cost $1.3 million to make. Although nominated for four Academy Awards (best picture, script, story, and best actress), it did not receive any. But *Ninotchka* has demonstrated impressive staying power, and is today considered one of the classics of 1930s Hollywood comedy, as well as one of the most perceptive films ever made about Communism. That it has been widely imitated and was even turned into a 1955 Broadway musical called *Silk Stockings*, with words and lyrics by Cole Porter (made into a 1957 film directed by Rouben Mamoulian) only proves how perceptive and prophetic *Ninotchka* was.

When the USSR collapsed in 1991, Communism almost instantly yielded to capitalism, East Germans hurried across the wall to go shopping, and we saw just how right Lubitsch was about human nature.

★ *Comrade X*, released in late 1940 when U.S.-Soviet relations were very tense, tried to emulate the success of *Ninotchka*. It is also the first mainstream Hollywood feature to be set almost entirely in the present-day USSR, which it portrays in an extremely unflattering light. Several of the creative people connected with *Ninotchka* were involved with the making of *Comrade X:* producer Gottfried Reinhardt, and writer Walter Reisch, credited with the story. American director King Vidor (1894–1982) was given a high-profile cast that included Clark Gable at his peak as the swashbuckling American Moscow correspondent "Mac" Thompson (he had appeared in *Gone with the Wind* the preceding year) and Hedy Lamarr as his romantic interest, Theodore, the daughter of Mac's valet. Lamarr, an Austrian sex-goddess with a scandalous past, had come to Hollywood in 1938. (In casting actors to play Russian characters, Hollywood producers continued to show a preference for Germanic/Nordic types.) Also featured in the cast are Eve Arden (in her familiar WASP wise-cracking sidekick mode as Mac's old friend Jane Wilson) and several Russian émigrés in small parts (Vladimir Sokoloff as Commissar Bastakoff, and Mikhail Rasumny as a Russian officer).

There was a strong Viennese influence in the cast and crew: besides Reisch and Lamarr, masterful character actor Oscar Homolka (1898–1978), trained by Gottfried Reinhardt's father, Max Reinhardt, took the role of the heavy, the censor Commissar Vasiliev. Homolka would play Russian several more times in his career, notably in *Mission to Moscow* (as the Soviet Foreign Minister Litvinov) and *War and Peace* (as General Kutuzov).

As an American journalist (he works for the *Topeka Bugle* in the heartland) posted in Moscow, Clark Gable plays Mac Thompson as a lusty, hard-drinking, and swaggering fellow, firmly in the "I don't give a damn" persona he developed in *Gone with the Wind* and elsewhere. The profanity and

FIGURE 16.

Comrade X. MGM 1940. Clark Gable as "Mac" Thompson and Hedy Lamarr as
Theodore. Courtesy of the Margaret Herrick Library, Academy of Motion
Picture Arts and Sciences.

drinking of the original script was too much for the Production Code Administration, which claimed to be concerned about the reputation of journalists: "These scenes of drinking are particularly questionable because of your principal character being a newspaper man, and the persistent characterization in pictures of newspaper men as drunks is only causing further severe condemnation from the newspaper fraternity."[67]

Mac is strongly established in the script as a red-blooded American with an unfailing sense of adventure and humor, and disgusted by the lack of personal freedom and expression he encounters in the USSR. Although the action is set in Russia, the psychological arc of the narrative is very similar to that of *Ninotchka:* a Soviet woman, a dedicated Communist, is lured away from her ideology by the charms of an unabashed capitalist and spirited away to the West. In *Comrade X,* however, the seducer is strongly identified as an American, unlike Count Leon in *Ninotchka.* The ideological clash between Soviet Communism and American capitalism is therefore much more clearly articulated.

A title that appears at the film's opening states its political position. "Russia: The Never Never Land of Steppes, Samovars and Spies—Beards, Bears, Bombs and Borscht—where almost anything can happen—and usually does." *Comrade X* perpetuates many common stereotypes about Russians— they kiss too much (Mac tells his cab driver, "Don't kiss me, please, go tend your pigs"), they are crude, gullible, and stupid. Mac's secretary, Olga, starts singing folk songs when she is drunk, and declares, "Russia has a soul. It is suffering and beauty." Most of the Russian characters speak heavily accented, faulty, and yet humorous English, mangling conversational idioms: "He is washing himself in a bathtub."

Mac, on the other hand, dismisses Communism as hogwash, and proclaims that it would never be tolerated in the United States: "You can't have a Revolution with people who believe in hot dogs and boogie woogie." He also refuses to take seriously the Communist convictions of Theodore, mainly because of her gender: "You'd be better than Karl Marx. You're prettier." Just as in *Ninotchka,* Theodore, a streetcar conductor, is "converted" through a piece of clothing, in this case a sexy nightgown that Mac gives her to replace her homely Russian one after they are married in a hilarious scene at a Soviet marriage bureau, where the impersonal ceremony requires nothing more than an exchange of postcards.

Mac's conversion of Theodore is not only a selfish act so he can possess her as a marital/sexual partner; he is also saving her from possible persecution or even death at the hands of the Party Commissars who are carrying out ideological purges. As Theodore's father, Vanya, explains to Mac, "The Communists are being executed so that Communism will succeed." Vanya (Felix Bressart) blackmails Mac into taking Theodore out of the USSR by threatening to reveal his identity as Comrade X, the journalist who has been secretly subverting Soviet censorship and sending highly unflattering stories about the USSR abroad. Further complications ensue, culminating in an extended chase scene that begins in a car, moves to a train, and then to a tank, in which Mac (at the wheel) and Theodore escape to the Rumanian border to give themselves up to American forces. The final short sequence shifts abruptly to the United States. Some time has passed, and Mac, Theodore, and Vanya are shown in the stands at a Brooklyn Dodgers baseball game, enjoying the quintessential American pastime. "The Dodgers are murdering the Reds!" Theodore exclaims. "The counterrevolution!" her father replies with a smile.

With *Comrade X,* Hollywood films about the USSR entered a new phase. The uncertainty about Communism reflected in films of the 1930s is replaced by a much more negative message, stimulated by the threatening Soviet-Nazi alliance and the deteriorating situation in Europe. "In a way, this film might be regarded as counter-propaganda comedy," wrote the author of a film preview in *Variety.* "It pokes fun at practices alien to American fundamentals. It skims laughs off the top of tragic matters. It holds up pompous or hideous inconsistencies to ridicule. Under its hearty laughter some of the more acute antagonism in the world's warring politics seethe uneasily in pointed reminders."[68] Hollywood was still most comfortable dealing with the grim realities of Soviet Communism as material for comedy.

And yet the more stridently critical attitude toward the USSR conveyed by *Comrade X* would not last long. A new phase would begin in Hollywood's representation of Russia six months after the film's premiere, in June 1941, when Hitler broke his pact with Stalin and invaded the USSR, inflicting incredible losses. After the Japanese attack on Pearl Harbor on December 7, and Germany's declaration of war on the United States on December 11, the American relationship with Stalin and his country was turned upside down. Now we were friends.

Temporary Comrades

"Messages are for Western Union."
Samuel Goldwyn

After the events of late 1941 brought the United States and the USSR together as wartime allies against Nazi Germany, Hollywood's portrayal of
the USSR underwent a complete transformation. Suddenly it was no
longer appropriate to belittle and ridicule the Soviet people or even Communism. The Roosevelt administration decided that German fascism was
far worse, and represented, at least in the short run, a much graver threat
to the American way of life. By late 1941, representatives of the Roosevelt
administration and the Office of War Information were approaching the
heads of the major Hollywood studios, urging them to make films that
would help the American public better understand our new ally Russia and
its people. The studio chiefs were willing to comply, and over the next few
years, until the end of the war in 1945, pro-Soviet feature films were produced by most of the leading studios. It also helped that many prominent
Hollywood producers, such as Sam Goldwyn, were Jews born in Eastern
Europe whose abhorrence of Nazi policies of anti-Semitism led them to
embrace the Soviet Union as the lesser of two evils.[1]

From Warner Brothers came *Mission to Moscow,* based on the controversial memoirs of former American ambassador to the USSR Joseph
Davies, released in April 1943. (Warner Brothers' campaign for *Mission to
Moscow* set "a company record for expenditure for national advertising
and exploitation of a single motion picture"; the original promotional
budget of $250,000 was raised a few months later to $500,000.)[2] Also released in 1943 was *Three Russian Girls,* starring the Russian-American actress Anna Sten, and produced by United Artists. From RKO came two
major pro-Soviet features: *The North Star,* a story of heroism set in a Soviet
farm village, directed by Lewis Milestone with screenplay by Lillian Hellman and music by Aaron Copland, released in November 1943, and *Days*

of Glory, starring Gregory Peck, in his first major screen role, as the leader
of a band of Soviet partisans, released in June 1944. From MGM came the
musical extravaganza *Song of Russia,* directed by Gregory Ratoff, released
in June 1944. Just how quickly and apparently easily many Hollywood
figures adapted to the changed situation is evident in the fact that the same
writer, Melchior Lengyel, supplied the original story both for *Ninotchka*
(before) and for *Days of Glory* (after). What a difference a war can make. In
a similar process of ideological turnabout, *North Star* would be recut and
reissued as an anti-Soviet film, *Armored Attack,* during the post-war era.

In addition to these commercial films made by Hollywood studios, several pro-Soviet documentaries using Hollywood behind-the-camera talent were produced and widely distributed by the United States military
and affiliated organizations. The most important were *Our Russian Front,*
produced by Lewis Milestone for Artkino Studios and the Russian Relief
Organization in 1942, and the 1943 *Battle of Russia,* directed by Anatole
Litvak and Frank Capra as part of the *Why We Fight* series produced by the
United States Army Signal Corps. The feature films borrowed heavily from
these documentaries for talent and material, including newsreel footage,
and in fact frequently veered over the line separating feature from documentary. As Andre Bazin writes in "On *Why We Fight:* History, Documentation, and the Newsreel": "War, with its harvest of dead bodies, its immense
destruction, its countless migrations, its concentration camps, and its
atomic bombs, leaves far behind the creative art that aims at reconstitut-
ing it."[3]

The Soviet-American love-in that began in 1941 was very short-lived,
however. Almost immediately after the end of World War II, anti-Soviet
and anti-Communist sentiment grew and rapidly intensified in the United
States, culminating, as has been well documented, in the era of so-called
McCarthyism (named after Wisconsin Senator Joseph McCarthy) that dominated the American political and cultural scene from 1949 to 1959. During this period, the House Un-American Activities Committee and its
related committees in the U.S. Congress summoned many prominent cultural figures to Washington to testify about their own alleged involved with
the Communist Party. The pro-Soviet films made at such great expense
and with such great fanfare during World War II suddenly became a terrible embarrassment for the studios and all the creative personnel involved with them. Indeed, these films were one of the main factors that led

to the launching of the campaign against alleged Communist influence in American culture and education of the postwar years. Numerous producers, directors, actors, screenwriters, and even composers who had worked on the pro-Soviet wartime Hollywood features were called up for questioning by HUAC—including Jack Warner, Louis B. Mayer, actor Robert Taylor, screenwriter Lillian Hellman, and composer Aaron Copland. Director Lewis Milestone (of *North Star*) was even a member of the so-called Hollywood Nineteen, the first group of "unfriendly" witnesses summoned in September 1947 to testify before HUAC about their alleged—and sometimes real—involvement with the Communist Party.[4] Another member of that group was German playwright Bertold Brecht. Only ten of these nineteen were actually called to testify, however, and Milestone was not among them.

Revisionist historians like Kenneth Lloyd Billingsley have also suggested that the not insignificant group of Communist Party members and sympathizers present in Hollywood before the war (which included a number of people born in the Russian or Soviet empire) happily contributed to the creation of pro-Soviet films, only to be caught a few years later in the anti-Communist backlash.[5] In *Hollywood Goes to War: How Politics, Profits and Propaganda Shaped World War II Movies,* Clayton R. Koppes and Gregory D. Black observe, "For a time the interests of communists in the film colony converged with the mainstream, but this was temporary, coincidental and not of their making."[6]

★   One striking feature of the major pro-Soviet wartime films is the recycling of particular creative talent. Walter Huston participates in no less than four of them: as off-screen narrator for *Our Russian Front* and *Why We Fight,* in the leading role of Ambassador Davies in *Mission to Moscow,* and in the supporting role of Dr. Kurin in *North Star.* (It is Kurin, the kindly and wise village doctor, who in *North Star* kills the evil German doctors who are taking blood from the village children.) No doubt it was Huston's association with roles carrying authority and moral rectitude, such as the title role in D. W. Griffith's *Abraham Lincoln* and as another American president in *Gabriel Over the White House,* that made him suitable to be the voice of national pride, confidence, and bravery, whether American or Russian. A profile of Huston in the *New York Times* in connection with the upcoming premiere of *Mission to Moscow* declares that he "has an ambassadorial look about him. He stands well over six feet, has an impressive head of graying hair and his manners are as indigenously American as apple pie."[7] Later, after the film's release, he even appeared together with Ambassador Davies to defend its historical veracity.

Lewis Milestone directed two of the films, one documentary and one feature: *Our Russian Front* and *North Star*. Indeed, his experience at handling combat footage in the documentary proved very useful in the feature. Earlier in his career, of course, Milestone had won an Oscar for his direction of another war film, *All Quiet on the Western Front*, and he was associated with this genre forever after. Although he emigrated from Russia before the Russian Revolution and never actually lived in the USSR, he apparently supported Communism, which made these two projects even more congenial to him.[8]

Nor was Milestone the only member of Hollywood's large Russian-speaking community to participate in the making of Hollywood's pro-Soviet wartime films. Veteran character actor Vladimir Sokoloff (1889–1962) plays both living Communist Party Politburo member Mikhail Kalinin in the docudrama *Mission to Moscow* and Meschkov (head of the local music school) in *Song of Russia*. Gregory Ratoff (1897–1960), who as it happens did service in the Tsar's army before leaving Soviet Russia, directed *Song of Russia*. Anatole Litvak (1902–1974), director of *Tovarich*, which celebrates the outmoded values of the ruined Russian aristocracy, co-directed the heroically pro-Soviet *Battle of Russia*. The cast of *Song of Russia* also includes cameo appearances by two prominent members of the Hollywood Russian community, Michael Chekhov (1891–1955) and Feodor Chaliapin, Jr. That these Russian-born actors had fled Bolshevik Russia for the warmer climate of southern California, and had no apparent desire to return to live there, did not prevent directors from casting them as characters who embodied Soviet patriotism. This sort of politically blind casting would be a bit like giving the role of Lenin to John Wayne or Ronald Reagan.

Significantly, however, Russian-American actors were given only minor character roles, while the leading roles in the feature films were given to red-blooded Americans. Walter Huston and Robert Taylor both play Americans abroad in the USSR at crucial historical moments, while American actors Gregory Peck, Dana Andrews, Walter Huston (again), Walter Brennan, and Farley Granger play "Russian." The starring female roles are also given exclusively to Americans: Susan Peters is the romantic lead,

FIGURE 17.

North Star. RKO 1943. Director Lewis Milestone seated behind the camera
during shooting. At extreme right is cinematographer James Wong Howe.
Courtesy of the Margaret Herrick Library, Academy of Motion Picture Arts and
Sciences. Gift of Lewis Milestone.

playing Russian concert pianist Nadya Stepanova, in *Song of Russia*, while Maria Palmer plays Russian in two of the films, as the martyred Yelena in *Days of Glory*, and as Tanya Litvinov, daughter of foreign minister Maxim Litvinov, in *Mission to Moscow*. The casting of Americans in the major Russian roles helped to promote the propaganda point that Soviets were just like Americans—here, in fact, they actually are Americans!

The way in which Hollywood deals with the issue of language in these films similarly serves to minimize perceptions of cultural difference between Russians and Americans. In the war documentaries, an authoritative American voice interprets the visual images—the Soviet soldiers or citizens never actually have the opportunity to speak for themselves. In the feature films, virtually no Russian words are heard, even though the action takes place almost exclusively on Russian-speaking territory. In *Mission to Moscow*, in keeping with the diplomatic setting, all conversations take place in fine literary American English. Although Huston/Davies admits that he does not speak any Russian, no interpreter is ever present for his exchanges with Soviet officials; even the suave Stalin (played by Manart Kippen) commands lovely unaccented English, which makes him appear even more sensible, intelligent, and "just like us."

In *Song of Russia*, too, the American pianist John Meredith (played by Robert Taylor) miraculously communicates without the slightest difficulty in English with characters on every rung of the social-economic ladder. In *North Star* and *Days of Glory*, where no American characters are present, the screenwriters make numerous attempts to make the spoken English sound somehow Russian, mainly through the use of diminutives and folksy turns of phrase. In *Days of Glory*, the partisans incessantly call each other "little brother," "little sister," "little mother," and even "little comrade," which would translate back into Russian as something like "*tovarischyok*," a term of address that even the most patriotic Soviet Russian-speakers might find comical. Peasant characters are also heard to utter such vivid phrases as "Our land—it's our mother." One of the partisans, a professor, has conveniently studied in England and speaks with an impeccable Oxford precision.

While the Soviet/Russian characters speak fine English to minimize the perception of their "otherness," the German characters (especially in *Days of Glory*), on the other hand, speak either German or heavily accented English to emphasize their otherness. One of the best examples occurs when German soldiers uncover the hiding place of the Soviet partisans (led by

Gregory Peck) in *Days of Glory. "Was ist das? Ein guerilla-nest?"* the commander proclaims as he enters. In *North Star,* Erich von Stroheim lays his German accent on heavily in his role as the perverted doctor who oversees the taking of blood from Russian children, but Walter Huston as the heroic Russian village doctor is allowed to speak in easy American English.

In attempting to make Soviet citizens as nonforeign as possible, these films also minimize and even falsify territorial and linguistic distinctions within the Soviet Union. The documentary *The Battle of Russia* deals with combat in Ukraine and the Caucasus as well as within the Russian Soviet Republic, but makes no attempt to distinguish between the regions or their cultures. Even worse is the confusion in the screenplay for *North Star.* Lillian Hellman initially wrote a scenario for what she called a "semi-documentary." She completed it by summer 1942, when Russia's military fortunes were at their lowest ebb, which profoundly affected American public opinion toward the USSR in a positive direction. Although Hellman (whose strong pro-Communist convictions were well known in Hollywood) later charged that Sam Goldwyn ruined her concept, and "phonied up" the film, her published screenplay in fact is quite close to the characters and story line of the completed film. For the details of life on a Soviet collective farm, she relied heavily on her visit to a model collective farm near Moscow in 1937. But there was one big problem that she and her collaborators overlooked. The film is set in Ukraine, near Moldova, not in Russia. And yet the title page of the screenplay bears the pretentious subtitle "A Motion Picture About Some Russian People." Ukrainians, as we know, are not Russians. They speak a different language, and have a different religious, cultural, and political history—as well as different music. These differences are completely ignored in the screenplay and in the film.

Even more, many Ukrainians, especially under Stalin, were extremely anti-Russian and anti-Soviet. Collectivization was forced upon Ukrainian peasants in the 1930s with terrible loss of life and property. Many Ukrainian peasants burned their own property rather than give it up to the Soviet state. When Hitler's forces entered Ukraine in June 1941, a significant portion of the population—especially in Western Ukraine, where this film is set, actually greeted the Nazi army with open arms, since they saw them as bringing their land back into the Austro-Hungarian orbit, and as saviors from Stalin's brutality.

Lillian Hellman saw or knew none of this, however, from her supposedly exhaustive research, which was confined to genteel nineteenth-century Russian novels, official falsified *Pravda* accounts of the triumphs of the Soviet economy, and cocktail lounge conversations in Moscow hotels with foreign journalists and official government spokesmen. The film's director, Lewis Milestone, who grew up in Moldova, later fumed that "Hellman knew nothing about Russia—especially the villages."[9]

Since they had been asked by President Roosevelt to make Russians as attractive as possible to American audiences, Hollywood producers and their studio personnel stressed "universal" values and the aspects of Russian culture that were the most familiar and nonthreatening. This meant, as we have seen, minimizing the diversity of the Soviet Union and presenting Great Russian nationalism as dominant and triumphant. This meant, in *Mission to Moscow,* presenting (as Joseph Davies did in the book on which the film is based) Stalin as a completely rational and dignified statesman, and the terrible Soviet purge trials of the late 1930s—directed against those who had at some point disagreed with Stalin over aspects of Communism in theory or practice—as justified and necessary.

This also meant, in the fictionalized features, omitting almost any reference to Soviet ideology or political life. One looks in vain for any visual evidence of Soviet power (such as the hammer and sickle, or prominent portraits of Lenin) in *The North Star, Days of Glory,* or *Song of Russia.* There is no discussion by any of the characters of the Soviet system, or of the ideals of Communism. Even more, Christian ritual is shown to be tolerated and practiced: Nadya and John have a religious wedding in *Song of Russia,* and Yelena is given a religious funeral in *Days of Glory.* There are also repeated shots of Soviet citizens crossing themselves in thanks or terror. Such presentation of religious freedom was clearly calculated to reassure American audiences that their Soviet allies could go to church, too. Once again, it is the Germans who are shown as heathen barbarians, most obviously in the opening sequence of *The Battle of Russia,* where footage from Eisenstein's classic 1938 film *Alexander Nevsky* (the Germans attacking Orthodox symbols) is presented (without identification) as historical background to the current situation.

In all of Hollywood's wartime portrayals of Russia, what is shown as worthy of preservation and defense is the legacy of pre-Revolutionary nineteenth-century Russian culture. This tendency is especially pronounced in *Days of Glory.* (Perhaps it is worth noting that the film's screenwriter, Casey Robinson, also wrote the screenplay for *Tovarich*.) The Soviet partisans' underground hideout becomes a veritable museum of highly prized objects of elite Russian culture: a dancer from the Bolshoi Ballet who was lost while making her way to the front line to entertain the troops (played by real-life Ballets Russes ballerina Tamara Toumanova) and who gives dance demonstrations to her "little comrades"; manuscripts rescued by the professor from Tolstoy's house nearby at Yasnaya Polyana; impassioned readings from Pushkin's *Eugene Onegin* (Tatiana's letter scene, in which she professes her naïve love for Onegin), and Lermontov's *Hero of Our Times;* even the spontaneous performance of a Russian folk song by the entire cast as they sit at their various useful tasks. (The score for *Days of Glory* was written by Hollywood veteran Daniele Amfiteatrof, a Russian-Italian born and raised in Russia.) There is nary a mention of any product of Soviet culture—these folks are shown to be fighting for Tolstoy, Dostoyevsky, and Tchaikovsky, not socialism.

Song of Russia promotes the same message, although here it is focused on music. The heroine, Nadya, comes from the village of Tchaikovskoe, named after the composer, which suits our American hero John Meredith just fine, since the reason he came to Russia was to better understand what inspired Tchaikovsky to write his Sixth Symphony. Nadya's dream is to perform Tchaikovsky's Piano Concerto No.1 in Carnegie Hall—which is what happens in the film's last shot, an apotheosis of Russian-American intimacy and cultural exchange. Tchaikovsky's music as arranged by Herbert Stothart provides the soundtrack throughout the film. (There is also an original popular song, "Russia is Her Name," by Jerome Kern and E. Y. Harburg.) A scene of threshing takes place to the accompaniment of the peasants' song (*"bolyat moyi belyie ruchenki"*) from the opening of Act I of *Eugene Onegin,* while the village children play to the children's marching song from Act I of *The Queen of Spades.* Later, scenes of post-invasion devastation unfold against the background of the final movement of the Sixth Symphony (*Pathétique*), and John searches for Nadya to the strains of *Romeo and Juliet.* After the Nazi assault, the music professor (Vladimir Sokoloff) announces defiantly, "The culture, the music we've been building will never die." This culture, this music, means Tchaikovsky, a "safe" composer American audiences had embraced ever since he conducted at the opening of Carnegie Hall in 1891, and who had served as the model for Hollywood film composers for decades.

Tchaikovsky also plays a major role in the documentary *Battle of Russia,* whose musical director was the Russian-born Dmitri Tiomkin, one of the most successful film composers in Hollywood history. Most of the music for the film is taken from Tchaikovsky scores, with repeated use of excerpts from the Fifth and Sixth Symphonies and the First Piano Concerto. An extended newsreel sequence shows the destruction of Tchaikovsky's house/museum at Klin. *The Battle of Russia* also exploits Tchaikovsky for its emotional climactic scene, in which American, British, and Soviet flags mingle as a chorus sings an English text to the military theme of the third movement of the Sixth Symphony: "On the land, on sea, and in the skies forever, / Man shall live proud and free."

Max Steiner, the composer of the score for *Mission to Moscow,* also ends that film with a hymn to international brotherhood, with the lyrics, "Are you your brother's keeper, yes you are, now and forever you are," sung as a processional into what looks like a cloudy heaven. Elsewhere, Steiner (who used various national and patriotic music with great success in the 1942 film *Casablanca,* which was directed by Michael Curtiz, also the director of *Mission to Moscow*) uses the old Russian folk tune "*Slava*" ("Glory") to convey the idea of Russian authority and cultural continuity. This tune, used by Musorgsky in the coronation scene of *Boris Godunov,* is heard early in the film with a panoramic view of the Kremlin, and returns later, very significantly, at the end of the scene of the conversation between Stalin and Davies. Stalin, the music is telling us, is worthy of the same respect accorded to the great Russian Romanov Tsars.

In *North Star,* too, the music plays an essential role in making the characters palatable and accessible to an American audience. Its composer, Aaron Copland, was deeply associated in the public mind with images of Americana, for he had already written such scores as *Lincoln Portrait,* the ballets *Rodeo* and *Billy the Kid,* and the music for two film adaptations of novels by John Steinbeck, *Our Town* and *Of Mice and Men* (both directed by Lewis Milestone). Like Hellman and Steinbeck, Copland also possessed strong pro-Communist sympathies. Copland's score for *North Star* includes eight songs whose lyrics were written by another quintessentially American artist, Ira Gershwin. The first half of the film, before the German invasion, employs a song-and-dance style that seems far more Broadway than Ukraine. During his preparatory work on *North Star,* Copland consulted several published collections of Russian folk and popular songs.

One was entitled *Russian Folksongs from the Voronezh Region*—even though Voronezh is in south-central Russia, very far from the supposed site of the film's action, and in a region with an entirely different tradition of folk music and dance.

For the scene of the high school graduation that takes place on the eve of the Nazi invasion, Copland made a piano-choral arrangement of what has become one of the most popular Soviet "mass songs," "How Wide is My Country" ("*Shiroka strana moya rodnaya*"), written by Isaac Dunayevsky for the Soviet film *Circus* in 1936. Ironically, of course, the film for which the song was written deals with an American circus performer who flees the United States to escape persecution for having given birth out of wedlock to a child fathered by a black man. In Moscow, she finds acceptance, happiness, and true love in the arms of a Russian acrobat. So this tune from an anti-capitalist Soviet film was recycled in a pro-Soviet American film. (This song is heard in the score of *Mission to Moscow,* too.) Copland's score also includes an orchestration of the Communist anthem, the *Internationale,* heard broadcast over the radio after the official announcement of the Nazi assault—but without the text, whose sentiments could upset American audiences.

★   Today, *The North Star,* like all the pro-Soviet films made during World War II, seems primitive, heavy-handed, emotionally insincere, and historically false. Pauline Kael joked that the film "romanticizes the Russians so fondly that they're turned into Andy Hardy's neighbors." Even Lillian Hellman later virtually disowned the film. In her memoirs, *An Unfinished Woman,* she admits: "It could have been a good picture instead of the big-time, sentimental, badly directed, badly acted mess it turned out to be."[10] Despite the film's all-too-obvious aesthetic shortcomings, however, the political climate in 1943 was such that *The North Star* was nominated for four Academy Awards, for Lillian Hellman's screenplay, for Copland's score, for cinematography, and for art direction. The same year, *Mission to Moscow* received an Academy Award nomination for art direction.

But Hollywood's pro-Soviet films provoked political controversy as soon as they were released. In particular, *Mission to Moscow* came in for severe criticism for its portrayal of the purge trials. The fact that *Mission to Moscow* (with its on-screen introduction by former Ambassador Davies) presented itself more as documentary than feature made it an easier target for those who found fault with its historical accuracy. On May 9, 1943, just ten days after Bosley Crowther's lukewarm review of *Mission to Moscow* appeared in the *New York Times,* the newspaper published Crowther's lengthy essay raising questions about the film's political and historical veracity, as well as its intentions: "It is just as ridiculous to pretend that Russia has been a paradise of purity as it is to say the same thing of ourselves."[11] In the same issue, a long letter by John Dewey, Professor of Philosophy at Columbia University, and Suzanne La Follette, cousin of Senator Robert M. La Follette, attacked *Mission to Moscow* as "the first instance in our country of totalitarian propaganda for mass consumption."[12]

Other letters to the newspaper on both sides of the issue appeared over the coming weeks. The director of the National Department of Americanism of the Veterans of Foreign Wars charged that "renegade Communists" were attempting to suppress the film.[13] On May 20, a statement signed by fifty-two leading American educators, historians, writers, and trade union leaders denounced the film as propaganda. The same day, at a rally held in Carnegie Hall (where else?), Ambassador Davies and Walter Huston were awarded a certificate of appreciation by the National Council of American-Soviet Friendship. On May 28, the New York City Board of Transportation ordered that placards placed in subway and elevated cars announcing *Mission to Moscow* as the "motion picture of the month" be removed after complaints were received about its distortion of "the facts upon which it is supposedly based."[14] So heated did the controversy become that Howard Koch, the screenwriter of *Mission to Moscow* (and, not incidentally, of *Casablanca*) felt called upon to defend himself in a long letter to the *New York Times:* "History provides us with the materials of drama, but it doesn't conveniently arrange them into scenes or bind them to any unifying theme. That is the province of the dramatist as distinct from the historian."[15]

Boston also had to get into the act. On June 15, the Boston City Council asked the Mayor to ban *Mission to Moscow* on the grounds it is "outright Communistic propaganda . . . of distorted truth, with an ulterior motive of glorifying a dictatorship government."[16] Meanwhile, in Moscow itself, *Mission to Moscow* was screened for Stalin and released for public consumption in the USSR. The film even became a useful tool of American propaganda in the USSR, although it was reported by American correspondents that Soviet audiences found the representation of Soviet life "slightly comical."[17]

As this documentation shows, then, the pro-Soviet Hollywood wartime features (and especially *Mission to Moscow*) provoked controversy almost immediately upon release, even at the height of pro-Soviet public opinion in 1943. It seems not at all surprising, then, that politicians at the beginning of the Cold War era would return to this debate and see these films as evidence of persistent and dangerous pro-Communist sentiment in Hollywood studios.

★   Russian music was extremely popular in Hollywood during World War II. Tchaikovsky's music, a favorite among directors for film scoring from the earliest days of Hollywood, acquired added patriotic resonance, and figured prominently (as noted above) in several of the large wartime pro-Soviet features. Tchaikovsky also furnished much of the emotional pathos in a classic wartime feature, *Now Voyager* (1942), starring Bette Davis as a Boston spinster who falls in love late in life. An on-screen performance of Tchaikovsky's Sixth Symphony (*Pathétique*) by what we presume to be the Boston Symphony (since the action is set in Boston) occurs at the emotional and dramatic climax. Charlotte (Davis) has decided finally to marry the respectable widower who has been decorously courting her when she suddenly comes face to face with the sexy married architect with whom she had an affair on a South American cruise earlier in the story. At the concert, Charlotte sits between the two men, and the music, the lyrical and wilting second theme of the first movement of the *Pathétique*, expresses her state of hypersensitivity and passion, which will lead her in the next scene to break off her engagement with the boring Boston gentleman. This music also returns later in the film, as Charlotte is listening to a radio broadcast of the same excerpt. The descriptive title of the *Pathétique* refers to a state of heightened emotion and receptivity—not to anything "pathetic" in the English sense of the word.

The use of this particular music in *Now Voyager* is also symbolic of how Charlotte's once closed and introverted emotional world has opened to great feeling through her work with the psychoanalyst played by Claude Rains. Max Steiner, the composer for *Now Voyager,* won an Academy Award for the film, although his contribution, as in *Casablanca,* amounts more to arrangement than to original composition. As William Darby and Jack DuBois write in their history of American film music, "One cannot avoid the impression that Steiner (or some later editor) merely plunked in the familiar Russian classic because the scene needed a good tune."[18]

Even living Russian composers found a warm welcome in Hollywood during World War II. Sergei Prokofiev's brilliant score (also arranged into a concert cantata) for Sergei Eisenstein's anti-German epic *Alexander Nevsky* became well known, since the film was frequently screened to promote the U.S.-Soviet military alliance and to demonize the Nazi enemy. By now, both Prokofiev and Eisenstein were back in Russia, their days of western travel ended, but Prokofiev's music continued to exert a significant influence on Hollywood film composers, including such figures as John Williams (particularly in the *Star Wars* films).

Prokofiev's countryman and frequent rival Igor Stravinsky arrived in Hollywood in 1940, searching for a more peaceful creative climate than Europe could provide at the moment. Los Angeles would be his home for the next thirty years. Esa-Pekka Salonen, conductor of the Los Angeles Philharmonic and a great champion of Stravinsky's music, likes to point out that Stravinsky lived as long in Los Angeles as he did in Russia. "If there ever was a home for Stravinsky, it was the house in West Hollywood," he has said. "And Stravinsky is maybe the most important figure in the world of the classical arts ever to have lived in Los Angeles, even though there's still very little appreciation of this fact, even in Los Angeles."[19] Salonen seems to be trying hard to raise the consciousness of his fellow Los Angelenos, judging by the high frequency with which he programs Stravinsky's works; his ballet *The Rite of Spring* has even become a kind of signature piece for the LA Philharmonic in its spectacular new home, Walt Disney Hall.

During the 1940s, Stravinsky was asked to write scores for several films, but he and the directors repeatedly encountered "artistic differences." In 1942, Stravinsky was commissioned to produce a score for a film about the Nazi invasion of Norway, *The Commandos Strike at Dawn,* but he balked at changes requested by Columbia and was eventually replaced by Louis Gruenberg, whose score was nominated for an Academy Award. Stravinsky did recycle the music he had written into *Four Norwegian Moods,* a marvelously evocative piece for orchestra. In many ways, this warm, nostalgic, and highly accessible piece makes a bridge to the earlier "Russian" phase of Stravinsky's career, with its witty treatment of folk material and bewildering "off-center" rhythms. The use of the English horn in the lyrical and sparely scored second movement also seems to recall the lonely Nordic world of the symphonies of Sibelius, a composer with a retrograde aesthetic radically different from Stravinsky's. Thousands of miles away from Russia under the palm trees of southern California, perhaps Stravinsky was reconnecting emotionally with the Baltic landscape of his childhood.

In 1943, Stravinsky was hired for another film score, for *Song of Bernadette,* a religious tearjerker set at the shrine of Lourdes, but again his music was not used; veteran film composer Alfred Newman replaced Stravinsky and won his third Academy Award. Stravinsky recycled his "Bernadette" music into the second movement of *Symphony in Three Movements,* where the heavenly harp from the "Apparition of the Virgin" scene figures prominently. After the 1940s, Stravinsky steered clear of the film industry. He always demanded complete creative control, an impossibility in the producer-controlled, harshly commercial, formulaic, and money-driven world of Hollywood movies.

Also in the early 1940s, another Russian musical giant moved to Los Angeles: Sergei Rachmaninoff (1873–1943). Rachmaninoff, who had been living in emigration from his beloved Russia since 1918, was by then wealthy and very famous as a result of his extensive tours as pianist throughout the United States over the preceding decades, and his association with the Philadelphia Orchestra, for which he wrote several new works. In 1939 he left Europe and took up residence in Long Island. When he decided to settle in Los Angeles in early 1942, he was seriously ill, suffering from sclerosis, lumbago, neuralgia, high blood pressure, and headaches. At first he leased a house in the hills on Tower Road, complete with swimming pool, garden, sweeping views, and a music room that could accommodate two pianos. There he loved to play two-piano works and adaptations with his friend virtuoso Vladimir Horowitz, another Russian who had sought refuge in Los Angeles. On occasion, the two pianists hosted domestic recitals. Rachmaninoff's friend Sergei Bertensson attended a particularly memorable one on June 15, 1942, with a program of works by Mozart and Rachmaninoff (the second suite for two pianos). "After the last note no one spoke—time seemed to have stopped. I, for one, forgot that I was living in Hollywood, where the word 'art' has a habit of slipping from one's memory."[20]

Rachmaninoff and his guests also did lots of talking, especially about the worsening situation in Europe and its impact on their family and friends. "Over dinner with the Horowitzes and other expatriate friends, the composer would talk about his feelings of guilt that he should be living in such luxury."[21] A few months later, Rachmaninoff bought a small house on Elm Drive, where he continued to host musical evenings. Around the same time, Rachmaninoff, an experienced and admired conductor, was offered the position of conductor of the Los Angeles Philharmonic, but his precarious health made it impossible for him to accept. Indeed, Rachmaninoff only lived in his new house for a few months. He died of cancer in Los Angeles on March 28, 1943, and his funeral was held in the tiny Russian Orthodox Church on Micheltorena Street in the Silver Lake neighborhood.

When Rachmaninoff moved to Los Angeles, he was much better known in the United States than Stravinsky. Rachmaninoff was the first composer Walt Disney thought of when he was planning the animated musical feature that became *Fantasia;* he wanted to include Rachmaninoff playing his Second Piano Concerto. "I don't know anything about music," Disney is alleged to have told Leopold Stokowski, longtime conductor of the Philadelphia Orchestra, "but I have heard of Rachmaninoff for a long time."[22] Although Rachmaninoff never worked on any film projects, his late romantic musical style exerted an enormous influence on the mainstream of Hollywood film music. Miklos Rosza even incorporated Rachmaninoff's *Rhapsody on a Theme of Paganini* into his original score for *The Story of Three Loves* (1953), co-directed by Gottfried Reinhardt and Vincente Minelli.

By the time Stravinsky and Rachmaninoff arrived in Hollywood, another Russian had already established himself there as one of the leading creators of film scores: Dmitri Tiomkin (1894–1979). Born in Ukraine and educated as a pianist and conductor at St. Petersburg Conservatory, where he crossed paths with Sergei Prokofiev, Tiomkin had no illusions about his talent or about the nature of the work he did: "I am no Prokofiev, I am no Tchaikovsky. But what I write is good for what I write for. So please, boys, help me."[23] When Tiomkin gave his acceptance speech upon receiving an Oscar for his score for *The High and the Mighty* in 1955, he mischievously thanked Brahms, Johann Strauss, Richard Strauss, Wagner, Beethoven, and Rimsky-Korsakoff. But Tiomkin was brilliant at what he did, one of the most consistently successful film composers of all time. In St. Petersburg, Tiomkin received an excellent academic training from such pedagogues as Felix Blumenfeld (Vladimir Horowitz's teacher) and Alexander Glazunov (mentor to Prokofiev and Shostakovich) and played piano accompaniment for silent film screenings. After leaving Russia, Tiomkin made his way through Berlin and Paris before coming to New York in 1925. Like many others, he left New York after a few years to find greater employment opportunities in the film industry in Los Angeles.

Tiomkin scored the film *Alice in Wonderland* (with W. C. Fields as Humpty Dumpty and Cary Grant as the Mock Turtle) for Paramount in 1933, and made his breakthrough in 1937 with the music for Frank Capra's *Lost Horizon,* for which he received the first of his twenty-three Academy Award nominations. In 1939 he scored *Mr. Smith Goes to Washington,* and in 1944, *The Bridge of San Luis Rey* (featuring fellow Russians Akim Tamiroff as the theatrical impresario Uncle Pio, and Alla Nazimova as the Marquesa). Tiomkin won his first Academy Award for the score for the classic 1952 film *High Noon,* a tale of cowardice and conformity in a small Western town, starring Gary Cooper as a quietly courageous sheriff who has to face alone the return of a band of hoodlums imprisoned years ago largely due to his efforts and now newly released from prison. Like the film, Tiomkin's score is unconventional and unheroic, built entirely around a single western-style ballad, "Do Not Forsake Me, O My Darling," sung by the country western star Tex Ritter.

Tiomkin breaks most of the rules of Hollywood film-scoring in his groundbreaking music for *High Noon.* Most important, perhaps, he eliminates the violins from the ensemble. The resulting combination of lower strings, brass, wind, and piano, with the harmonica heard while Tex Ritter is singing, creates a rustic, deglamorized sound that suits the anti-heroic sentiments of the film. Also, the score opens and closes very softly, with guitar, accordion, and drums—in most classic Hollywood films, the overture tends to be big and string-heavy, with a climax just as the director's name appears on the screen. The unusual concept of building the score around a single folk tune recalls the way Russian classical composers employ folk tunes; a good example is Mikhail Glinka's *Kamarinskaya,* where a folk tune is subjected to increasingly fanciful and ornate variations. Indeed, it was long rumored that the tune of "Do Not Forsake Me, O My Darling" was Russian or Ukrainian, but this has never been proven.

In his excellent book *The Composer in Hollywood,* Christopher Palmer speculates on the reasons why a Russian-born conservatory-educated figure like Tiomkin could have been so successful in the American movie business.

He came from a Big Country, too, and in America's vastness, particularly its vast all-embracingness of sky and plain, he must have seen a reflection of the steppes of his native Ukraine. So the cowboy becomes a mirror-image of the Cossack: both are primitives and innocents, etched on and dwarfed by a landscape of soul-stirring immensity and rugged masculine beauty. And as an exile himself, Tiomkin would have identified with the cowboys, pioneers and early settlers who people the world of the Western. . . . [T]hose like Tiomkin who blazed a trail in Hollywood were actually winning the West all over again.[24]

Palmer also tries to explain why Russian music (in the widest sense) was so often used for film scores: "It is as natural for a Russian to think episodically as for a Frenchman to think logically. Now episodic thinking is an essential qualification for any film composer."[25]

Tiomkin once observed, "A steppe is a steppe is a steppe. . . . The problems of the cowboy and the Cossack are very similar. They share a love of nature and a love of animals. Their courage and their philosophical attitudes are similar, and the steppes of Russia are much like the prairies of America."[26]

Especially since he was not trained as a composer, Tiomkin never possessed the technical expertise of a Prokofiev or a Stravinsky. His genius lay in coming up with themes and finding vivid ways of creating sonic color appropriate to the story and visual image, not in his ability to combine the themes into a complex symphonic structure that could stand on its own.

Tiomkin did not work on feature films set in Russia, with a single exception, the unfortunate bio-pic *Tchaikovsky* which he also co-produced in 1971, a Soviet-American project for which he acted more as compiler/arranger/musical director than as composer. For the most part, the scoring of Hollywood features dealing with Russia or the USSR was left to non-Russians, often to composers of German or Austrian background. There were a number of Russian musicians in the studio orchestras, however, and in production positions. Max Rabinowitz, for example, the former pianist for operatic bass Fyodor Chaliapin, settled in LA and made his living by dubbing piano parts for movie scores, and by having his hands photographed in close-up shots for piano-playing scenes.

Probably the most visible and influential of these production people was Constantine Bakaleinikoff, who spent his entire adult career as a conductor working in the movie business in Los Angeles. Born in Moscow in 1896, he graduated from the Moscow Conservatory in 1916 as a cellist and composer. Like so many other musicians and artists, Bakaleinikoff left Russia and ended up in California in 1920, where he played the cello briefly in the Los Angeles Philharmonic before being hired by the producer Sid Grauman as musical director for his movie theaters, conducting the orchestra for silent films shown at such palaces as the Egyptian and the legendary Grauman's Chinese Theater. So familiar was he with movie audiences that they started calling him by the nickname "Backy." With the advent of sound, he moved to Paramount, where he stayed until 1935, then went to MGM for six years, and finally worked at RKO in the powerful and demanding position of musical director from 1941 to 1957.

Bakaleinikoff also composed scores for a number of films. Several of Bakaleinikoff's numerous brothers were also musicians; Mischa started out playing double bass in studio orchestras (including the one that recorded Tiomkin's score for *Lost Horizon*) and then served for many years as the musical director at Columbia Studios. Vladimir was a conductor who appeared with the symphony orchestras of Cincinnati and Pittsburgh. Constantin's house in Bouquet Canyon was apparently a gathering place for Russian émigrés, at least according to a complaint made by his wife, the actress Fritzi Ridgway, to the *Los Angeles Examiner* that "whenever he brought friends home . . . they would exclude her from their conversation by talking entirely in Russian."[27]

"Tschaikowsky," a zany song in the 1941 Broadway musical *Lady in the Dark*—created by the dream team of composer Kurt Weill, lyricist Ira Gershwin, and writer Moss Hart—celebrates the fad for Russian composers in a tongue-twisting cascade of syllables. In the original Broadway show, which received its premiere just a few months before the Nazi invasion of the USSR, the song was sung by Danny Kaye in the role of Russell Paxton, a fey fashion photographer and the ringmaster of an imaginary circus. After declaring "I love Russian composers!" Paxton launches into one of the most well-educated patter songs ever written, a litany of fifty Russian composers in thirty-nine seconds:

There's Malichevsky, Rubinstein, Arensky and Tschaikowsky,
Sapelnikoff, Dimitrieff, Tscherepnin, Kryjanowsky,
Godowsky, Arteibojucheff, Moniuszko, Akimenko,

Solovieff, Prokofieff, Tiomkin, Korestchencko.
There's Glinka, Winkler, Bortniansky, Rebikoff, Ilyinsky,
There's Medtner, Balakireff, Zolotareff and Kvoschinsky.
And Sokoloff and Kopyloff, Dukelsky and Klenofsky,
And Shostakovitsch, Borodine, Gliere and Nowakofski.
There's Liadoff and Karganoff, Markievitch, Pantschenko
And Dargomyzski, Stcherbatcheff, Scriabine, Vassilenko,
Stravinsky, Rimsky-Korsakoff, Mussorgsky and Gretchaninoff
And Glazounoff and Caesar Cui, Kalinikoff, Rachmaninoff,
Stravinsky and Gretchaninoff, Rumshinsky and Rachmaninoff,
I really have to stop, The subject has been dwelt upon enough!
Stravinsky, Gretchaninoff, Kvoschinsky, Rachmaninoff!
I really have to stop because you all have undergone enough!

Sadly, when Paramount made *Lady in the Dark* into a film in 1944, most of the songs were eliminated, including this one. Mischa Auer took the role of the effete photographer, in an ensemble that included Ginger Rogers and Ray Milland.

Another popular wartime film version of a Broadway show, *Cabin in the Sky,* not only featured a song *about* Russian composers—it was composed by one: Vernon Duke (1903–1969). That a Russian composer should write the music for one of the first all-black musicals is a peculiar and telling fact, no less intriguing than Tiomkin's central role in creating the sound track for the classic American film western. Known to millions as the American composer of such popular song hits as "Autumn in New York," "April in Paris," and "Taking a Chance on Love" (from *Cabin in the Sky*), Duke also had another identity. As Vladimir Dukelsky (his real name), he composed respectable "classical" ballets, symphonies, concerti, sonatas, oratorios, and chamber music. Born in Russia and educated at the Kiev Conservatory, Dukelsky came to the United States in 1921. For the rest of his life, Dukelsky/Duke led a double creative life, writing "serious" music for such imposing impresarios as Serge Koussevitsky and Serge Diaghilev with one hand, and collaborating with Ira Gershwin, Bob Hope, and the Ziegfeld Follies with the other.

Duke was also a longtime friend of Sergei Prokofiev. They met in Paris in 1924 when both were working on ballets for Diaghilev. In the spring of 1928, it was Duke who brought George Gershwin to Prokofiev's Paris apartment, where the American composer "played his head off," impressing Prokofiev with his facility, although Gershwin's enjoyment of "dollars and dinners"—a vice shared by Duke—made him wary.[28] As time went on, the creative paths Prokofiev and Duke followed came to diverge more and more. Duke followed up the commercial success of his 1932 "April in Paris" (written for the show *Walk a Little Faster*) in 1934 with another standard, "Autumn in New York" (written for the show *Thumbs Up*). In 1940 he produced the music for the groundbreaking stage musical *Cabin in the Sky*, made into a film by MGM in 1943, directed by Vincente Minelli and featuring Ethel Waters, Lena Horne, and Louis Armstrong. Was it easier for a Russian émigré like Duke, a cultural outsider, to appreciate and convey the value of black musical culture to a mainstream American audience?

Although he continued to compose "classical" works, Duke became known primarily as a "popular" composer, an identity he did not attempt to cast off. It was Duke, too, who arranged for his agent to make an offer to Sergei Prokofiev, on his last visit to Hollywood in 1938, to write music for the movies at $2500 a week. Prokofiev's reaction, as recorded by Duke (Prokofiev's nickname for him was "Dima," from his first name, Vladimir), shows just how deeply Russians abroad were divided by the presence of the Communist regime in the USSR.

> I showed Serge the telegram exultantly; there was a flicker of interest for a mere instant, then, his face set, his oversize lips petulant, he said gruffly: "That's nice bait, but I won't swallow it. I've got to go back to Moscow, to my music and my children. And now that that's settled, will you come to Macy's with me? I've got to buy a whole roomful of things you can't get in Russia. . . .
>
> The list was imposing, and we went to Macy's department store, another sample of capitalistic bait designed by the lackeys of Wall Street to be swallowed by oppressed workers. Although he wouldn't admit it, Serge enjoyed himself hugely in the store—he loved gadgets and trinkets of every description. Suddenly he turned to me, his eyes peculiarly moist, his voice even gruffer than usual: "You know, Dima, it occurred to me that I may not be back for quite some time. . . . I don't suppose it would be wise for you to come to Russia, would it?" "No, I don't suppose it would," I answered, smiling bravely, my happiness abruptly gone. I never saw Prokofiev again.[29]

★   There was a strong feeling of solidarity among the Russian émigré
community in Hollywood. Those more successful and affluent frequently
helped others to become established and helped them through difficult
times. Before his death in 1943, Sergei Rachmaninoff often used his
money and influence to assist friends and colleagues. One of his last gestures of this kind was directed toward the actor/director/pedagogue Michael
Chekhov (1891–1955).

Considered one of the greatest Russian actors of his generation, Chekhov had long struggled under the psychological burden of being Anton
Chekhov's nephew. Chekhov studied with many of the leading figures of
the early twentieth-century Russian theater, including Stanislavsky and
Yevgeny Vakhtangov, and made his reputation in leading and supporting
roles at Stanislavsky's Moscow Art Theater between 1913 and 1923. (He
was particularly acclaimed as Khlestakov in Gogol's satirical play *The Inspector General.*) Eventually Chekhov came to disagree with Stanislavsky's
theory and teaching methods, particularly his reliance on psychological
memory at the expense of imagination in creating a role. As director of the
second Moscow Art Theater from 1924 to 1927, he put his own ideas into
practice. Eventually, however, he fell afoul of the Soviet cultural bureaucrats, who branded him a "sick artist" staging "alien and reactionary" productions in the increasingly oppressive cultural environment that developed after Lenin's death. In 1928, Chekhov accepted Max Reinhardt's
invitation to perform in Berlin and never returned to Russia.

For the next few years, Chekhov, like so many other Russian artistic
émigrés, took on all sorts of work. He starred in German-language comedies and silent films in Berlin and set up acting studios in Paris, Latvia,
and Lithuania. Soon his work came to the attention of impresarios, including the Russian-American Sol Hurok. In early 1935, Hurok brought
Chekhov and his company—the Moscow Art Players—to the Majestic Theatre in New York with a production of *The Inspector General.*

By the time Chekhov came to America in 1935, he already had a devoted
(if small) following there among the members of the Group Theatre. This
ensemble had been formed in 1931 by a group of actors and producers devoted to Stanislavsky's theories and teachings. They greeted Chekhov enthusiastically, as a disciple of the master, and even offered him a job. New
York's critics had more difficulty appreciating his work, probably because
the productions he brought were performed in Russian. Harold Clurman,

one of the leading theater critics of the day and a founding member of the Group Theatre, complained that the New York press had "been unable to recognize" Chekhov's genius. After the New York engagement, the Moscow Art Players went on to perform in Philadelphia and Boston.

Hurok lost money on the Moscow Art Players and did not bring them back to the United States again. But the tour was a turning point for Chekhov, because it gave him the opportunity to meet American actress Beatrice Straight, who proposed to him that he start a theater-studio at Dartington Hall, the English estate of her stepfather and mother. Chekhov set up shop there and further refined his acting and pedagagogical methods with students and instructors recruited from all over the world.

When war with Germany threatened in 1939, he relocated his Chekhov Studio Theatre to Ridgefield, Connecticut, and then opened a studio in Manhattan in 1941. Here he worked with some of the leading figures in the American theater—Stella Adler, Bobby Lewis, Sandy Meisner. Later, in their own work as teachers, they further disseminated Chekhov's ideas about imagination and the "psychological gesture," which they saw as a strong counterweight to the dominant interpretation of the Stanislavsky "Method" championed in America by Lee Strasberg. By 1943, Chekhov's Ridgefield operation was in trouble. The financial subsidies that had supported the school were coming to an end, and the draft was taking away most of the talented male members of the company. It was at this moment that Rachmaninoff, who had only a few months to live, and Gregory Ratoff came to Chekhov's rescue.

Chekhov had known Rachmaninoff since before the 1917 Revolution, and they frequently met in Europe in the 1930s. Rachmaninoff held a high opinion of Chekhov's talent and abilities, and treasured his serious and passionate devotion to Russian literature, music, and theater. When the composer heard of Chekhov's precarious situation, as Chekhov later wrote in his memoirs, he "began to make plans for my subsequent fate—without saying a word to me."

At that time he was in Hollywood. Through his boundless generosity Sergei Vasilevich spared neither time nor energy in reaching his goal, and did not cease his efforts until my arrival in Hollywood was assured. He appealed to Ratoff . . . and Ratoff did everything in his power to fulfill Sergei Vasilevich's request. And several times, already ailing,

Sergei Vasilevich asked about my situation. I kept waiting for the day when I could personally thank him for his indispensable help, but he was quickly slipping away, and I did not have the opportunity to see him. Just a few days before his death I did manage to send him a short note and a bouquet of red roses. I thanked him in my thoughts when I kissed his cold, beautiful hand at the funeral service in the small Russian church.[30]

Almost immediately after arriving in Hollywood in 1943, Michael Chekhov began giving acting classes. His reputation as an inspiring and exacting teacher had preceded him, and it wasn't long before both aspiring and established film actors were flocking to the "professor" (as he was called by his admirers) for instruction. Among his students were Yul Brynner, Ingrid Bergman, Gary Cooper, James Dean, Rex Harrison, Gene Kelly, Marilyn Monroe, Patricia Neal, Paul Newman, Gregory Peck, Tyrone Power, Anthony Quinn, and Robert Taylor. Upon meeting Chekhov for the first time, many of the actors were surprised to encounter (in the words of Anthony Quinn) a "tiny little man, very frail, with a high-pitched, breathy voice. *This* is the great Russian actor?"[31] But they soon came to see that within this fragile physique dwelt a powerhouse of energy and advice. For Marilyn Monroe, who began taking classes with Chekhov in 1951, Chekhov was an invaluable source of objective feedback; he helped her understand how she was being manipulated by the studios and to "assert an independence that had been bubbling up in her for many months."[32] They became both creatively and personally close during the last few years of Chekhov's life. Monroe even gave her mentor an engraving of Abraham Lincoln, explaining, "Lincoln was the man I admired most all through school. Now that man is you."[33]

Not long after moving to Hollywood, Chekhov bought a house in the San Fernando Valley, where he and his Russian wife Xenia would entertain their circle of Russian friends, who included Akim Tamiroff and Lewis Milestone. In 1948, his success as a teacher and in supporting acting roles in a few films allowed him to buy a home in Beverly Hills. The climate he found "marvelous" and good for his delicate health. But Chekhov, an intellectual deeply grounded in literature and the theater, never really got used to (or accepted) the blatant commercialism and superficiality of Hollywood. In a letter to his friend, the artist M. V. Dobuzhinsky, written in 1944, Chekhov confessed, "I have seen and experienced so much that is good in the theater in my time that film, with its crude and stupid people, can hardly be of much interest to me."[34]

Chekhov's career as a film actor began almost immediately after he arrived in Hollywood, with *Song of Russia*, directed by his friend and benefactor Gregory Ratoff. Here, he was cast as a teacher (a role he knew well), Ivan Stepanov, the kindly director of the village music school in the village of Tchaikovskoye and mentor to the pianist heroine Nadya. (Chekhov's involvement with *Song of Russia* cast a shadow over his career in the late 1940s, when the film was severely criticized by Ayn Rand and others as blatant pro-Soviet propaganda in hearings before the House Un-American Activities Committee.) Alfred Hitchcock also cast Chekhov as a mentor-figure in *Spellbound* (1945), the best and most important film in which he appeared. In his film work, Chekhov (who still had a strong Russian accent in English) always feared becoming what he disparagingly called an "accent clown," something he avoided in his strong and nuanced performance in *Spellbound*.

As the psychoanalyst Dr. Alex Brullov, Chekhov unlocks the puzzle of the amnesia that has been afflicting Dr. Edwards (Gregory Peck), a noted psychiatrist and the newly appointed Chief of Staff at the hospital where Ingrid Bergman also works. She falls in love with and marries the troubled newcomer, and brings him to visit her mentor Dr. Brullov for his advice. Chekhov's Brullov (who lives in snowy Rochester) is closely modeled on Sigmund Freud—he wears the same kind of spectacles, and adopts a vaguely Viennese accent ("Do you think Alex Brullov can't tell that two and two come out four?"), a humorous self-deprecating manner ("Good night and happy dreams, which we will analyze at breakfast") and the stereotype of the absent-minded professor ("I'm always late, always forgetting"). Brullov's relationship with his former student Constance (Bergman) is paternal and loving, although he is clearly dazzled by her beauty and charm. It is Brullov who leads Edwards through the labyrinth of his dreams (in a famous surreal sequence designed by artist Salvador Dali) to discover the cause of his amnesia: he was the accidental cause of his brother's death when they were children, and is traumatized by the memory. Cured of his affliction, Edwards can now enjoy his marriage to Constance, and their union is blessed by Brullov in the last scene as they wait to board a train. For Chekhov, the role of Dr. Brullov provided many points of contact with his own experience of psychoanalysis, which he used as an important element in his theory of acting. He had also been psycho-analyzed at the request of Stanislavsky earlier in his career.

In a review for *Tomorrow* magazine, Harold Clurman wrote that the "only vitality" in *Spellbound* was generated by Chekhov. "He was not a cog in the machine of the story but a living person. . . . Through him we learn once more that we have but to watch any moment of concentrated behavior to be fascinated. The smallest action thoroughly carried out seems to contain a kind of universal essence."[35] One of the best examples is the improvised business Chekhov came up with for the scene where he has to light his pipe while conversing with Bergman. After repeated failures to coordinate the words and action, he struck the matchbox so hard that he scattered the matches in all directions as he spoke, symbolizing his irritation and concentration in one physical gesture that seems completely natural in the context.

In the assessment of fellow Russian actor Leonid Kinskey, Chekhov never completely understood how film acting was different from stage acting. When Chekhov was given strong direction, as in *Spellbound* by Hitchcock, he excelled. "But when he was given complete freedom, Misha did everything he wanted to do and it was too much. He did not understand that the camera, the audience is here, right in front of you. They can see your teeth. And he was playing for the audience way out there, and this is what pictures cannot accept. But he helped a tremendous lot of actors who believed in him like you believe in God. He coached them. And he was wonderful in explaining things."[36]

Chekhov was nominated for an Oscar for best supporting actor for his work in *Spellbound,* but Leo McCarey won for *Going My Way.* Even this early success in film did not make Chekhov feel more comfortable in Hollywood. He still focused on his work as a teacher and writer. In 1946, his book *O tekhnike aktera* (On the Actor's Technique) was published in Russian, an accomplishment he considered far more important than anything he ever did in the movies. In 1953, it appeared in English along with an earlier book as *To the Actor—On the Technique of Acting,* and became a handbook for aspiring Hollywood actors.

Chekhov's last years in Hollywood were overshadowed by illness. Just as the filming of *Arch of Triumph,* directed by Lewis Milestone, was to begin in 1948, Chekhov, cast as a Gestapo agent, had a second heart attack. He was replaced by Charles Laughton, and made no films for the next several years. In a letter to his friend Mark Aldanov written in January 1951, Chekhov admitted that his financial situation was very difficult. Aldanov had offered to recommend Chekhov for a Guggenheim fellowship.

"My illness, from which I have almost completely recovered, has created a devastating impression in Hollywood: all the studios are convinced that I am still gravely ill, and for nearly two years no one has invited me to appear anywhere as an actor. It seems impossible to change their minds, even my agent has been powerless. That is fate. I support myself on my paltry lessons, but how it will all end I cannot even allow myself to imagine. Therefore the Guggenheim fellowship is my last and only hope. I will receive the news in March."[37] But Chekhov—like Arnold Schoenberg—did not receive a Guggenheim award.

Despite his ambivalent feelings about Hollywood, Chekhov did not have any desire to return to Europe: "it would be too terrible to see the destruction."[38] So he lived out his days in a kind of existential limbo, pouring his enormous energy into his teaching and his students, but expressing deep frustration and alienation to his Russian émigré friends. For Americans, Chekhov was adept at adopting kindly old-world mannerisms, delivered with a sweet smile, what he jokingly called in private his "Russian sugar" that he poured on in social situations.[39] Like Maria Ouspenskaya, Chekhov was a heavy smoker, and refused to give up the habit even after the doctor advised him to. On September 30, 1955, Chekhov died from a heart seizure as he was reaching over to light up a cigarette. Among those who attended the memorial service were Marilyn Monroe and a number of Russian émigrés, including Fyodor Chaliapin, Jr.

★ Chaliapin (1905–1992) was the son, the youngest of six children, of the great Russian operatic bass Fyodor Chaliapin (1873–1938). Imposing, warm, and mercurial, with (in the words of the impresario Sol Hurok) a "zest for good eating and good drinking and good talk," Fyodor Chaliapin, Sr., was the lusty Russian basso par excellence, a sturdy Volga peasant with a huge voice and personality to match, whose talent and fortitude led him from a miserable childhood of beatings and desperate poverty to one of the greatest stage careers of all time. "When Chaliapin sang," the ballerina Galina Ulanova has written, "it seemed like Russia herself was singing." Tsar Boris in Mussorgsky's opera *Boris Godunov* was one of Chaliapin, Sr.'s, most famous roles; when he sang that role at the Metropolitan Opera in New York for the first time in 1921, the audience nearly rioted in its excitement. It was Chaliapin's talent as an actor, and his relentless pursuit of the inner truth of the characters he portrayed, that set him apart from other opera stars of his day. Chaliapin didn't just "play" the guilty Tsar usurper—he *became* Boris, in every gesture and intonation. When he was finally ready to go on stage, after extensive research and preparation, Chaliapin's metamorphosis was so total as to terrify his co-stars. Even Stanislavsky learned from observing his longtime friend at work.

Chaliapin emigrated from Soviet Russia in 1922, and spent most of his time in Paris after that, but with frequent trips to the United States. Chaliapin's first wife (and the mother of his children) was Italian, so his son Fyodor Chaliapin, Jr., had a very international upbringing. He learned English well at his father's insistence, a skill that came in very handy later when he moved to America. In 1924, Fyodor Chaliapin, Jr., left Russia and settled in France. Having such a famous and larger-than-life father can be a burden, so it is not surprising that Jr. eventually struck out on his own, creating a new life in faraway Hollywood. Just before and during World War II, he appeared in numerous films—*Balalaika, Mission to Moscow, Three Russian Girls, Song of Russia, A Royal Scandal*—in bit parts, cast as a Russian.

But his breakthrough role came as the bomb-throwing partisan Kashkin in *For Whom the Bell Tolls* (1943), an expensive and star-studded adaptation of Ernest Hemingway's novel about the Spanish Civil War. It is Fyodor Chaliapin, Jr., who appears in the film's opening sequence, along with Gary Cooper, blowing up a train. Wounded in the aftermath, he begs Cooper to shoot him, as they had previously agreed. Chaliapin was hardly the only Russian cast in *For Whom the Bell Tolls*—he was joined by a whole battery of Russian émigré character actors, all of them playing Spanish partisans, supporters of the Republican government overthrown by General Franco. Most prominent among them is Akim Tamiroff as the partisan chief Pablo, who was nominated for an Academy Award for his performance. Vladimir Sokoloff is Anselmo, Mikhail Rasumny is Rafael, Leonid Snegoff is Ignacio, Leo Bulgakov is General Golz, and Michael Visaroff is a Staff Officer.

Politically, the idea of having Russian émigrés (most of them anti-Soviet in their own political persuasions) play Spanish partisans who were allied with the USSR in their opposition to General Franco and his fascist government was confused, to say the least. But it was a job, and the Russians were happy to have the work. Tamiroff in particular made a mini-career of playing Spanish-accented roles, especially during World War II, when he appeared in *For Whom the Bell Tolls*, *Tortilla Flat* (1942), and *The Bridge of San Luis Rey* (1944).

As for Fyodor Chaliapin, Jr., he had a long and prolific career both in Hollywood and in Italy, where he moved after World War II, appearing in many films. As an old man, he returned to Hollywood and (in his early 80s) scored one of his biggest successes as the crazy dogwalking grandfather ("*La luna! La luna!*") in *Moonstruck*. In 1991, not long before his death, he played Russian, as the survivor Prof. Bartnev, in Andrei Konchalovsky's underrated film about Stalin's projectionist, *The Inner Circle*. Like most of the other Russian actors in Hollywood, he was valued for his professionalism and flexibility.

The Russian émigré community was briefly joined during World War II by an official representative of the Soviet film industry, the distinguished director Mikhail Kalatozov (1903–1973). A Communist Party member and the chief administrator since 1939 of Soviet feature-film production, Kalatozov arrived in late 1943 and remained in Los Angeles for a year and a half as "the Soviet Union's official ambassador to the movie industry."[40] A Georgian born in Tbilisi (his real name was Kalatozishvili), Kalatozov was already famous for his controversial early avant-garde surrealist film *Salt for Svanetia* (1930) and for his popular film biography *Valery Chkalov* (1941), about the celebrated Soviet aviator who flew from the USSR across the North Pole to the United States, where he was greeted with wild enthusiasm. In a cameo appearance in that film, Kalatozov himself played one of the Americans who welcomed Chkalov.

Upon his arrival in Los Angeles in 1943, Kalatozov (who spoke very little English) was welcomed by what *Time* magazine described as "a suitably distinguished gathering of Hollywood liberals. The occasion was celebrated by a 'drinking' thrown at Hollywood's swankiest nightclub, Mocambo." Although exactly what Kalatozov was doing in Hollywood remained something of a mystery, he told *Time* halfway through his stay that he had screened 120 movies, of which nine had been sent back to Russia: *Young Tom Edison*, *Bambi*, *The Little Foxes*, *Hurricane*, *The North Star*, *Der Fuehrer's Face*, *Saludos Amigos*, *Mission to Moscow*, and *Sun Valley Serenade*. Kalatozov also "opened negotiations for setting up a film exchange between the U.S.

and Russia which will send at least 40 U.S. films a year to Russia," and sought to expand distribution of Soviet films in the American market.[41] After returning to the USSR, Kalatozov eventually resumed his career as a director. His brilliant, sophisticated, and innovative film *The Cranes Are Flying* (1957), a moving war story of a young Muscovite who copes less than heroically with the disappearance of her boyfriend at the front, was a landmark film of the post-Stalin "Thaw" era, and became one of the best-known Soviet films in America. In 1969, Kalatozov directed *The Red Tent*, an Italian-Soviet joint production starring Sean Connery as famed polar explorer Raold Amundsen.[42]

★ Ever mindful of social and political trends, Hollywood during World War II embraced Russianness as never before, both on and off screen. It was in 1941 that a new restaurant called Romanoff's opened on North Rodeo Drive in Beverly Hills. Soon it was one of the hottest spots to be seen. Romanoff's was the dream of a celebrated Hollywood impostor and "rogue of uncertain nationality," Harry F. Gerguson, who had passed himself off under various names during a career as a kind of "latter-day Robin Hood, extracting cash from the wealthy and joyfully sharing the benefits accruing therefrom with his friends."[43]

Inspired by the story of Anastasia, one of Gerguson's favorite identities was as a relative of the murdered Tsar Nicholas II. "Sometimes he was the czar's nephew, occasionally his half brother, often he was the son of Prince Yusupov, who had pumped booze and bullets into Rasputin, and on particularly low-risk occasions, he became Yusupov himself."[44] In star-crazy Hollywood, where many film people used fictitious names designed to make them sound more glamorous, and theatrical truth was much more powerful than reality, it was less preposterous for Gerguson to present himself as Prince Michael Alexandrovich Dmitri Obolensky Romanoff than it would have been in other locales. The studios even used Romanoff as an adviser on films set in Russia. Self-invention is the engine of the Hollywood dream factory. The façade was what mattered—just like the manufactured building fronts of New York or Paris or London that stood nearby on the studio lots and substituted for the real thing. After he was denounced in the newspapers as an impostor by a real friend of the late tsar, Gerguson "went straight," but continued to use the Romanov name as a kind of joke that was accepted by his wide circle of friends and associates, becoming "more widely admired, feted, and entertained as a famous impostor than he ever had been in the days when he was accepted as the real thing."[45] That he chose a Romanov identity shows the special cachet that the idea of Russian aristocracy occupied in the Hollywood mentality, combining wealth and status with mystery and tragedy.

Soon after it opened, Romanoff's, serving French cuisine, began to attract an A-list crowd—Humphrey Bogart, Alfred Hitchcock, Clark Gable, Gary Cooper, Cole Porter, Frank Sinatra, Jack Benny, Billy Wilder. On the front door an imperial R welcomed patrons to a fantasy world where their whims were indulged and they were made to feel glamorous and elegant. Gerguson was an unapologetic snob and admitted only those he deemed worthy of the Russian royal treatment. Romanoff's did such a good business that it moved to another location on South Rodeo Drive in 1951, and Gerguson opened a satellite establishment near Palm Springs that he called Romanoff on the Rocks. In his later years, Gerguson became a vocal ultraconservative and nurtured a close friendship with FBI Chief J. Edgar Hoover, alienating many of his former buddies.

Romanoff's closed its doors on New Year's Eve in 1962, as a new, more democratic spirit swept into Hollywood and the realities of the Cold War intruded upon tsarist fantasy.

Russians Don't Smile Like That

"The great advantage of history is that it's adaptable."
Peter Ustinov, *Romanoff and Juliet*

Red Danube, a star-studded feature released in 1950 by MGM, the same studio that had produced *Song of Russia,* illustrates vividly just how radically and quickly Hollywood's representation of the USSR and Russians changed after World War II.

Young Janet Leigh, who had only recently won hearts as Meg March in *Little Women* (as sister to Elizabeth Taylor), plays a fugitive Russian ballerina living in Vienna in 1946. She is trying desperately to escape being repatriated to the USSR as part of a controversial secret 1945 agreement on exchange of prisoners of war between the British government and Stalin. (This agreement affected Soviet citizens located in Europe after the War who had been born within the pre-1939 boundaries of the USSR.) Combining innocence and artistic skill recognizable to American audiences, fugitive ballerinas had long found favor with Hollywood producers. Only a few years earlier, in *Days of Glory,* Tamara Toumanova (a real-life ballerina) had played one with the reverse ideological agenda, seeking protection from the Nazis in the arms of heroic anti-Nazi Soviet partisan Gregory Peck. In years to come, fugitive ballerinas (and male dancers, too) would continue to figure prominently in Hollywood's representation of Russians, since they combined entertainment value with topical political commentary.

Actually, Janet Leigh's character, Maria Buhlen, is a German who was born in Russia, her ancestors having immigrated to Russia generations earlier. As she reveals to British army Major John "Twingo" McPhimister (Peter Lawford), a member of the allied occupation army who immediately takes a shine to her, she was a dancer at the ballet in Moscow. Because they were ethnically German, she and her parents were deported during World War II to Siberia, where her parents died. Maria escaped to Vienna, adopted a new identity as a Russian, Olga Alexandrova, and found a job dancing in the ballet of the Vienna Opera. (Conveniently, Maria also speaks fluent English.) She seeks refuge, in a convent run by a typically imperious and upright Ethel Barrymore, from Soviet officials intent on finding her and sending her back to Moscow. Desperate to avoid that fate, she begs Twingo to help her: "You do not know the Russians. Millions of Russians no longer believe what they are told officially, but they can do no more about it than I can." When the dour and unappealing Soviet Lieutenant Piniev comes to the convent looking for her, he explains to Mother Superior that Stalin wants Maria/Olga back so she can dance for Stalin: "You know we Russians have always loved our artists."

The moral dilemma of *Red Danube* (adapted from the novel *Vespers in Vienna* by Bruce Marshall) turns on the age-old conflict between love and duty beloved of Mozart and Beethoven. Should Twingo, as a loyal servant of the British crown, turn Olga over to the Soviet officials, as he is obligated to do under the controversial repatriation agreement between the Soviet army and its Western allies? Or will he yield to his own feelings of affection for the defenseless ballerina, a maiden in distress in need of his chivalric assistance?

When Lt. Piniev (Louis Calhern) returns a second time to the convent to fetch Maria, Twingo is powerless to stop him. The Soviet officer tries to soothe them by asserting that she will become the "prima ballerina of the Bolshoi." Maria is taken away to be deported along with thousands of other Russians residing in Austria. Twingo's superior, Colonel Nicobar (Walter Pidgeon), must also locate other Russians in the British sector and inform them that they are to be returned to the USSR.

One of these is a Professor Brullov (played by Russian émigré Konstantin Shayne). Upon learning of his fate, he goes to the bedroom to pack and shoots himself. (In reality, suicides were common among those scheduled to be repatriated.) His wife, of mixed Hungarian-Norwegian-Polish heritage as she explains, sobs in horror at the thought of being returned to Russia. She and Maria are both loaded onto trucks that will transport them eastward, but Maria manages to escape and return to Twingo. Overcome by a moral obligation to help her, he and Nicobar and the Mother Superior take her secretly by car to southern Austria. When Nicobar returns to Vienna, he is again confronted by Colonel Piniev, who demands the return of Maria. In an act of moral courage, Nicobar refuses and is removed from command, but retains his humanity. Tracked down by the British, Maria is returned to Vienna for deportation. Attempting to jump through a second-floor window to escape, she falls to her death.

In a brief epilogue, director George Sidney works to mitigate the sadness of what has preceded by having Nicobar (now restored to favor), Twingo, and their chatty assistant Audrey (Angela Lansbury) sing a hearty round of "Row, row, row your boat" as they are flying off to London for their next (presumably more cheerful) assignment.

In *Red Danube,* the chummy ("The Russians are just like us") spirit of the pro-Soviet World War II movies is replaced by a demonization of the Soviet military and of the Soviet/Communist way of life. So terrible for former Soviet citizens is the prospect of being forcibly sent to the USSR that they prefer death. (In fact, those who were sent back faced either execution or, even worse, long sentences in Soviet forced-labor camps.) Personal choice is one of the essential ingredients of the American way of life. That Janet Leigh, the girl next door, could have been so cruelly denied her freedom made the anti-Soviet message more powerful and personalized. The ideological message of *Red Danube* leaves no room for the ambivalence concerning the Soviet system that was typical of Hollywood films made before World II. In the atmosphere of the Cold War, the only good Russian as far as Hollywood was concerned was one who wanted to defect to the capitalist West.

★ Between 1946 and 1962, the production of films featuring Russian characters declined precipitously. During this period, international events drove the USSR and the United States further and further apart. The division of postwar Europe into two spheres, the eastern, Communist half dominated by Moscow and the western, capitalist half by Washington, polarized popular feelings about Russia. These feelings became more intense after Czechoslovakia, a former democracy that had been established in 1918 with the help of Woodrow Wilson, became Communist in 1948. The splitting of Berlin, and the drama of the Berlin airlift in 1948–1949, made the Soviet-American conflict dramatic and immediate, with massive media coverage. When China proclaimed itself a Communist People's Republic closely allied with the USSR in 1949, Americans began to fear that they were being encircled globally by powers hostile to the American way of life. In 1950, these fears broke into open conflict with the start of the Korean War, the first driven by the American-Soviet ideological rift. Adding to the tensions was the nuclear arms race, with both sides now capable of annihilating the other. On both sides of the superpower confrontation, propaganda encouraged hostility and dehumanization of the new enemy.

As the art form reaching by far the largest audience, films played an important role in solidifying and perpetuating negative images that developed between 1945 and 1950. For the first time in American history, Russia came to be seen as our primary military, economic, and ideological adversary, Enemy Number One. In the American popular consciousness, Russians "became inseparable from the Soviet system."[1]

So intense was anti-Soviet paranoia that the Hollywood studios came under attack for having produced pro-Soviet films during World War II. When the House Un-American Activities Committee (HUAC) initiated hearings into alleged Communist influence in the film business in 1947, after the Republicans had gained control of Congress in the 1946 elections, one of the early targets of the HUAC chairman, J. Parnell Thomas, and his Committee, was films such as *Mission to Moscow, North Star,* and *Song of Russia.* One of the first called to appear before a committee hearing held at the Biltmore Hotel in Los Angeles in May 1947 was Robert Taylor, who played the American conductor in MGM's *Song of Russia.* Taylor was known to be sympathetic to the HUAC investigation. In his testimony, he claimed he had been pressured by the White House to appear in the film—a charge he later partially retracted. Also called was Louis B. Mayer of MGM studios. He denied that *Song of Russia* ever intended to be a realistic portrait of the USSR, that it was just another film. Claiming falsely that "I never was in Russia" (Mayer was born in Minsk, in Belorussia, part of the Russian empire), Mayer dismissed the film as a musical love story not to be taken seriously, and reminded the Committee members that MGM had also made *Ninotchka* and *Comrade X,* both of which used the Soviet system as material for jokes.[2]

In an attempt to receive a more objective analysis of *Song of Russia,* the Committee summoned a young screenwriter and novelist, Ayn Rand. One of the main sources of Rand's special expertise was the fact that she was Russian. Rand (1905–1982) was born in St. Petersburg as Alissa Rosenbaum. The 1917 Bolshevik Revolution and its aftermath ruined the Rosenbaum's family business, and they were reduced to living in squalid poverty, an experience she later described in her powerful, if melodramatic, novel *We the Living* (1936), the graphic story of a young woman's struggle to maintain dignity, independence, and economic security amid the chaos, corruption, and political repression of the post-Revolutionary era. This early confrontation with Communism also instilled in Rand the fiercely anti-Communist and pro-capitalist (even libertarian) sentiments that she later developed into a philosophical system.

In 1926, Rand came to the United States to stay with a relative in Chicago and never returned to Russia. After a brief time in Chicago, she moved to Hollywood, where she found various jobs associated with the film industry. Her novel *The Fountainhead* (1943) established her as a serious writer and political thinker, and as the center of a cult of admirers and disciples. She also wrote widely on the dangers of Communist influence in the film industry, notably in the *Screen Guide for Americans* published by the Motion Picture Alliance. "Red propaganda has been put over in some films produced by innocent men, often by loyal Americans who deplore the spread of Communism throughout the world and wonder why it is spreading."[3]

When she was called to testify before the HUAC on *Song of Russia,* Rand had never seen the film, so a special screening was arranged for her. Before the Committee, she ridiculed *Song of Russia* as an inaccurate and highly romanticized depiction of the country in which she was born. The film made Moscow look more prosperous and clean than it really was, she argued (although Rand herself had not been in Russia at that point for more than twenty years). And the village where Taylor's new love resides is full of happy and smiling faces—an impossibility, Rand insisted to Pennsylvania Republican John McDowell, because people in the USSR don't really smile. To the relentless Rand, "the mere presentation of that kind of happy existence in a country of slavery and horror is terrible because it is propaganda."[4]

What Rand and the members of the HUAC failed to appreciate, however, was that *Song of Russia* and the other pro-Soviet films made during World War II were not documentaries, but feature films—works of fiction. As Otto Friedrich writes, "When Louis B. Mayer of Minsk decided to make a movie about Russia, he would inevitably make it the Russia of Andy Hardy, accompanied by Tchaikovsky."[5] If Hollywood producers and directors were to be consistently held to the standard of accuracy in depiction demanded by Rand, then hundreds of films dealing with real locales and historical events would need to be censured. How about Cecil B. DeMille's shlocky epic *King of Kings,* in which Ayn Rand appeared as an extra soon after arriving in Hollywood? Would that conform to the same standard of historical accuracy she was demanding of *Song of Russia?* Debates over historical and biographical accuracy have raged in Hollywood for years—a recent example is the controversy over the content of *The DaVinci Code.* In "investigating" films set in Russia, HUAC's main goal was to establish the strong anti-Communist convictions of its members. One of the results was to discourage Hollywood studios from making more films set in the USSR, lest they encounter further political criticism and negative publicity.

Besides examining films for excessively pro-Communist sentiments, HUAC launched a campaign to expose Communist political activity among prominent people in the film industry. This campaign and its destructive consequences have been exhaustively chronicled from various political viewpoints, and need no further description here. It is notable, however, that among the original nineteen "unfriendly" (uncooperative) individuals subpoenaed to give testimony was the Russian émigré director Lewis Milestone. In fact it was at Milestone's house that these nineteen gathered for a strategy session. Other members of the group were writers Bertolt Brecht, Ring Lardner, Jr., and Dalton Trumbo. In interviews conducted by Joel Greenberg for an American Film Institute oral history project, Milestone recalled the unpleasant atmosphere of those years.

> I was subpoenaed by the Un-American Activities Committee, which was, I guess, part of McCarthy's outfit, to come to Washington. By the time I tried to reason out what the hell it was all about I got another telegram from Washington canceling the invitation; I didn't have to go. By that time they'd called nineteen people; I was one of them, which left eighteen others. Anyway, some were going and two or three were cancelled and didn't have to go. By then the people who were called had had a couple of meetings to see if we could collectively get legal representation to fight this thing. So we were already sort of in one boat. . . .[6]

Although his "invitation" was withdrawn, Milestone decided to accompany his colleagues to Washington, and even to help organize a fund for those in the group who needed money. He attended all the Committee sessions in the Capitol, and was particularly impressed with the young California Representative Richard Nixon. "From watching him sitting with the Committee on the stand, I knew he was headed for a career." For Milestone and others who had been initially "named" but not called to testify, the situation was ambiguous, uncomfortable, and threatening. For several years, Milestone was visited at home by government representatives who would question him about people they considered suspicious and his knowledge of them. Finally he was cleared. In jittery Cold War Hollywood this was more than enough to tarnish Milestone's reputation, to land him not on a blacklist, but on "something worse, a grey list—which was bad enough. It took a long, long time to get rid of it. You had adversaries, you see, but you never knew who they were, so you couldn't face them." Those on the "grey list" found that they were no longer being hired. "You couldn't put your finger on it; you couldn't accuse anybody because they were all looking out the window—everybody was innocent. That's when I went to Europe. I left in 1950, and I didn't come back until the middle of 1955."[7]

Nor was Milestone the only Russian who felt unwelcome in Hollywood in the rabidly anti-Russian and anti-Communist atmosphere of the early 1950s. His friend Akim Tamiroff also left the United States to live in Europe from 1953 to 1956; he and Milestone even worked on a film (*They Who Dare*) together in England in 1954. Fyodor Chaliapin, Jr., settled in Rome. Suddenly, being a Russian in the Hollywood film industry had become a liability, not the asset it had been from the late 1920s through World War II.

There were a few exceptions. One was Dmitri Tiomkin, who continued to turn out film scores with undiminished success. (*High Noon*, for which he won two Oscars, for score and best song, has been seen as an allegory for the anti-Communist witch hunt led by Senator Joseph McCarthy and HUAC.) Two others were actor Yul Brynner and cinematographer Boris Kaufman.

★ Brynner was Hollywood's first Russian émigré leading man. Born in the Russian far east, in Vladivostok, to a Swiss-Mongolian father and a Russian mother, Brynner liked to pass himself off as a gypsy, perhaps because he had first found a creative community with gypsies in Paris as a young man. Taken by his mother as a child to Harbin, China, where there was a large and thriving Russian émigré community after the Bolshevik Revolution, Brynner moved to Paris in 1934, where he first began working in the theater and was befriended by Jean Cocteau and other leading bohemians. In 1940, Brynner, who spoke English, Russian, French, Chinese, Mongolian, Romany gypsy, and Korean, came to the United States to study with Michael Chekhov. From Chekhov Brynner learned his craft well, and was soon appearing in prestigious theatrical productions and on television in its early days.

Brynner came to Hollywood at least in part to continue his study with Michael Chekhov. By then, they had worked together successfully on several plays, including *Twelfth Night,* in which Brynner took the role of Fabian at the Little Theater in New York in 1941. In the early years, Brynner even drove the company truck for Chekhov's itinerant troupe, before being cast in the early TV series *Mr. Jones and His Neighbors.* His big break came when he appeared as Tsai-Yong opposite Mary Martin in 1946 in the Broadway show *Lute Song,* based on the classic Chinese drama *Pi-Pi-Ki.* With his exotic features, high cheek bones (inherited from his half-Mongolian father), and slight accent, he enjoyed particular success in Asian roles.

It was Mary Martin who recommended him for the role of The King in the Rodgers and Hammerstein musical *The King and I,* which opened on Broadway in March 1951. From this time on, The King became the role most closely associated with Brynner, and one that he continued to reprise throughout his career, nearly to his deathbed. For his work in the film version, released by 20th Century Fox in 1956, he won his first Oscar. That same year he also appeared in *Anastasia* (his first time on screen as a Russian character) and as the Egyptian Pharoah Ramses in the Cecil B. DeMille epic *The Ten Commandments* (with Charlton Heston and Anne Baxter), gliding above the masses in a splendid chariot with what looks like a powder blue crash helmet on his bald head.

In 1958, Brynner starred in the MGM adaptation of *The Brothers Karamazov* and as the pirate Jean Lafitte in *The Buccaneer.* A departure from his usual historical roles was his portrayal of a Soviet general (Major Surov) in *The Journey* (1959), directed by fellow émigré Anatole Litvak. Set during the 1956 Hungarian uprising (an event that further intensified anti-Soviet feeling in the United States), the film tells the story of a group of people—including Deborah Kerr, his co-star in *The King and I*—attempting to flee from Hungary to Austria. Acting against orders, Major Surov refuses to prevent their departure, delivering such lines as "All people should be allowed to live and love freely." In *Solomon and Sheba* (also 1959), Brynner returned again to antiquity, playing opposite Gina Lollobrigida as Sheba in what many consider one of the worst movies ever made. Even Brynner considered the script ludicrous. But his macho bearing, imperious arrogance, and undeniable sex appeal won over most of his detractors, including writer Dorothy Parker, who proclaimed, "He's the sexiest man I've ever met."[8] Brynner was a shrewd manipulator of his own image, and advised Steve McQueen on the set of *The Magnificent Seven*, a cowboy remake of Kurosawa's *Seven Samurai:* "Always try to play a bastard with a heart of gold."[9]

In his later years, Brynner even enjoyed poking fun at his own macho gunslinging image. In *Westworld* (1973), written and directed by Michael Crichton, he played a robot modeled on his character of the gang leader Chris in *The Magnificent Seven*. So well received was his performance that he followed it up with a similar role in his final screen appearance, in *Futureworld* (1975), another flop that one reviewer said "was as much fun as running barefoot through Astroturf."[10]

Despite his serious dramatic training with Michael Chekhov, Brynner participated in a large number of artistically inferior films, including several considered among the most outrageous bombs ever produced by Hollywood. Apparently content to play the off-screen role of a wealthy playboy, Brynner loved to make money and, according to Eli Wallach, took on roles in weak projects because he "honestly believed that his mere presence could improve a bad plot."[11]

When questioned about his past and Russian origins, Brynner often became combative and abusive, but he did not hesitate to capitalize on the image of the hard-drinking, chain-smoking gypsy lover, strong and impervious to misfortune, ever able to defend himself and his loved ones. He was famous for his performance of Russian gypsy songs, especially "*Ochi chernye*" ("Black Eyes"). (Unlike Mischa Auer as Carlo in *My Man Godfrey*, Brynner did know all the words.) And yet he avoided strong identification with Russia (after all, he had lived there only briefly in his very early youth), instead passing himself off as "a mysterious person from almost nowhere."[12]

When Brynner portrayed Russians on screen, he was careful to take roles that would not challenge the intensely anti-Soviet sentiments of the 1950s American audience. In *Anastasia*, he played a Tsarist general who wanted to resurrect the glory of the Romanov dynasty. In *The Brothers Karamazov*, he was a lovable ruffian who also lived in the remote nineteenth century. In *The Journey*, he played an unexpectedly compassionate Soviet officer. In *Taras Bulba*, he was an anti-Russian Ukrainian chief of the distant past fighting to protect the existence of his homeland from powerful and greedy foreign powers. The film's message resonated comfortably in the Cold War context of the repressive Soviet domination of the small countries of Eastern Europe.

Brynner's trademark was his shaved bald head, an innovation in Hollywood, where leading men had always been expected to have a full head of hair. This highly individualistic style was associated more with Asia than with Russia. Having lived in many different countries and societies, Brynner skillfully changed his persona to fit the circumstances and the times. In this way, he projected an important aspect of Russian society, its ability to absorb influences from the different civilizations that surround it— Europe, Central Asia, China. Brynner knew how to impress his audiences without scaring them. He was the quintessential King—wise, inquisitive, generous, stern, physically dominant, but capable of ferocious acts of revenge when his pride or authority were challenged. Both on and off screen, Brynner embodied the concept of individualism and individual expression that during the Cold War became a particularly potent symbol of the American way of life.

★   Like Yul Brynner, cinematographer Boris Kaufman (1906–1980) had led a nomadic and eventful career. By the time Kaufman made his belated Hollywood debut as a feature-film cinematographer in 1954 shooting *On the Waterfront*, one of the most beloved American movies, for director Elia Kazan, he had already been working in the film business for more than twenty years, in three different countries (France, Canada, and the United States).

Born in Bialystok, Poland, when Poland was still part of the Russian Tsarist empire, Kaufman belonged to a remarkable cinematic family. His older brothers Denis (known under his pseudonym Dziga Vertov) and Mikhail were among the most important pioneers in the lively Soviet film industry during the 1920s. Vertov (1896–1954) directed the still astonishing avant-garde textless and plotless documentary *The Man with the Movie Camera* (1929), a fascinating and influential excursion into the realm of pure cinematic formalism and experimentation; brother Mikhail was the cameraman. After Stalin consolidated his control over the Soviet film industry in the 1930s, however, Vertov's aestheticism became anathema, and the director gradually slid into suspicion and obscurity.

Considerably younger than his brothers, Kaufman was sent off to Paris around the time of the Russian Revolution to be educated. He immigrated officially to France in 1927 and never returned to Russia. After corresponding with his brother Mikhail, who taught him the fundamentals of cinematography, Kaufman began working as cameraman with the French director Jean Vigo in 1930. Their first collaboration was *A propos de Nice* (1930), followed by the classic schoolroom tale *Zéro de conduite* (1933) and *L'Atalante* (1934). Kaufman was serving in the French army at the time of the Nazi invasion, but soon fled to Canada as a war refugee. After working briefly in Canada, Kaufman moved to the United States in 1942.

For more than ten years, Kaufman was blocked from working on big features in Hollywood by the rigid union structure and (in the postwar years) because of his Soviet/Russian origins. It took a director with the clout of Elia Kazan to bring him into the mainstream as the cinematographer for *On the Waterfront*, a gritty tale of union corruption that is also a thinly veiled anti-Communist parable for the Cold War McCarthy era. Kazan's friend Marlon Brando was persuaded to play the role of Terry Malloy, a former prizefighter, now a longshoreman on the rough docks of New York harbor. Initially acting as a stool pigeon for the corrupt union bosses, Malloy decides—after falling in love with a girl whose brother was killed by the union for opposing their tactics—to testify against the bosses in court, bringing an end to their reign of terror. The structure and operation of the union is intended to resemble that of the Communist Party, which threatened and punished those in the Party rank and file who dared to challenge the judgment of their ideological leaders.

For Kazan, the story of *On the Waterfront* also had intense personal resonance. Shortly before starting to work on the film, he had testified (after considerable hesitation and reflection) as a friendly witness before HUAC, naming those he had known as a member of the Communist Party in the 1930s, an act that outraged many of his friends and associates. *On the Waterfront*, then, can be seen as an apology for the act of informing and a warning about the dangers of the enforced group mentality demanded of Party members.

That Boris Kaufman, whose brothers were among the most prominent of committed Soviet Communist filmmakers, and who was himself the victim of heavy-handed union tactics in the United States, should have been selected to work on this anti-Communist feature, is both ironic and appropriate. Even more important, Kaufman brought to the project many years of experience working in the black-and-white medium (his favorite). He and Kazan worked very well together, and as the filming progressed, the director came to place great trust in his cinematographer's subtle visual instincts.

Kaufman's treatment of the urban industrial landscape of On the Waterfront—the forest of rooftop antennas, the hulking ocean liners, the chaotic and hypnotic movement of cars and trucks and cranes—often recalls the way in which his brother Dziga Vertov portrayed Moscow in The Man with a Movie Camera. The city becomes a breathing, living character, with its own organic rhythmns and personality, changing with the light and weather. Against this oversized, overwhelming urban machine, the tender but sparely photographed intimate scenes between Terry Molloy and his fragile sweetheart Edie (a very young Eva Marie-Saint) carry even greater emotional power and pathos.

At the start of production, Kazan had doubts whether Kaufman was up to the demands of the job, as he remembered later in his autobiography: "The cameraman, Boris Kaufman, whom I would come to admire enormously, seemed on first view awfully soft for the job ahead of us and the place where the job was to be done."[13] As filming progressed, however, Kaufman was able to feed off the feeling of tension that Kazan wanted to create. He was also able to improvise under difficult circumstances. One of the most memorable examples is the brilliant scene in the taxi between Terry Molloy and his crooked brother Charlie the Gent (Rod Steiger), when Charlie halfheartedly pulls a gun on Terry in an unsuccessful attempt to prevent him from testifying against the bosses. (It is in this scene that Brando utters with abject despair one of the most famous lines in American cinema: "I could have been a contender!")

Originally, Kazan intended to shoot the scene in a real taxi in traffic. In order to cut costs, however, the producer Sam Spiegel instead provided a "shabby old taxicab shell, which he had placed in a small, shabby studio." Since rear-projection equipment that would create the image of traffic through the rear window had not been provided, Kaufman covered the window with a venetian blind and shot "straight in to avoid the side windows, except for an edge that he caught with a flickering light to suggest traffic going by. We had some of the crew shake the taxi shell to suggest movement, and that was it; we thought it a crude, primitive solution, but we got by with it. The audience watches the actors, not the taxi, not the traffic outside."[14]

Kaufman's moody, precise, naturalistic style contributed mightily to the artistic success of *On the Waterfront,* and won the cinematographer an Oscar for his first Hollywood feature. In the coming years, Kaufman worked again several times with Kazan, most notably on *Baby Doll* (1956) and *Splendor in the Grass* (1961). Kaufman also teamed up with director Sidney Lumet for a series of imposing dramatic features including *Long Day's Journey into Night* (1962), *The Pawnbroker* (1964), and *The Group* (1966).

The presence of Kaufman on the crew was not the only Russian ingredient in *On the Waterfront.* Here, as in all his films, Kazan draws heavily on his deep familiarity with the Russian theatrical tradition of Konstantin Stanislavsky and Vsevolod Meyerhold, the directors whose work provided the artistic foundation for the Group Theatre created and led by Lee Strasberg and Harold Clurman in the 1930s. Even long after he had parted ways with the Group Theatre (of which he was a founding member) and with his Depression-era infatuation with Communism, Kazan retained his belief in the importance of the psychological naturalism that was an essential part of the Stanislavsky "Method." Several of the actors cast in *On the Waterfront,* especially Marlon Brando and Karl Malden, shared Kazan's enthusiasm for the "Method," and had even studied with Stanislavsky's latter-day interpreter Michael Chekhov. So what was perceived as one of the most clearly anti-Communist American films of the Russophobic McCarthy era in fact represented an eloquent tribute to the lasting influence of the Russian theatrical and cinematic heritage.

★   During the 1950s, Hollywood was most comfortable dealing with the Russia that existed before the Russian Revolution. That Russia could be contained and admired at a distance, like the paintings in the Hermitage.

Even the Russian presence in Alaska in the nineteenth century (before the sale of Alaska to the United States) was more palatable to Hollywood producers than the real scary Russia of the Cold War era. *The World in His Arms,* released by Universal in 1952, was based on a popular novel by Rex Beach. Directed by Raoul Walsh, it is set in San Francisco and Alaska around 1850, starring a swashbuckling Gregory Peck as Jonathan Clark from Boston (the Russians call him "The Boston Man" and his ship is the *Pilgrim of Salem*), a sailor and adventurer embodying the American values of humor, self-reliance, quick thinking, and hatred of oppression. "A salty sea captain, a beautiful Russian countess, and the love that would span an ocean," reads the film's promotional copy.

The first half of the film unfolds in Gold Rush San Francisco. Here, Peck meets the lovely Russian aristocrat Marina (Ann Blyth), daughter of a Russian countess (played with delicious arrogance by the Russian émigré actress Eugenie Leontovich, speaking exclusively in Russian) eager for a desirable match for Marina. Marina lets it be known to Clark that she detests the life of royalty and is really a democrat at heart ("I'm just a Russian girl"), and reveals that she will soon be sent to Russian-controlled Alaska to be married against her wishes to the unpalatable arranged fiancé Prince Semyon. The film provides a colorful picture of the life of Russian San Francisco ("This is a mad city, this San Francisco of yours") centered upon the obligatory Russian cabaret/restaurant, where the *maître d'hotel* Nicholas (Leo Mostovoy) is Clark's buddy. When Clark expresses his enjoyment of the entertainment, Nicholas is surprised: "But I thought you didn't like Russians. And these people are Russians." Clark replies: "Once upon a time, but they're all good Yankees now."

Just like Ninotchka, they have converted from their bad Russian values.

Once she has met Clark, Marina wants to partake fully in American life, as she tells him: "We are going to be Americans. We're going to learn to sing and be happy and never be afraid." (In the end, even Marina's status-conscious mother comes to prefer Clark as a match for her daughter.) But she is fetched from San Francisco by the repressive governor of Alaska, her uncle, who is intent on marrying her to Prince Semyon, whom she has already spurned back home.

A well-filmed race at sea (between Clark and his rival, a manic Portuguese mariner played by Anthony Quinn) from San Francisco to Sitka takes the action to Alaska. There, the Russians are shown to be repressive not only toward their own people but also to the native Aleuts, whom they mistreat and use as slaves. Even worse, the Russians are decimating the seal population and despoiling the environment, unlike Clark, an advocate of killing seals "only as nature does" (whatever that means). When Clark comes into port, his ship is shelled and he is taken captive and imprisoned, even as the celebration of Marina's forced marriage to Prince

Semyon begins. But Clark manages to escape from jail, and the film concludes with a cowboys vs. Cossacks shoot-out, complete with horses, as Clark and his men vanquish the Russians, blow up Prince Semyon, and free Marina.

The negative portrayal of the Russian administration of Alaska on the eve of the American purchase of the territory in 1867 is clearly motivated by the tense ideological situation that prevailed when the film was made in the early 1950s, at the height of the Korean War and of anti-Soviet and anti-Communist sentiment in the United States. The character of Marina acts as a surrogate for the "oppressed people" behind the Iron Curtain, who are not allowed to exercise their freedom of choice, even in the most personal matters. (The 1952 film *California Conquest*, set between the years 1825 and 1841, about the Russian colonization of California, provides a similar example of the use of nineteenth-century history to teach Cold War—era lessons.)

To create the necessary Russian emotional and sonic atmosphere, the musical score (by Frank Skinner) for *The World in His Arms* draws heavily on Russian folk music, using the sadly nostalgic tune "*Severnyi veter*" (The North Wind) as part of the story line (Marina sings it with a violinist in the cabaret for Clark, thereby setting up their romance) and as a leit-motif for dramatic emphasis. Its lyrics are also the source for the film's title. Before it is interrupted by Clark's leap through the church window, the marriage ceremony unfolds to the singing of an Orthodox choir.

The art director of *The World in His Arms*, Alexander Golitzen, was another Russian émigré with many Hollywood credits. Golitzen (1908–2005) had been brought to the United States as a teenager by his family fleeing the Revolution. After studying architecture at the University of Washington, he came to Hollywood, where he broke into the business as an assistant to another famous Russian set designer, Alexander Toluboff (1882–1940), on *Queen Christina* (directed by fellow émigré Rouben Mamoulian). In the course of his amazingly prolific career, Golitzen, appointed Supervising Art Director at Universal in 1954, did the sets for hundreds of films, including *To Kill a Mockingbird* (like *The World in His Arms*, starring Gregory Peck), *Spartacus, Flower Drum Song, Airport*, and *Earthquake*. In 1963, Golitzen was nominated for two Academy Awards in the same year, for *To Kill a Mockingbird* (for which he won) and for *That Touch of Mink*. Golitzen was especially famous for his work in color films, and he brings just the right touch of cheap glamour to the San Francisco scenes, and elegant *hauteur* to the surroundings of the cruel Russian ruling aristocracy.

★ Two other major Russian movies of the 1950s—*War and Peace* and *The Brothers Karamazov*—celebrated bigness and classical values, remote and safe from viewers being advised to build bomb shelters in the event of a nuclear attack by Soviet forces.

Because of its enormous scope, and the obvious problem of reducing a novel of well over a thousand pages to a manageable film script, Tolstoy's novel *War and Peace* posed daunting logistical and casting problems for Hollywood filmmakers, although they were long tempted by its spectacular scale and the presence of recognizable historical figures like Napoleon who had already proved appealing at the box office. Such prominent film moguls as D. W. Griffith, Ernst Lubitsch, Erich von Stroheim, and Irving Thalberg had all considered making a screen version of *War and Peace,* but never got past the conception stage. In the mid-1950s, at a time when lavish technicolor epics were in fashion, the idea resurfaced, and numerous producers suddenly wanted to tackle Tolstoy's novel. But it was Italian producer Dino DeLaurentiis who actually made it happen, by enlisting producer Carlo Ponti and hiring Mel Ferrer to play Prince Andrei. Then he signed Audrey Hepburn to play Natasha, and King Vidor to direct. Henry Fonda was cast as Pierre. It cost $6 million to make the film, which was shot in Italy and released in 1956.

DeLaurentiis paid huge bribes to gather 15,000 Italian soldiers, 8,000 horses, and 3,000 cannons for the filming of the battles of Austerlitz and Borodino. For King Vidor, it was the character of Pierre Bezukhov—the aristocrat in search of the meaning of life in the midst of Napoleon's assault upon Russia—that attracted him to the project. "The strange thing about it is that the character of Pierre was the same character I had been trying to put on the screen through many of my own films," he said. "My favorite theme is the search for truth. It's also the essence of Tolstoy's book. It's Pierre who strives to discover it. He goes to observe the battle so as to observe what lies in the heart of man."[15]

It was hard for Vidor to express his ideas in the film, however, because of the enormity and logistical challenges of the subject. (Vidor even had to defend himself from charges of cruelty to the horses used during the battle

FIGURE 18.

War and Peace. Paramount 1956. Jeremy Brett, Sean Barett, May Britt, director King Vidor, and Audrey Hepburn (left to right), work out the details of the first scenes of *War and Peace,* which has begun production in Rome. This set, representing the home of the Rostovs, was built at a cost of $150,000 and occupies the whole of the second largest sound stage in Europe. Courtesy of the Margaret Herrick Library, Academy of Motion Picture Arts and Sciences.

scenes.) Six different writers—including Vidor—worked on the screen-play, and Irwin Shaw demanded that his name be removed from the billing because of Vidor's repeated changes to the script. The atmosphere of the film is strangely remote, and more Italian than Russian. There are few close-ups, and many extended tracking shots, so that the intense psychological relationships of the novel are not successfully rendered visually. And the international cast seems often to be acting past one another without making contact.

Audrey Hepburn, having convinced everyone (including those who bestowed the Oscar) that she could play a princess in *Roman Holiday* (1953), makes a visually compelling Natasha Rostova, but her interaction with Ferrer's petulant Andrei Bolkonsky and the Pierre of Henry Fonda (adopting an American homespun "aw-shucks" demeanor that creates a credibility and culture gap) does not come alive, and she fails to mature and change as a result of the tragedies she experiences. Throughout, she remains an ingénue, strangely untouched by everything that is happening around her. Hepburn and Fonda make no attempt to disguise their natural speaking styles, but the resourceful Oscar Homolka, another "accent clown," assumes the manner of what sounds something like a Russian native speaker trying to speak English in the role of the heroic General Kutuzov.

The reviews of *War and Peace* were for the most part negative; one called it "the least Russian movie ever made," while the *Manchester Guardian* quipped that it had "length without depth." *Variety* complained that the actors' mismatched accents "make for a curious infidelity of speech. Homolka is very Akim Tamiroff as the Russian general, but some of his aides speak in clipped British English. That was true also of Napoleon, as played by Lom. Some of the lesser principals, of native Italian lineage, also found themselves dubbed into British English."[16] The most successful sequences were the battle scenes, although the countryside looks much too Mediterranean (there are no cypress trees in this part of Russia) to pass for Borodino.

In his score, composer Nino Rota (having begun his legendary collaboration with Frederico Fellini three years earlier) avoided Russian folk-music clichés, instead imitating (like so many other Hollywood composers in search of battle music) the modernist-epic sound of the music Sergei Prokofiev wrote for the battle on the ice sequence in Sergei Eisenstein's *Alexander Nevsky* (1938), a film that was widely seen and admired by filmmakers and film composers all over the world.

★ Not to be outdone, in 1958 MGM released its own big "Russia picture," *The Brothers Karamazov,* adapted from Dostoyevsky's dense novel examining (among many other matters) fraternal envy and parricide. Yul Brynner was given the starring role of the wildest brother, Dmitri. In his biography of Michael Chekhov, Charles Marowitz relates that when Chekhov found out that Brynner had been cast as Dmitri in the upcoming film of *The Brothers Karamazov,* he urged Brynner to get Monroe cast for the role of Dmitri's love interest, the prostitute Grushenka. But the idea was laughed off by the studio heavyweights, and director Billy Wilder joked that "he would be happy to direct Marilyn in 'a whole series of Karamazov sequels, such as *The Brothers Karamazov Meet Abbott and Costello.'"* [17] In the end, the role of Grushenka went to the Austrian-born actress Maria Schell, who had a more impressive intellectual pedigree and had given a noted performance in an Italian film based on Dostoyevsky, Visconti's *White Nights,* the preceding year. Joining her were Lee J. Cobb as the loathsome father Fyodor and, as the religious youngest son Alyosha, 27-year old William Shatner in his film debut.

In his *Brothers Karamazov,* director Richard Brooks takes the opposite approach from von Sternberg in *Crime and Punishment,* stressing the Russian flavor of the subject at the expense of psychological depth. The script (adapted from the novel by Julius J. and Philip G. Epstein of *Casablanca* fame) and shooting were built around Yul Brynner, so the role of Dmitri was beefed up accordingly to give him maximum screen time. The character of the third brother, Ivan, who is crucial for the novel's philosophical message, is nearly eliminated in the film, and Dmitri becomes a much more conventional hero. From the very opening, Brooks tries to convey "Russianness" with lots of wild singing and dancing and drinking, with a very aggressive score by Bronislau Kaper, a Polish-born veteran Hollywood film composer.

Not incidentally, this was also the moment in American cultural history when Russian musicians (David Oistrakh, Mstislav Rostropovich, Emil Gillels, Sviatoslav Richter) and theatrical attractions like the Moiseyev Dance Company and the Bolshoi Ballet were first finding an audience,

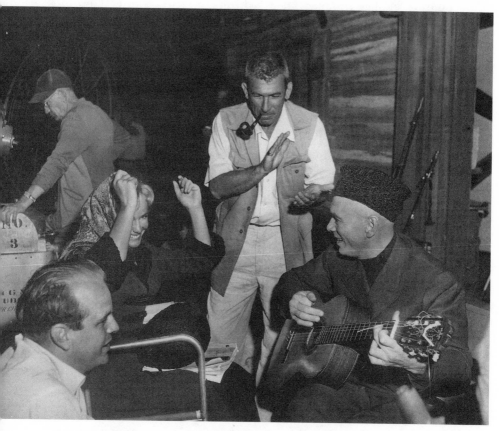

FIGURE 19.

The Brothers Karamazov. MGM 1958. Yul Brynner (right, as Dmitri Karamazov) plays guitar on the set for Maria Schell (left, as Grushenka) and director Richard Brooks (center). Courtesy of the Margaret Herrick Library, Academy of Motion Picture Arts and Sciences.

during the thaw in American-Soviet cultural relations that followed the death of Stalin in 1953. What results is a picture-postcard Russia that overshadows the violence, blood, and squalor of Dostoyevsky's novel, as well as its spiritual message—the character of Father Zossima, brother Alyosha's Orthodox guru, hardly makes any impression here.

Yul Brynner is also at the center of another major Hollywood Technicolor recreation of nineteenth-century Russia, *Taras Bulba*. Based on a novel of the same name by Ukrainian/Russian writer Nikolai Gogol, it was released in 1962 by United Artists. The filming took place in Argentina, which looks considerably more dessicated than the prairies of Ukraine. Playing opposite Brynner, the fierce Cossack chieftain Taras Bulba, devoted to the cause of winning independence for Ukraine, is Tony Curtis as his son, who is hard-pressed to live up to his father's unrealistic and violent expectations. He further infuriates Taras by falling in love with a Polish noblewoman. The villains are the Poles, who have dominated Ukraine ruthlessly and are loathe to give it up. (We know the Poles are villains in this film because they speak with a high-class British accent.)

One of the most memorable aspects of *Taras Bulba* is the score by Franz Waxman, who created the music for *Sunset Boulevard*. In order to produce an identifiably "Russian" or "Ukrainian" sound for what was his last major score, Waxman relied heavily on imitation of the music of Soviet composers Sergei Prokofiev and Dmitri Shostakovich, and on use of folk music, both real and imitation. As part of the recently initiated program of Soviet-American cultural exchange, Waxman had been invited to visit Russia and Ukraine, and he brought back copies of Ukrainian folk music. There are numerous scenes of Cossacks drinking and singing with riotous abandon, obviously calculated to cash in on Brynner's box-office reputation as a musical talent. In one of the more memorable ones, the traditional Russian folk song *Kalinka*, a sexy flirtation song, is turned into a drinking song with English lyrics that have nothing to do with the original meaning: "If we drink we will die / If we don't drink we will die / So we might as well say what the hell and let our glasses clink / Whatever you name you'll be dying just the same / So as long as we're going to die/ It's better if we drink . . ."

Taras Bulba was not a critical success. *Variety* observed that Brynner is "allowed plenty of space in which to chew the scenery and there's precious little of it in which he doesn't leave teethmarks," and that Christine Kauf-

FIGURE 20.

Taras Bulba. United Artists 1962. Yul Brynner (center, as Taras Bulba)
with Tony Curtis (right, as Andrei Bulba) and Perry Lopez (left, as Ostap
Bulba). Courtesy of the Margaret Herrick Library,
Academy of Motion Picture Arts and Sciences.

man as the Polish noblewoman "never makes credible her wholesale and immediate capitulation to Curtis' charms and, during a siege, never shows the least sign of starvation, disease or dirt."[18] In *Saturday Review,* Hollis Alpert wrote that Brynner "loves his son with such fierce, affectionate pride that he is constantly knocking him down. Mr. Curtis is active, but seems unhappy."

★ So scary was the threat of the real Russia/USSR that many films of the 1950s dealt with Russians in the allegorical guise of alien invaders. In the sci-fi classic *The Day the Earth Stood Still* (1951), one of the residents of the boarding house where Patricia Neal and her son live remarks that the flying saucer that has landed on the mall in Washington, D.C., must be "from there"—meaning the USSR. The mutant monsters and zombies who in so many films of this era (the 1956 *Invasion of the Body Snatchers* is a particularly good example) appeared to terrorize, abduct, and inhabit the innocent people of small-town America materialized the fears of Marxist brainwashing that arose from the Korean War and highly publicized spying cases, like that of Julius and Ethel Rosenberg, sentenced to death for atomic espionage in 1951.

A few films, such as *Red Menace* (Republic, 1949), dealt directly with the Soviet Communist threat to American society through infiltration and recruitment of vulnerable individuals. In *Red Menace,* a feature film that uses many documentary conventions, especially an editorial voice-over narration, the naïve American World War II vet Bill Jones is lured to a Party cell through a phony real-estate scam. He is ultimately saved by Nina Petrovka, a reluctant Party member whose father was killed because he disagreed with the tactics of the Party leaders. They narrowly escape the tyrannical female commissar, a Party automaton who goes mad when she is finally brought to the police for questioning, and flee to Texas, where a kindly sheriff listens to their story, gives them a second chance ("You folks have been running away from yourselves"), and advises them to "get yourself hitched and raise a couple of good kids." In this and many other films of the era, Communists, with Russian backing, are portrayed as literally insane for believing in Marxist ideology. The only way to find mental health is to accept the American dream, like Nina in *Red Menace.*

Defection of the female protagonist from Communism to capitalism drives the plot of several other prominent films of the 1950s. *Never Let Me*

Go (1953) is a remake of *Comrade X,* again starring Clark Gable as an American journalist in Moscow. This time he falls in love with (surprise, surprise) a ballerina (Gene Tierney) and rescues her from a performance of *Swan Lake* to emigration and freedom.

★   Two films released in 1957—*Jet Pilot* and *Silk Stockings*—remake that master narrative of East-West relations, *Ninotchka.*

Jet Pilot was a high-profile project involving two of Hollywood's most prominent and mercurial personalities: producer Howard Hughes and director Josef von Sternberg. In 1949, Hughes approached von Sternberg, whose flair for Russian subjects was already well established in *The Scarlet Empress* and *Crime and Punishment,* to work on a film about flying, "the *Hell's Angels* of the jet age."[19] At the time, the eccentric and adventurous Hughes was deeply involved in the burgeoning aircraft industry, and was also the owner of RKO studios. The script was written by Jules Furthman. Production began in 1950 with a cast that included two hot stars: Janet Leigh and John Wayne.

Leigh (having just appeared as a German/Russian ballerina in *Red Danube*) was cast as a Russian jet pilot, Anna Marladovna, and Wayne as the American fighter pilot Major Shannon. As the film opens, Anna is flying across the Bering Strait to Alaska, where she lands at an Air Force base and announces she is seeking asylum because she disobeyed orders back home. (For unknown reasons, she speaks perfectly beautiful unaccented English.) Major Shannon is wary, but immediately takes a shine to the sexy newcomer, who is actually only pretending to be a refugee in order to spy for the USSR. Anna removes her flight suit after arriving, in what amounts to a strip tease, then showers while singing the Soviet World War II army song "*Polyushka, polye*" (also known as "The Song of the Red Army.") Shannon's superiors encourage him to woo Anna so as to gain more information from her ("Washington wants us to find out what interests her the most"), so he gladly shows her around the base and the new state-of-the-art aircraft. Their conversations are heavy with sexual innuendo and banter, and they perform flying duets filmed like elaborate mating rituals, complete with arcane cockpit jargon. Hughes's love of aircraft technology is evident from the outstart, with many shots of gleaming wings and sparkling skies crisscrossed with jet trails. Much of the dialogue occurs over the radio. At last, after the foreplay of aerial maneuvers, Shannon and

FIGURE 21.

Jet Pilot. United Artists/RKO 1957. Michael Mark, Janet Leigh (as Anna
Marladovna), and John Wayne (Colonel Shannon). Courtesy of the Margaret
Herrick Library, Academy of Motion Picture Arts and Sciences.

a very willing Anna lock in a kiss—"a perfect example of teamwork"—and Anna has to admit (just as Ninotchka does at a similar moment) that "capitalism has certain dangerous advantages."

These advantages become even more obvious to her when they arrive in Palm Springs, a luxurious oasis of bright color and consumerism in the midst of the desert. In a sequence lifted directly from *Ninotchka,* they go shopping, first to a swimsuit store and then to a hat store, where she buys a hat and exclaims, "It's perfectly silly and I adore it," demonstrating the start of her conversion from Communist ideals. In the swimsuit store she marvels at the technology behind the manufacture of the items on sale, particularly the breast cups, and he lamely jokes: "We both believe in uplifting the masses."

So saturated with double-entendre and sex are the conversations between Shannon and Anna, and so provocative are her breast-hugging outfits, that Joseph Breen of the Production Code Administration warned the producers to be careful.

"At the outset, we direct your particular attention to the need for the greatest possible care in the selection and photographing of the dresses and costumes of your women. The Production Code makes it mandatory that the intimate parts of the body—specifically, the breasts of women—be fully covered at all times. Any compromise with this regulation will compel us to withhold approval of your picture." Breen also warned that a line spoken by Major Rexford—"I love all kinds of equipment"—would be "unacceptable if it refers to Anna's breasts. His look accompanying this line should not be leering or leacherous."[20] As usual, von Sternberg emphasized the underlying sexual tension in the story as a primary motivating factor, although not as obviously and pervasively as in *The Scarlet Empress.*

The crowning moment of their visit to Palm Springs is a dinner in a swank restaurant where a succulent steak is grilled to perfection at the table. Already a bit drunk from the cocktails they have consumed while listening in the lounge, she asks wistfully, "How can we compete with this propaganda?"

But their Palm Springs idyll is interrupted when they are informed that the General has decided to deport Anna back to the USSR. On the way to deliver her to U.S. officials, fulfilling his duty, Shannon takes a detour to Yuma, Arizona, where they are married. Upon returning to headquarters, he learns that Anna is an agent sent to obtain secret information for the

Soviet government. His superiors ask him to bring her back to Russia in order to gain valuable information, so he pretends he cannot be parted from his new wife and wants to be with her there. Until the end, von Sternberg deftly maintains uncertainty over the real motivations of the leading characters, whether they are actually in love or only acting out their roles as undercover spies.

The extended sequence set at a Russian airbase in Siberia was shot at George Air Force Base outside Victorville, California. The living conditions of the Soviet military are shown as shabby, dreary, and shoddy—doorknobs fall off, the furniture is sparse and uncomfortable, lights don't work. Anna's superiors are ruthless, demanding that she obtain immediate results from Shannon and threatening to use mind-altering drugs on him so that he will forget his loyalty "to his dirty rotten capitalist country." When a new, vicious commanding officer replaces the one with whom Anna had been working, she impulsively decides to defect, this time for real. A spectacular aerial sequence follows, as she shoots down Soviet jets and is reunited with Shannon in a *pas de deux* for aircraft. They evade the pursuing fighters, rising into the clouds, and find asylum in Palm Springs, where the last shot shows them happily consuming another steak at table. "If only I could make my people realize things like this are more important than all the guns in the world," says Anna, as meat juice dribbles from Shannon's chin. Steak, swimsuits, and sex have prevailed over socialism.

Compared to most of Sternberg's earlier films, *Jet Pilot* is unreflective and superficial, but visually it has many stunning moments, as one of the first features to celebrate in color the beauty of high-speed jet flight—a favorite theme of films of the later 1950s and 1960s in both the United States and the USSR. The shooting was completed quickly, in only seven weeks, but post-production dragged on for months, and then years. Hughes, a notorious perfectionist famous for extended and extremely expensive reworking and re-editing, did not consider *Jet Pilot* ready for release, although the airplane technology it showcased was rapidly being superseded. A few months after Hughes sold RKO studios in 1955, he bought back the rights to *Jet Pilot* and updated it with new footage provided by the USAF. More scenes were filmed with the stars, and the entire film recut and reprocessed for the newly available wide-screen projection. Finally, in September 1957, the film was released. In the seven years since it was begun, the Korean War had ended, Josef Stalin had died (on March 5,

1953), and Nikita Khrushchev had become the new leader of the USSR, opening a new and somewhat less confrontational era in Soviet-American relations.

The gently satirical spirit of *Silk Stockings,* shot for MGM between November 1956 and January 1957 and released in July 1957, reflects a less fearful and anxious perception of the East-West superpower standoff. It was based on a moderately successful Broadway musical of the same title, with music by Cole Porter and book by veteran George S. Kaufman (*You Can't Take It With You, Guys and Dolls, Dinner at Eight, Stage Door*), Leueen McGrath, and Abe Burrows that opened on Broadway on February 24, 1955, and ran for 478 performances. Porter's musical was in turn inspired by the film *Ninotchka.*

Set in present-day Paris, the action still revolves around the ideological conversion through romance of a Soviet commissar sent on a state mission—in this case, to bring to heel a wayward Soviet pianist and composer, Peter Ilych Boroff, and his three sidekicks—Brankov, Ivanov, and Bibinski. (Boroff's name intentionally recalls that of Peter Ilych Tchaikovsky.) The man who "turns" Nina (Cyd Charisse) is an American director-choreographer, Steve Canfield (Fred Astaire), who has come to Paris to work with Boroff and down-home American movie star Peggy Dainton (Janis Paige), famous for her on-screen swimming (obviously modeled on Esther Williams). They are developing a new film musical based on *War and Peace* ("The title is going to have to go") but starring Dainton as Napoleon's overdressed wife, Josephine. The musical and film add a strong American flavor through the characters of the upbeat Canfield and the wholesome if dim Dainton. Boroff is a mostly comic character, the dreamy artist in danger of losing his Soviet Communist ideals while collaborating with carefree Americans in the decadent surroundings of Paris. "Oh yes, Tchaikovsky and Borodin," Boroff observes wryly. "They have a great advantage in Russian music today. They are dead." Peter Lorre shows a manic comic gift as Commissar Bibinski, particularly in the hilarious trio "Siberia," about the horrors that await them at home. If the show's creators had known more about what was really happening in Stalin's gulag at the time, they might have thought better of making light of the matter.

To direct *Silk Stockings,* MGM engaged Rouben Mamoulian. Since working on the Tolstoy-inspired film *We Live Again* in 1934, Mamoulian had produced a small number of high-quality films, including the dramas

Golden Boy, The Mark of Zorro, Blood and Sand, and the musicals *High, Wide and Handsome* and *Summer Holiday.* Perhaps as a result of his early training in the Russian theater, where productions were usually rehearsed for very extended periods before being staged, Mamoulian had also developed a bad reputation among Hollywood studios for taking too long and spending too much. Prickly, patronizing, and autocratic, he had been out of work as a film director for a decade when he was hired for *Silk Stockings.* Mamoulian's vocal opposition in October 1947 to the campaign of Cecil B. DeMille (in response to the HUAC investigation into Communist influence in Hollywood) to require all members of the Screen Directors Guild to sign a loyalty oath also won him few friends among producers. After 1950, the only project (on either film or stage) that Mamoulian completed was *Silk Stockings.*[21]

To *Silk Stockings* Mamoulian brought deep experience with the genre of musical comedy. After immigrating to the United States, he spent a number of years with the American Opera Company in Rochester, New York, staging opera and musicals. In 1927 he directed the play *Porgy* by Dorothy and DuBose Heyward (based on DuBose Heyward's novel) for The Theatre Guild in New York and in 1935 at the Alvin Theatre, the world premiere of the opera based on *Porgy,* Gershwin's landmark *Porgy and Bess.* That an Armenian from Russia who had emigrated to the United States as an adult should have directed the premiere of what is today regarded as the quintessential American opera is a tribute to the idea of the American melting-pot, and to the high regard in which Mamoulian was held by the theatrical community. As an immigrant and outsider, he could see things about America—especially the rituals and myths of American life, its spectacle—more clearly.

To Mamoulian also fell (in 1943) the honor of directing the premiere of the show that revolutionized the Broadway musical, *Oklahoma,* and ran for the unprecedented number of 2,248 performances. Two years later, Rodgers and Hammerstein entrusted him with the premiere of another big new show—*Carousel.* With such credentials behind him, it is not surprising that Mamoulian often expressed impatience with the compromises required of a film director in Hollywood.

Compared to these masterpieces, *Silk Stockings* appears rather slight. And yet the film has many charming and entertaining moments. For Mamoulian, the main message of the film was that "all people are alike deep down." According to his biographer Mark Spergel, he wanted to show that "people are basically good and yearn to act on their higher impulses and dreams, but that evil influences in the environment test people's willpower to rise above outside pressures and listen to their inner voices, like Joan of Arc. For Mamoulian, this was a lifelong struggle and the essence of every conflict he chose to dramatize."[22]

The ideological aspects of *Ninotchka* are somewhat toned down in *Silk Stockings;* the highly stylized spectacle of song-and-dance takes over. This was inevitable with dancers Cyd Charisse and Fred Astaire in the main roles. In the brilliant opening sequence, the camera self-consciously follows Astaire's feet from a taxi to a hotel lobby. His courtship of Nina unfolds choreographically and musically. The most memorable song in the show and film is Canfield's "All of You," whose witty and suggestive lyrics prompted the following warning from the Production Code Administration. "The following lyrics must be delivered in a non-suggestive manner: 'I'd love to make a tour of you, / The arms and yes the mouth of you, / The east, west, north and the south of you.'"[23]

When Nina is irretrievably converted to the joys of consumerism and capitalism, the process unfolds sensually through ingenious choreography (by Eugene Loring, a former Balanchine dancer who came to Los Angeles in the 1940s). Canfield awakens in her the ability to dance, to jettison the robot-like behavior she brings with her from the USSR, to move freely and sensually. Here, the material token of her conversion is the silk stockings she at first ridicules for their uselessness, but later cherishes for their luxury and style. *Silk Stockings* celebrates entertainment, fantasy, and theatricality more than realism or ideology, using the Soviet-American relationship as a pretext rather than a premise. Since the habitually apolitical Mamoulian had left Russia before or around the time of the Bolshevik Revolution (he was always vague about the subject and all other biographical information), did not experience life in the USSR, never returned to visit (even Ernst Lubitsch had more first-hand information), and showed very little interest in what was going on there, his knowledge of Soviet reality was abstract and limited.

For Mamoulian, reality was the theater—his adopted homeland—and America was nothing more than a stage set.

The critical and commercial success of *Silk Stockings* rescued Mamoulian's career, at least temporarily. In autumn 1957, Sam Goldwyn (with whom Mamoulian had collaborated less than amicably on *We Live Again* in 1934) offered him a big new picture—the film version of *Porgy and Bess*. But after eight months of work on the project, disaster struck when a fire at Goldwyn Studios destroyed the sets and costumes. Apparently dissatisfied with Mamoulian's preparatory work, Goldwyn used the interruption to terminate his contract and replace him with Otto Preminger, belittling the director's talent and abilities, as Goldwyn's biographer Arthur Marx has written: "What did a Russian know about life on Catfish Row?"[24]

Enraged by Goldwyn's treachery, Mamoulian launched an unsuccessful lawsuit that dragged on for months and further damaged his reputation. Even so, in 1959, Mamoulian was engaged to direct a wide-screen epic of *Cleopatra* for 20th Century Fox. It was Mamoulian who insisted that Elizabeth Taylor should be cast in the lead, for which she received over $1 million, but it was Taylor who later helped to have Mamoulian removed as director. After two years of frustration and delays, Mamoulian resigned and was replaced by Joseph L. Mankiewicz. Mamoulian's film career had come to a sad and humiliating end. His formalism and extravagant stylization, products of his early experience in the world of pre-Revolutionary avant-garde Russian theater, had never really meshed with the commercial demands of the Hollywood studios.

Like Sergei Eisenstein (born just one year later), Mamoulian was an aesthete who never really understood or accepted the vulgar rules of the game.

Not All Russians Are Blond

*"Somewhere, my love, there will be songs to sing
Although the snow covers the hope of spring."*
Paul F. Webster

Just a few months after *Jet Pilot* flew onto American movie screens, the Cold War soared into outer space. Stunned disbelief was the reaction all over the world when, on October 4, 1957, the first artificial earth satellite, the Soviet Sputnik I, well equipped with instruments, climbed into orbit, presenting a startling challenge to the presumed superiority of American science and technology.

As a result of the Sputnik launch, respect for the USSR—hitherto regarded as a secretive, remote, and underdeveloped nation—rose dramatically in the United States. Resources were suddenly mobilized to study the Soviet Union and Eastern Europe. A new awareness grew that the two postwar atomic superpowers would have to work together in whatever areas they could agree upon if nuclear war were to be avoided in the shrinking global village. This awareness had led directly to the signing of the first Soviet-American cultural exchange agreement in January 1958. Notwithstanding the fears expressed by Secretary of State Dulles in testimony to the Senate Foreign Relations Committee that the Bolshoi Ballet was used by the Soviet government to strengthen international Communism, interest in all areas of Russia life and culture burgeoned. Russia was the forbidden other, as terrifying and alluring as sex to a teenager. Russian was hot. Red-hot.

American attitudes toward the USSR in the late 1950s were also influenced by the death of Josef Stalin on March 5, 1953, and the change in leadership in the Kremlin. After an initial period of collective leadership, Nikita Khrushchev emerged as the new Communist Party chief. In February 1956 Khrushchev delivered a dramatic speech to the Twentieth Congress of the Soviet Communist Party in which he denounced the repressive and cruel policies of his predecessor, Stalin. A period of political and cultural liberalization, known as "The Thaw," followed, lasting until the removal of Khrushchev from power in October 1964. Khrushchev also reached out to Western leaders in a way no other Soviet leader had ever done. He met with President Eisenhower in Geneva in July 1955, and opened the door to further superpower dialogue.

The initiation of cultural exchange did a great deal to humanize Russia for the average American. Heavily publicized, the first performance by the Moiseyev Folk Dance Ensemble at the Metropolitan Opera House in New York on April 14, 1958, was a sensation, both artistically and politically. By the end of its cross-country tour, the Moiseyev had appeared before an estimated 450,000 spectators. Also on April 14, the news broke on front pages all over the United States that a 23-year-old American pianist named Van Cliburn had won first prize in the prestigious Tchaikovsky Competition in Moscow. He became an instant celebrity and American folk hero, and a powerful symbol of peaceful cooperation between Russia and the United States.

One year later, this optimistic spirit was boosted by the arrival in New York of the Bolshoi Ballet for an extended tour arranged by the Russian-born impresario Sol Hurok. Hurok had already been immortalized in *Tonight We Sing,* a kitschy and highly inaccurate film made under his supervision by 20th Century Fox, released in 1953 and starring David Wayne as Hurok and a young Anne Bancroft as his adoring wife. It also features opera star Ezio Pinza as Fyodor Chaliapin, Mikhail Rasumny as Chaliapin's long-suffering valet, and Tamara Toumanova as Hurok's favorite client, ballerina extraordinaire Anna Pavlova. One reviewer of *Tonight We Sing* joked that, as Hurok, Wayne "fights a losing battle with a Russian accent."[1] In response to the anti-Communist mood, the film contains no reference to Hurok's early work for the Socialist party or any mention of his deep involvement in left-wing politics throughout his career.[2]

Throughout the Bolshoi's tour, public interest in the company and its dancers ran sky-high. In most cities, policemen had to be called out to hold back the throngs of those eager to see and touch and feel real Russians. Anti-Soviet demonstrations were also frequent, but the dancers tried not to pay attention. These tours by Russian ensembles and soloists stimulated heightened interest in Russian culture, and led Hollywood producers and directors to see films about Russia as a more marketable commodity.

★ Hollywood's relationship with the USSR took on a stunning new immediacy in September 1959 when Nikita Khrushchev paid a visit to Los Angeles as part of his tour of the United States, the first ever by a Soviet premier. Although he spent only a single day (September 19) in Los Angeles, it was a very memorable one. Preparations had gone on for weeks, with Hollywood's movers and shakers engaging in an all-out power struggle to gain access to the various planned events, especially a lunch at 20th Century Fox studios to be hosted by Fox chief Spyros Skouras, an immigrant from Greece. As Murray Schumach wrote in the *New York Times,* "Movie executives are more worried where they will sit than what they stand for."[3]

When Khrushchev finally arrived at the studio, he was greeted by such stars as Elizabeth Taylor, Bing Crosby, Marlon Brando, Deborah Kerr, Gary Cooper, Doris Day, Bob Hope, James Cagney, Danny Kaye, Rock Hudson, Kim Novak, Debbie Reynolds, and Marilyn Monroe. Monroe wore her "tightest, sexiest dress" and left her husband Arthur Miller at home. "I could tell Khrushchev liked me," she confided to her maid. "He smiled more when he was introduced to me than for anybody else. . . ."[4] One of the few actors who displayed political principles was staunch anti-Communist Ronald Reagan; he chose to boycott the affair.

At the lunch, Skouras chose to make a rather provocative speech in which he extolled the glories of the American dream by describing his own inspiring saga from impoverished boyhood to wealth and power. Khrushchev, always a volatile personality with a fiery and unpredictable temper, countered testily by telling the audience of his own rise from sheep-herding to the Kremlin. After lunch, the premier was given the opportunity to watch some of the filming of *Can-Can,* but found the skirt-raising dance routines (as he told labor leaders in San Francisco the following day) nearly pornographic. Shirley MacLaine spoke a few words of welcome in primitive Russian, and thanked Khrushchev for permitting Soviet performing artists to come to America.

Khrushchev's irritable mood was not helped by the extreme heat or by the refusal of local authorities to let him visit Disneyland. The denial of Disneyland threatened to explode into a full-blown scandal, with Khrushchev venting his frustration and disappointment in characteristically colorful fashion. "What is it? Is there an epidemic of cholera there or something? Or have gangsters taken hold of the place that can destroy me?" he asked.[5] For their part, the authorities insisted that the matter had been discussed long before Khrushchev's visit with his staff, and that it was too late to make the necessary security arrangements.

Piqued, Khrushchev let loose in the evening at a banquet in his honor at the Ambassador Hotel ballroom. When the Mayor of Los Angeles, Norris Poulson, referred to Khrushchev's famous phrase about the inevitable victory of Communism over capitalism—"We will bury you"—in his remarks, Khrushchev became angry and combative. Poulson decided to appear patriotic by stating, "You can't bury us, Mr. Khrushchev, so don't try. If challenged we shall fight to the death." In his reply, a defensive Khrushchev charged that there were some in the audience who had invited him only to embarrass him, to assert the superiority of the United States and to make him "a little shaky in his knees."[6] In that case, he said, he could turn around and return to the USSR at any moment.

"You may say that you can live without such visits," he continued, "but it is much better to live in peace than to live with loaded pistols and guns aimed at objectives. It's much better to live in peace and be sure that your sleep will not be disturbed and that the peace will be eternal." According to Harrison Salisbury, who was covering the event for the *New York Times,* "Mr. Khrushchev delivered his words in tones of the utmost gravity. He made it plain that he felt that he was being received in a manner that was light and frivolous."[7] Khrushchev's encounter with Hollywood was full of tension and jockeying for power, but it put a human face (flawed though it may be) on the Soviet leadership, and confirmed the crucial role played by the mass media and the movies in depicting and defining the Cold War. Just before Khrushchev arrived, it was also announced that a program of Soviet-American film exchange had been initiated. On November 10, 1959, a selected audience in Washington, D.C., would see the Soviet anti-war film *The Cranes Are Flying,* while the American film *Marty* would be shown in Moscow.

★   One of the hottest spots in the Cold War was Berlin. Ever since the end of World War II, when the Red Army liberated the city from the east, the fate of Berlin had been one of the most contentious issues in the difficult Soviet-American relationship. It was also the place, especially after the division of the former Germany into two countries—the capitalist West and the Communist East—where the superpowers maintained their closest proximity. In 1948, the allies mounted a massive airlift to the western part of jointly occupied Berlin in response to a Soviet blockade. Henceforth, the city, deep into East Germany, was divided into two halves. For four decades, West Berlin was a strange island of capitalism in a sea of Communism, and a place where intrigue and espionage flourished. Through the 1950s, although East and West Germany were separated by a heavily fortified barrier, Berliners could still move freely from one part of the city to another. A steady flow of refugees from East Berlin kept arriving in the West, a situation that was increasingly humiliating and aggravating to the Soviet and East German leaders.

When Khrushchev and Kennedy met for another summit in Vienna in 1961, the status of Berlin was one of the main items of discussion. Neither man would yield, Kennedy refusing to abandon the people of West Berlin and asserting the right of the Western powers to maintain a presence there. Finally the East German government, with the support of the USSR, did what had long been feared: it began to erect a wall in August 1961. The historic Brandenburg Gate at the head of the stylish Unter den Linden, where the wall cut the city in two, became the most powerful single symbol of the Cold War for the next thirty-eight years, until November 1989, when the wall was breeched by crowds of elated Germans celebrating the end of the East German state.

Not surprisingly, divided Berlin also became the focus and inspiration for many films. Directors and producers were attracted by the city's special combination of decadence and despair, of conspicuous capitalist consumption and utopian socialist planning gone awry. The fact that Berlin became the center for Cold War espionage on both sides made it a natural setting for the spy-film genre. Such films as *The Spy Who Came in from the Cold, Funeral in Berlin, The Enigma,* and Hitchcock's *Torn Curtain* and many others all capitalize (excuse the pun) on the city's special atmosphere of fear and euphoria, of a nihilistic life lived on the edge of a precipice. For several decades, many believed that World War III would start in Berlin.

Leave it to Billy Wilder, then, to use these economic and ideological tensions as material for comedy.

Wilder had served in the U.S. Army in Berlin after World War II, helping in the reorganization and de-Nazification of the German film industry. He also lost his mother in the Holocaust; she vanished without a trace, like millions of others. Even so, he retained his sense of humor in treating the strange aftermath of the war in the sarcastic comedy he directed (and co-wrote) for Parmount, *A Foreign Affair* (1948), starring Jean Arthur as Phoebe Frost, a naïve American senator from Iowa who is investigating the reconstruction of the German economy, and Marlene Dietrich as Erika von Schlutow, a seductive former Nazi and cabaret singer with easy morals and a gift for hooking up with powerful men, whatever their political persuasions. (In real life Dietrich was outspoken and brave in her condemnation of the Nazis.) In the end, the prim Frost and the depraved von Schultow find they have something in common: they are in love with the same man, an American officer. And the Soviet and American soldiers are happy to carouse together at the Lorelei café, where the black market reigns.

In 1961, Wilder revisited Berlin and the ideological war between Communism and capitalism in the zany feature *One, Two, Three.* By now, Wilder had established himself as one of the greatest Hollywood directors of all time, with such films as *Sunset Boulevard, Stalag 17, Sabrina, The Seven Year Itch, Love in the Afternoon, Some Like It Hot,* and *The Apartment* to his credit. *One, Two, Three,* which Wilder directed, and co-wrote with I. A. L. Diamond, is loosely based on a farce by the Hungarian Ferenc Molnar that played in Berlin (as *Ein, Zwei, Drei*) in 1929.

In their adaptation, Wilder and Diamond made that quintessential American product, Coca-Cola, the symbol of the East-West conflict, constructing around it a Romeo-and-Juliet style plot involving the daughter of an American Coca-Cola executive and the East German boy with whom she falls in love. For the leading role of the hard-driving, frenetic American soft drink executive MacNamara, Wilder made an unlikely casting choice: James Cagney. As a placid foil for Cagney's energy, Wilder cast Arlene Francis, best known as a regular on the television show *What's My Line,* who had last appeared in a film in 1948 (*All My Sons*). Pamela Tiffin played the role of Scarlett, the wayward daughter of Cagney's boss, and the German actor Horst Buchholz was cast as her boyfriend Otto.

With an affectionate nod to *Ninotchka,* three comic Russian characters enliven the proceedings: the trade commissars Peripetchikoff, Borodenko, and Mishkin, who drive around Berlin in a beat-up Moskvich ("just like a 1937 Nash"). They have been sent to investigate making a deal for Coca-Cola distribution in the USSR, and are forever spouting folksy nonsensical proverbs like "You can't milk a cow with your hands in your pockets." MacNamara brags that he will defeat Russia through commerce: "Napoleon blew it, Hitler blew it, but Coca-Cola will pull it off." For their part, the three Russian commissars prove no less susceptible to the lures of consumerism than their predecessors in *Ninotchka*—and no less pragmatic:

BORODENKO: Well, comrades, what are we going to do? He's got it, we want it. Are we going to accept this blackmailing capitalist deal?

MISHKIN: Let's take a vote.

BORODENKO: I vote yes!

MISHKIN: I vote yes?

BORODENKO: Two out of three—deal is on.

PERIPETCHIKOFF: Comrades, before you get in trouble I must warn you—I am not really from Soft-Drink Secretariat. I am undercover agent assigned to watch you.

MISHKIN: In that case, I vote no. Deal is off.

PERIPETCHIKOFF: But I vote yes!

BORODENKO: Two out of three again. Deal is on!

Wilder is merciless in his depiction of the inane regimentation of life in East Germany, where the citizens are forever singing the *Internationale* and are required to salute at all times, clicking their heels. But neither does he spare the ignorance of naïve Americans like the empty-headed Scarlett, who pleads with MacNamara not to condemn Otto: "He's not a Communist, he's a Republican. He comes from the Republic of East Germany." Through her love for Otto, Scarlett is at first politically transformed, and is even prepared to follow him to Moscow, where he is going to study. In the end, however, it is Otto who is converted from Communism to capitalism (just like Ninotchka) through his love for a capitalist, and his realization that he really enjoys the nice clothes and accessories (remember Ninotchka's hat) that MacNamara lends him to disguise him as a German aristocrat when Scarlett's parents unexpectedly pay a visit to Berlin from Atlanta ("Siberia with mint juleps"). Scarlett's father even gives Otto a job and sends him to the London office. One of the three Soviet trade commissars also defects to the West after he turns in his two comrades. In Wilder's Berlin, everyone is on the take: even the border guards can be bribed with bottles of Coke—"just return the empties."

In *One, Two, Three,* the musical score (arranged by Andre Previn) reinforces and even drives the East-West cultural divide. The "Sabre Dance," a wild Caucasian number from the socialist realist ballet *Gayane* by Soviet/Armenian composer Aram Khachaturian, propels the manic energy that drives the film. It is used with particular success in the madcap scene set in the ballroom of the Grand Hotel Potemkin, named for its association with the idea of the Russian Potemkin Village, a hastily constructed façade hiding shabby reality behind, a tactic allegedly used by Catherine the Great's minister Potemkin to impress visiting foreign dignitaries. For Wilder, the Potemkin Village syndrome also symbolized the Soviet attempt to conceal the increasingly obvious economic failure of Communist regimes in Russia and Eastern Europe. As the band plays relentlessly, MacNamara's secretary leaps onto the table with flaming skewers of *shashlik*—Caucasian shish kebab—and performs a crazed routine with a whip in the hopes of persuading MacNamara to buy her (yes, more consumerism) a new dress. In contrast, when Otto is detained by the East German police for riding a motorbike with an attached "Russki Go Home" balloon, he is tortured by being forced to listen repeatedly to a recording of the American pop song "She wore an itsy bitsy teeny weeny yellow polka dot bikini."

When Wilder started filming *One, Two, Three* on location in Berlin in June 1961, the East German leader Walter Ulbricht was denying publicly that his government planned to build a wall between East and West Berlin. But two months later, while filming was still going on, the Soviets and East Germans began to close the border and build a barrier of wire and cinder blocks. Wilder found that his film had become even more topical than he had expected. "We had to make continuous revisions to keep up with the headlines. It seemed to me that the whole thing could have been straightened out if Oleg Cassini had sent Mrs. Khrushchev a dress."[8] (The *Ninotchka* syndrome again.) Production had to be halted in Berlin and completed in Bavaria.

Although most critics dismissed *One, Two, Three* as an insignificant trifle unworthy of Wilder's talents, and the film lost more than $1.5 million, it was eerily prophetic of the future of the Berlin Wall and of Berlin. When The Wall finally came down in 1989, it was because the yearning of East Germans (along with the Russians and other East Europeans) for freedom of expression and choice had become so strong that it overwhelmed the promises of socialist equality and justice promoted by the Communist governments. One of the first things East Germans did after the Wall came down was to go shopping in the West. Like Ninotchka, they wanted to buy that silly hat.

★   *One, Two, Three* was not the only Romeo-and-Juliet Cold War comedy that came out in 1961. The other was *Romanoff and Juliet,* written and directed by Peter Ustinov and released by Universal International Pictures.

Ustinov (1921–2004) was born of Russian parents in England. His mother was Nadia Benois, an artist and niece of Alexandre Benois, a prominent stage designer for the Ballets Russes. (Among the many productions he designed was Stravinsky's *Petrouchka*.) Ustinov's father was an officer in the Tsar's army, forced to flee Russia after the Bolshevik Revolution. Brought up in England and fluent in several languages, Ustinov became involved with theater and film early in life, and worked successfully and prolifically as an author, director, and producer. In film, Ustinov excelled, according to Leonard Maltin, "in characterizations of vain, selfish, petulant characters."[9] His aristocratic and effete manners made him particularly suitable for the roles of supercilious patricians of ancient Rome, such as Nero in *Quo Vadis* (1951) and Lentulus Batiatus in Stanley Kubrick's *Spartacus* (1960), for which he won an Academy Award as Best Supporting Actor.

During the filming of *The Egyptian* (1954), directed by Michael Curtiz ("a film I never saw since I found it so profoundly silly while I was making it"), Ustinov and his wife had the time to become better acquainted with the Hollywood scene, at the height of the McCarthy era which had been so devastating to the film community.[10] Ustinov welcomed the chance to work with Michael Curtiz, "a tall and upright Hungarian who had come to Hollywood so long ago that he gazed over the palm trees and stucco castellations of its civilization with the blind, all-seeing faith of its prophet. He had never learned American, let alone English, and he had forgotten his Hungarian, which left him in a limbo of his own, both entertaining and wild."[11]

But the political atmosphere was depressing. "Some American friends I had made in England . . . had virtually disappeared, and asking after them seemed as dangerous as any request for the whereabouts of distinguished colleagues in a dictatorship."[12] This experience of American political repression gave Ustinov a new insight into the behind-the-scenes realities of the superpower conflict, the realization that despite their rhetoric about defending democratic freedoms, some members of the United States government were also prepared to censor and even persecute those perceived to hold dissident ideological beliefs. Ustinov's observation of the Hollywood scene in the early 1950s was a major source of material for a new political satire.

While in Hollywood for *The Egyptian,* Ustinov spent his spare time writing this new play, accompanied by the constant singing coming from Frank Sinatra in the neighboring apartment. The work was *Romanoff and Juliet,* "a three-act play absolutely neoclassical in form."

> I had always remembered the joy of playing in *The Rivals* with Edith Evans, and I wanted to try my hand at something as direct and as undisguisedly theatrical, ignoring the famous "fourth wall" and employing asides whenever expedient. I remembered that *The Rivals* had entertained troops, some of whom had never seen a play before, much more than the low farces specifically aimed at their intellect.
>
> The theme was a variation on the tragic love of Romeo and Juliet, with Romeo as the son of the Soviet ambassador and Juliet the daughter of the American ambassador. The intractable families, the Capulets and the Montagues, were replaced by the governments of the U.S.A. and the U.S.S.R., and the scene was a small neutral country, cringing in the center of the political arena, its economy largely dependent on printing stamps with deliberate anomalies.[13]

Romanoff and Juliet opened at the Piccadilly Theatre in London on May 17, 1956, and enjoyed an immediate and considerable success. The play was so well received that it was brought to Broadway by producer David Merrick soon after, opening in New York on October 10, 1957, where it was directed by the aging George S. Kaufman, with Ustinov (as in London) in the main role of the President of the tiny country of Concordia. It ran for a season on Broadway, and even received two Tony nominations, both for Ustinov, as Best Actor in a Dramatic Role and Best Play Author. Ustinov went on to Hollywood, where he worked on the filming of *Spartacus* for Universal. After he received his Oscar for *Spartacus,* grateful Universal executives told Ustinov they would

> be interested in a film version of my play *Romanoff and Juliet,* so long as it cost no more than $750,000. Those were the days.
>
> I have always found it difficult to digest the same meal twice, and perhaps I was too eager to keep those moments which had really worked in the play intact, even if it was part freewheeling fantasy and part photographed play. The leads, Sandra Dee and John Gavin, were then Universal contract stars, and they were given me for a small consideration,

but although they tried manfully, neither of them was ideally suited to the style of the text and the film suffered from an intrinsic incongruity, although it had many elements I was satisfied with.[14]

Joining Sandra Dee and Gavin were two veteran Hollywood Russians, Akim Tamiroff (as the Soviet ambassador Vadim Romanoff) and his wife Tamara Shayne (as the Soviet ambassador's wife Evdokia). Tamiroff's "jolly but menacing-looking" appearance well suited the role of the Soviet ambassador, who (like the real-life impresario Sol Hurok) insistently promises the people of Concordia that he will send them orchestras and ballet companies (even the Bolshoi!) in an attempt to compete with the economic aid being promised by the American ambassador. Using his gift for verbal and physical humor to superb effect, Tamiroff portrays the Soviet ambassador as a bumbling, well-meaning pawn of the powerful people in Moscow whom he fears and must obey. He and his wife also display their own susceptibility to the consumer attractions that happy Concordia (where "misery is a punishable crime") offers. In an affectionate homage to *Ninotchka,* Ustinov (who plays the President of Concordia and also directed the film) has Evdokia early in the story admire a hat in a shop window. Later, Romanoff finally buys it for her, in an act of love and generosity that runs counter to the image of the stern ideologue he likes to convey, symbolizing his acceptance (in true neoclassical fashion) of his son's choice of a mate.

Romanoff's subordinates are no less needy of positive emotional reinforcement. His political attaché is forever complaining that "no one likes me." On both sides, ideological rigidity is debunked and the combatants humanized.

Ustinov's screenplay stresses how both ambassadors, despite their status and political power, are unable to control their offspring, just like parents everywhere. When the American ambassador Hooper Moulsworth (John Phillips) learns that his daughter has fallen for Romanoff's son Igor, he wails, "Our daughter has fallen in love with a Commie!" In an attempt to derail their romance, Romanoff tries to set up Igor with a politically correct Russian fiancée, but this plan backfires when the imported fiancée meets the American boy who has been summoned as a marriage partner for Juliet Moulsworth on the plane and they fall in love with each other. The President of Concordia uses the cover of an elaborate history pageant performed in costume to marry Igor and Juliet—taking the role of Friar Lawrence in Shakespeare's *Romeo and Juliet*. Touched by the love and reconciliation, the top-ranking spy from the Russian Embassy (disguised as a cook) becomes a monk. The hostility and danger of the Soviet-American conflict vanish in a celebration of young love, future happiness, and the realization that people on both sides of the Iron Curtain share common human aspirations.

Most critics responded positively to the movie. In *The Reporter,* James Powers called it "one of the funniest pictures of the year, unpretentious but important. . . . *Romanoff and Juliet* seems a satire until one reads the daily headlines."[15]

By using the name Romanoff as the name for the Soviet ambassador, Ustinov stresses the continuity of Russian history, and cleverly creates an association with the highly marketable mystery of Tsar Nicholas II and his family—just like the impostor-creator of Romanoff's Restaurant in Beverly Hills. But like Billy Wilder, a frequent patron at Romanoff's, Ustinov was almost incapable of thinking tragically. (One prominent exception is his outstanding work on the 1962 film *Billy Budd,* which he wrote, produced, and starred in as Captain Vere.) Ustinov's version of Shakespeare's great love tragedy ends happily, with the reconciliation of the hostile families, just as his vision of the Cold War concludes with hugs and kisses across the ideological divide. As the idealistic and benevolent President of Concordia proclaims, "Our weapon is laughter, our cause, love." It was an escapist message anxious audiences desperately wanted to hear.

★   The noticeable thawing of relations between Moscow and Washington that had been progressing since the mid-1950s, following the death of Stalin and the rise of Nikita Khrushchev, was seriously jeopardized in 1962 by the Cuban Missile Crisis, "the most serious confrontation of the Cold War and perhaps its major turning-point."[16] In October, American surveillance cameras confirmed that nuclear missile sites were being constructed in Cuba, using equipment secretly imported on ships sent from the USSR. Since the revolutionary rise of Fidel Castro to the post of prime minister of Cuba in 1959, the country had been turning increasingly to the USSR for economic assistance, leading to fears that the new Cuban regime would become Communist. The United States broke off diplomatic relations with Cuba in 1961.

During the days that followed the discovery of the missile sites, the world came closer to a nuclear conflict than ever before. Thanks to shrewd diplomacy on the part of President Kennedy and his advisors (who had to discourage insistent calls for armed response on the part of certain members of the American military), and direct personal communication between Kennedy and Khrushchev, the crisis was peacefully resolved on October 28 when the USSR agreed to withdraw the missiles in exchange for promised secret concessions from the United States. For the moment, the threat had been deterred, but the crisis—beamed into the living rooms of most Americans through television—made the prospect of nuclear annihilation much more real, and renewed fears of Russia as an aggressive and dangerous power bent on spreading its influence throughout the globe. The Cold War was no longer confined to Europe and Asia; it had arrived in the Caribbean, on America's doorstep.

It seems oddly fitting that one of the most important—and most intensely ideological—films of the Cold War era should have been released in the midst of the Cuban Missile crisis. *The Manchurian Candidate,* directed by John Frankenheimer for United Artists, deals with the Soviet threat in an oblique manner, through a bizarre story of the aftermath of "brainwashing" of American soldiers during the Korean War. Set (with numerous flashbacks) on the eve of an American presidential election, it is one of the greatest political thrillers ever made, its ambiguous and multilayered "meaning" debated and analyzed by countless film historians, critics, and political scientists. The screenplay by George Axelrod is based on a 1959 novel by Richard Condon that was, in the words of critic Greil Marcus, "simultaneously a bestseller and a cult book."[17]

Frankheimer's film calls into question nearly all the assumptions underlying American Cold War attitudes of the 1950s. Instead of a crusader against Communism, Senator Joseph McCarthy (in the fictional character of Senator John Iselin) is an agent of the Soviets and Chinese, who hope to use him as a pawn for their own aims when he reaches higher office. Even more sinister is Iselin's wife, Eleanor, the brains of the team, who engineers his rise to power under the guise of strident anti-Communism. And her son, Raymond, a Korean War veteran, has been "brainwashed" so he can follow (robot-like) commands to kill those who stand in the way of the Communists' plans. Only Raymond's buddy from Korea, Major Bennet Marco (Frank Sinatra), is able to penetrate the complex puzzle of indoctrination and nightmares.

The film comes to a remarkable climax at the political convention in Madison Square Garden at which Iselin is to be nominated as candidate for vice-president. Eleanor has planned for the presidential candidate to be assassinated so that Iselin can take his place and usher in, after his election, a new era of Communist domination under her control, seizing "powers that will make martial law look like anarchy." But her plan goes dreadfully awry when the assassin Raymond either fails to follow instructions, or is mysteriously reprogrammed, and shoots his parents instead.

In *The Manchurian Candidate,* it is never entirely clear who is controlling whom, or what their motivations are. Even at the last moment, when Raymond is aiming his rifle at the podium from his hiding place high above the convention floor, we are not sure upon whose orders he is acting or whom he will shoot. (Just a year after the release of *The Manchurian Candidate,* President Kennedy was assassinated in circumstances that were not dissimilar to those depicted in the film. This close and disturbing resemblance was one factor that led to the film being withdrawn from distribution for the next twenty-five years.)

Frankenheimer's film exposes the politicians on both sides of the Cold War as power-hungry cynics intent above all else on self-aggrandizement. Ideology is only a tool to achieve personal ends. The black-and-white distinctions of the McCarthy era between Commies and non-Commies are blurred and collapsed. By portraying Raymond's mother (Angela Lansbury, in one of her greatest roles) as an evil and manipulative monster, the 1950s ideal of the happy American family requiring defense from the bad Communists is exploded into sharp pieces. Nothing is what it seems. The enemy is not only in Russia or China, but right here among us. The alien zombies of the *Invasion of the Body Snatchers* have taken on the identity of our own parents and children.

Russian characters occupy a muted but important presence in *The Manchurian Candidate.* In the film's innovative opening sequence, a flashback-dream, which shows Shaw and his fellow soldiers being captured in Korea, we hear vague Russian words being spoken in the background, apparently the conversation of those who are carrying out the ambush of the Americans. In the extended surreal dream of Major Marco, combining a scene at a ladies' garden party with a conference of brainwashing scientists, several Russians are in the audience and register observations about the course of Raymond's "brainwashing," a joint effort by Chinese and Soviet doctors that was carried out at a special center in Manchuria. Later, the Russian scientist Zilkov (Albert Paulsen) is a member of the team sent to reprogram Raymond: "his brain has not only been washed but dried clean." KGB agents roam the streets of New York. Portraits of Stalin hang on the walls of the conference room in Marco's dream (set in 1952), and Raymond shoots a soldier (in another dream) so that Stalin's face is splattered with gore, a shocking and unforgettable image. That the Soviets are involved in the "brainwashing" of the Americans is clear; they have trained the Chinese and Koreans in the latest techniques of mind control at the Pavlov Institute in Moscow. But their crimes seem no less reprehensible than those committed by the American politicians. Communism and anti-Communism are depicted as equally corrupt, repressive, and devious.

Frankenheimer's casting of Janet Leigh—known not only for her recent work in *Psycho* but also for her portrayal of Russian women in *Red Danube* (a repressed anti-Communist) and *Jet Pilot* (a loyal Communist converted to capitalism through love)—as Major Marco's new girlfriend Rosie brings yet another unusual resonance to *The Manchurian Candidate*. Rosie's political and personal loyalties and motivations also remain murky and uncertain. Is she, too, an agent? If so, who is she working for?

The pervasive ambiguity of ideological allegiances in the film was disturbing to many viewers, including Bosley Crowther of the *New York Times*, who wrote that he was troubled by a "grave sort of irresponsibility in its premises and tone." The Los Angeles *Herald-Examiner* also reported that the 23rd District of the American Legion charged that *The Manchurian Candidate* showed that "Communists are again infiltrating the film industry," and was urging the launching of a new probe by the House Un-American Activities Committee, a response that only seemed to validate Frankenheimer's interpretation of the paranoid ideological climate.[18]

Filmed in naturalistic black-and-white that adds to its harsh documentary-like believability, *The Manchurian Candidate* examines the implications of the Cold War from an existential perspective previously lacking in the American cinema, initiating a new era in the treatment of Russia and the USSR in film. For the rest of the 1960s, the demonization of the Soviet leadership and people gave way to a more evenhanded (and sometimes absurdist) portrayal that stressed the mutual danger facing both of the superpowers in the nuclear era. So awful and so beyond the range of past human experience was the specter of atomic annihilation that it stimulated several directors to treat it with absurd humor, with what can be called "comic surrealism."

One of the masters of this technique is Stanley Kubrick, whose film *Doctor Strangelove, or How I Learned to Stop Worrying and Love the Bomb*, uses the Soviet-American nuclear confrontation as material for brilliant black satire. Like another great satirist, Billy Wilder, Kubrick was descended from a family of German-speaking Jews from Galicia, a province of the former Austro-Hungarian empire located in what is today southern Poland. Wilder, however, spent his young adulthood in Europe (Vienna and Berlin), while Kubrick was born in America—in New York. That both directors were steeped in the European values of their families may help to explain why they were so adept at looking at American culture from a sharply comic perspective.

Throughout his career, Kubrick also had a special fondness for things Russian or with a Russian sensibility. His film *Lolita* (1962) was based on a celebrated and controversial novel by the Russian-American writer Vladimir Nabokov. *Doctor Strangelove* (1964) features several Russian characters and revolves around the Soviet-American relationship. In *2001* (1968), about the implications of space exploration, Soviet and American scientists collaborate to solve the mysteries of the cosmos. In *A Clockwork Orange* (1971), based on a novel by Anthony Burgess, characters chat in a manufactured futuristic language possessing many Russian words and phrases. Russian music figures prominently in the scores of Kubrick's films—notably Khachaturian's ballet *Gayane* in *2001* and piano music of Dmitri Shostakovich in *Eyes Wide Shut*.

Kubrick also read with considerable interest the works written on film theory and practice by the prominent directors of early Soviet cinema, especially Sergei Eisenstein and Vsevolod Pudovkin, finding the ideas of Pudovkin on editing particularly cogent. For Kubrick, it was editing (Eisenstein called it montage) that was the distinguishing feature of cinema as an art. "Editing is unique to film. You can see something from different points of view almost simultaneously, and it creates a new experience."[19]

Although the idea for what became *Doctor Strangelove* was already in the works before the Cuban Missile Crisis, and shooting had begun in October 1962, the reality of that event helped to convince Kubrick that a film about a nuclear attack launched by a mentally imbalanced American general could be made as a black comedy. The original script for *Strangelove* was adapted from the novel *Two Hours to Doom* by Peter George. Later, Kubrick called in the off-beat writer Terry Southern to rework it, telling him that "nuclear war was too outrageous, too fantastic to be treated in any conventional manner," and that he had decided to present it as "some kind of hideous joke."[20]

Since the film was financed with British money, it was shot in England, but released by Columbia. Columbia demanded that Kubrick use Peter Sellers, who had also appeared to considerable acclaim in *Lolita* (as Clare Quilty), in multiple roles. In the end, Sellers took three roles: as the impossibly courteous British Group Captain Lionel Mandrake, who attempts unsuccessfully to dissuade the crazed General Jack D. Ripper from carrying out his plan to launch nuclear missiles against the USSR; as American President Merkin Muffley; and as the German émigré and former Nazi scientist Dr. Strangelove. This casting choice heightened the film's strange sense of self-conscious theatricality and absurdity. Kubrick also gave the film's characters intentionally funny names heavy with double-entendre: Jack D. Ripper, "Buck" Turgidson, Major T. J. "King" Kong, Ambassador DeSadesky, Dr. Strangelove.

The plot of *Doctor Strangelove* is relatively straightforward—especially compared to *The Manchurian Candidate*. As the film opens, the mentally unbalanced American missile base commander Jack D. Ripper (Sterling Hayden), convinced that the threat of Communism is sapping the strength of his "bodily fluids," has used his authority to launch planes that will drop hydrogen bombs on targets in the USSR. The process can be reversed only by inserting a special code known only to Ripper, who commits suicide in his office bathroom. Most of the film depicts the comically inept efforts of the American President and his advisors (huddled in a futuristic war room) to recall the bombers, with the assistance of the Soviet Ambassador (present in the war room) and the Soviet Premier (on the telephone from Moscow). Finally they succeed in recalling all the bombers—except one (commanded by Major "King" Kong, played by Slim Pickens with heavy hillbilly manners and drawl) that has lost radio contact as the result of damage sustained from an enemy missile explosion. It continues against all obstacles. Even a broken door in the bomb bay cannot detain the gung-ho Kong; he manages to open the door, mounts the bomb and rides it to earth like a bucking bronco, setting off the Soviet "Doomsday Machine" and leading to complete and utter nuclear annihilation.

One of the comic highlights of *Doctor Strangelove* is the performance of Peter Bull as the Soviet Ambassador DeSadesky. (The character's name is clearly derived from that of the Marquis DeSade, and carries implications of sadism and aristocracy upon which Bull plays with hilarious panache.) In the hopes of averting a nuclear catastrophe, President Muffley invites DeSadesky into the inner sanctum of the war room, over the vigorous objections of General Turgidson, who cannot abide the idea of a "dirty Commie" present in this top-secret environment. DeSadesky and Turgidson even scuffle when Turgidson discovers that the Ambassador is carrying a tiny camera with which to take pictures of the top-secret equipment. When they start to wrestle, the ineffectual President orders them to stop with a brilliantly illogical command: "There is to be no fighting in the War Room!" Unlike other Soviet diplomats and military men who had appeared in American films up until this point, DeSadesky is shown to be no worse than his vain and self-important ideological foes on the American side. Plump and self-satisfied, DeSadesky seems most concerned about his own comfort and satisfying his appetite for fresh fish and Cuban cigars rather than averting the impending disaster. Originally, the film was to have ended with a pie-throwing fight in the War Room, initiated by DeSadesky, but this scene was eliminated from the final cut.

Although we do not see the Soviet Premier Dmitri Kissoff on camera, or hear his voice, his character is sharply delineated in his remarkably silly phone conversation with President Muffley. It is DeSadesky who gives the President the private phone number at which the Premier can be reached. (The direct "hot line" was set up only after the Cuban Missile Crisis.) DeSadesky has a short conversation with the Premier in (bad) Russian, without subtitles, then hands the phone to the President with the warning, "I think he's drunk." (Kubrick required Peter Bull to learn his entire role in both English and Russian.) President Muffley and the Premier then exchange a number of trivial pleasantries that sound completely absurd under the circumstances, with the clock ticking down to Armageddon: "Yes, I'm fine, Dmitri." "I'm glad you're fine, too." "It's nice that we are both fine." Neither Muffley nor the Premier exhibit anything resembling heroic behavior, instead they show themselves as petty, whining, little men with the same human concerns (food, drink, sex) as everyone else. Kubrick strips away the seriousness surrounding the issue of atomic weapons, and exposes how both leaders use the threat of nuclear war for their own personal and political purposes. The Soviet threat turns out to be less dangerous than the erratic behavior of individual generals.

The nihilistic message of *Dr. Strangelove* offended many critics. Bosley Crowther of the *New York Times* voiced his dismay over the irresponsibility of painting such a negative picture of the American military and defense establishment. "To make a terrible joke of this matter is not only defeatist and destructive of morale. It is to invite a kind of laughter that is only foolish and hysterical."[21] In response, Lewis Mumford wrote a letter to the editor charging that Crowther "still does not understand either the point of Stanley Kubrick's satiric method or the soundness of the film's morals. It is not this film that is sick: what is sick is our supposedly moral, democratic country which allowed this policy to be formulated and implemented without even the pretense of open public debate. This film is the first break in the catatonic cold war trance that has so long held our country in its rigid grip."[22] To critic Loudon Wainwright, the criticism of the message of *Doctor Strangelove* was all too reminiscent of the way Soviet commissars attacked Soviet artists for failing to provide a positive portrayal of Soviet life.

Two other major films with anti-bomb and antiwar messages similar to *Doctor Strangelove*'s were released in 1964: *Fail-Safe* and *Seven Days in May*. Neither of these competent films could compete artistically with the unconventional, nihilistic *Dr. Strangelove*, however.

★ The idea that both sides in the Cold War had become victims of powers over which they had little control also informs the 1963 James Bond film *From Russia with Love*, the second in the Bond series after *Dr. No*. Here, the villain is not the USSR, but an international terrorist conspiracy (SPECTRE) that plays the two parties in the superpower conflict against each other for its own evil ends. Instead of killing each other, James Bond (working for the British Secret Service and by extension for the Western NATO powers) and his Soviet counterpart Tatiana Romanova (Romanovs again!) fall in love and—after many complications and a long and eventful journey by train and boat from Istanbul—apparently live happily ever after in Venice. For most of the film, Bond (Sean Connery, in his second appearance as the suave and unflappable agent) believes that Romanova—a former ballet dancer, of course—is working for the Soviet side out of the Soviet Embassy in Istanbul. (As in *Ninotchka*, Istanbul functions as a neutral space between East and West.)

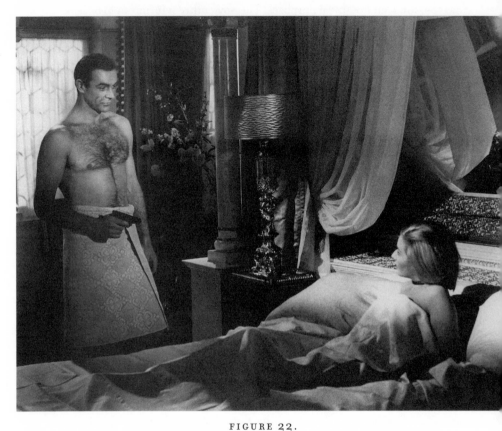

FIGURE 22.

From Russia with Love. United Artists/UK 1964. Sean Connery as James Bond
with Daniele Bianchi (as Tatiana Romanova). Courtesy of the Margaret Herrick
Library, Academy of Motion Picture Arts and Sciences.

Only toward the end does Bond learn that Tanya's superior, the voyeuristic and sadistic Rosa Klebb (legendary German-American actress Lotte Lenya, in a marvelously malevolent and perverse performance) has in fact secretly defected from the Soviet anti-espionage agency (SMERSH) to SPECTRE and is using Romanova as a pawn in a plot to obtain a highly coveted decoding machine from the Soviets. Tanya "thinks she is doing it all for Mother Russia," but in fact Klebb plans for her to be murdered by a SPECTRE agent after Tanya has ceased to be useful, after delivering the machine (a "lektor") to Bond, from whom SPECTRE then plans (but of course, fails) to seize it. Bond saves Tanya (played by Italian actress Daniela Bianchi) from this fate. In gratitude to him and out of disillusionment with Mother Russia, she, too, defects at the end, her mission, like Ninotchka's, subverted by contact with Westerners. West (Bond) and East (Tanya) become co-victims and find common ground against more sinister foes.

Although they were financed primarily with American money, and co-produced by an American based in Britain (Albert R. Broccoli), the James Bond films have a strong British sensibility. Shot at Pinewood Studios in Britain, they do not (for the most part) use Hollywood stars, and cannot be considered as reflecting the American cinematic response to Russia.

Indeed, in many ways, the Bond films, based on the novels of British writer Ian Fleming, celebrate Britishness—a bit defensively—in an era when British global influence was on the wane. "The Britishness of Bond," writes James Chapman in *Licence to Thrill: A Cultural History of the James Bond Films*, "has been central to the ideology of national identity which the films project; it also serves as a means of differentiating Bond from the All-American action heroes incarnated by the likes of Mel Gibson, Bruce Willis and Sylvester Stallone."[23] And yet, the Bond films became extremely popular with the American audience in the 1960s and 70s, and were widely imitated by American directors of spy and action movies. The films also strongly tone down the snobbish British tone of the novels, recasting "the source material so that the upperclass Englishness of Ian Fleming's original gives way to the more classless virility of the Hollywood action hero," to create "an image of Britishness carefully packaged for the international market."[24]

Few American characters appear in the Bond films, but there are, of course, numerous Russians. About half of the Bond films deal in some way with the USSR, notably *From Russia with Love, You Only Live Twice, The Spy Who Loved Me, For Your Eyes Only, Octopussy, A View to a Kill, GoldenEye* and *The World Is Not Enough*. In adapting the novels (most of them written in the 1950s) for the screen beginning in the 1960s, Ian Fleming (who died in 1964) and his collaborators decided to modify the strong anti-Soviet message, reflecting the improving relations between the USSR and the West after the late 1950s. The villains became members of an international band of terrorists who (as in *From Russia with Love*) victimize both Soviet and Western agents. In preparing the screenplay for *From Russia with Love*, Broccoli and his Canadian-born co-producer Harry Saltzman decided to make SPECTRE the enemy rather than the Soviet agency SMERSH because they felt "the Russians could no longer be the heavies."[25]

Fleming shared this view, as he explained concerning his decision to introduce an international criminal conspiracy in his novel *Thunderball* (1961). "I have always liked the Russians as people, and I enjoyed myself when I worked in Moscow. . . . I could not see any point in going on digging at them, especially when the coexistence thing seemed to be bearing some fruit. So I closed down SMERSH and thought up SPECTRE instead."[26] Throughout the 1960s and '70s, the conspiracy against which Bond struggles (and inevitably triumphs) comes from "a third party, either Red China or Spectre, taking advantage of the Cold War fears that divide the Soviet Union and the West."[27]

In *The Spy Who Loved Me* (1977), for example, Bond (now played by Roger Moore) and his Soviet counterpart Anya Amasova (Barbara Bach) are both victimized by the SPECTRE magnate and proto-Nazi Karl Stromberg (Curt Jurgens). Using a gigantic battleship with jaws, he sets about capturing Russian, American, and British nuclear missile submarines, hoping to start a world war out of which he and his organization will emerge victorious and capable of starting a new world order. The close personal and romantic relationship between Bond and Amasova symbolizes the era of détente in Soviet-Western relations, as Stromberg notes: "Well, well, well, a British agent in love with a Russian agent—détente indeed."

In the early 1980s, however, after the Soviet invasion of Afghanistan and the election of Ronald Reagan in the United States and Margaret Thatcher in Great Britain, the Soviets again became more villainous in the Bond films. In *For Your Eyes Only* (1981), a Greek gangster attempts to capture and sell to the Soviets a missile targeting system. In *Octopussy* (1983), the rogue Soviet General Orlov collaborates with an exiled Afghan prince in a complicated scheme to detonate a nuclear weapon on an American air force base in West Germany, making it look like an accident so as to encourage anti-nuclear groups in Europe and defeat the Soviet push for détente with the United States. In *A View to a Kill* (1985), a millionaire industrialist Max Zorn, an ex-KGB agent, plans to monopolize production of the world's microchips by destroying Silicon Valley. At its end, the Russian General Gogol offers Bond the Order of Lenin for defeating Zorn and saving Silicon Valley, since, as he jokes, "where would Russian research be without it?"

The collapse of the USSR at the end of the 1980s created a crisis for the makers of the Bond films, since it was no longer possible to use the superpower confrontation as a fundamental dramatic conflict. There was an unusual six-year hiatus between the release of *Licence to Kill* (1989), which deals with the international drug trade, and *GoldenEye* (1995).

In *GoldenEye,* written for the screen, Bond (now Pierce Brosnan) negotiates the tricky terrain of post-Communist Russia, where a former Soviet general has become a criminal plotting his own private conspiracy, in league with a former British agent who has turned against England to run an international crime syndicate. Bond is aided by a former antagonist from the KGB, Valentin Zukovsky (Robbie Coltrane), proving that it is difficult to predict how the collapse of the USSR will affect those who worked both for and against it. The opening credits (after a flashback sequence to 1986, when the USSR was still intact) show the symbols of Soviet power—hammer and sickle, statues of Lenin—being dismantled and smashed. *GoldenEye* was also the first of the Bond films to be filmed on location in Russia—in St. Petersburg. Despite the relaxation of ideological tensions between East and West, the Russia of *GoldenEye* remains "a mysterious and sinister enemy."[28]

The World Is Not Enough (1999) moves the action from Russia to Azerbaidzhan, where the heiress to an oil fortune is being threatened by criminals disenfranchised in the post-Soviet aftermath. In some ways, the new post-Communist world looks even more dangerous for James Bond than the old one, for it is no longer clear who is on which side and why.

★ Hollywood's blockbuster "Russia" film of the 1960s—the most ambitious "Russia" film produced to date—was the historical/romantic epic

Doctor Zhivago. Financed by MGM, directed by Englishman David Lean (1908–1991), produced by Italian Carlo Ponti, and shot in Spain and Finland, *Zhivago* was a thoroughly international project whose principal actors were Egyptian (Omar Sharif), British (Julie Christie, Tom Courtenay, Alec Guinness, Ralph Richardson), and American (Geraldine Chaplin, Rod Steiger). Ponti had acquired the screen rights to Boris Pasternak's novel *Doctor Zhivago,* and when he struck a deal with the recently appointed president of MGM, Robert O'Brien, O'Brien immediately began to pursue Lean, already a film legend, and particularly successful in working with big historical subjects, as he had proved in *The Bridge on the River Kwai* (1957) and *Lawrence of Arabia* (1962). For directing *Zhivago,* Lean was paid the highest salary ever given to a director.[29]

In filming *Zhivago,* Lean and his team were tackling a novel by a Nobel Prize-winning author that had already become world-famous for both political and literary reasons.

Boris Pasternak (1890–1960) was one of the great poets of the twentieth century and one of the very few Russian artists of his generation to survive both the Revolution and the Stalin era with body and soul intact. The son of a well-known artist, Pasternak was the member of a prominent family and grew up in a privileged, Bohemian milieu. Through his parents, he met many of the leading figures of Russian pre-Revolutionary culture, including Leo Tolstoy. Initially, Pasternak studied to be a composer, and was even encouraged in this aspiration by Alexander Scriabin, but eventually he decided that he had insufficient talent for that career and turned to the study of philosophy. For a time he studied in Germany, acquiring an excellent knowledge of German language and literature. During World War I, Pasternak spent some time in the Urals, and later used his knowledge of this region in the novel *Doctor Zhivago.* Like most liberal members of the Russian intelligentsia, Pasternak welcomed the revolutions of 1917, and confessed to a personal admiration for Vladimir Lenin, whom he saw in person at the Bolshoi Theater in 1921.

Like many Russians of their class and education, the Pasternaks found life under the Bolsheviks difficult and alien. Pasternak's parents and sisters left the USSR in 1921. Boris travelled abroad to visit them several times, but as a budding writer, he was loathe to leave the country of his native language and culture forever. His last trip abroad was in 1936, when he attended a writers' congress in Paris. In his early career, Pasternak focused on poetry, and soon became one of the most original and influential poets of his extremely talented literary generation.

Pasternak's attitude toward the Soviet regime was ambivalent and complex. He never embraced the role of a pro-Communist cheerleader like his contemporary and friend Vladimir Mayakovksy, but he also refrained from pointed criticism of the government. As time went on, he became the target of attacks from the Party bureaucrats for remaining too aloof from socialist reconstruction, and for continuing to write lyrical and philosophical verse dealing with highly personal and apolitical concerns. He was labeled a "fellow traveler" and "internal émigré," and encountered increasing difficulty in getting his poems published. After 1935, he virtually stopped publishing his own work and turned increasingly to the safer craft of translation, producing what are still regarded today as the best translations of the plays of Shakespeare.

In 1936, Pasternak made a speech in Minsk disagreeing with some of the tenets of Socialist Realism, the official doctrine of Soviet literature that required authors to write uplifting narratives of Communist progress revolving around the figure of a positive hero. Even so, Pasternak was not singled out for arrest, imprisonment, or execution during the terrible purges directed by Stalin against Russian artists and intellectuals during the late 1930s, which carried off many of his friends and colleagues. It appears that Stalin himself had decided that Pasternak should be spared, and he was even given a house in the prestigious writers' colony in Peredelkino outside Moscow, where he spent most of his time until his death.

In 1946, Pasternak began an extramarital affair with Olga Ivinskaya. She became the model for Lara Antipova, the heroine of his first and only novel, *Doctor Zhivago*, written between 1946 and 1955. (Because of her ambiguous association with the suspicious Pasternak, Ivinskaya was arrested— like the wives and lovers of many other prominent Soviet artists—in 1949 and sent to labor camp until 1953). Its hero, the doctor/poet Yuri Zhivago, is in many ways a self-portrait of Pasternak, an artist who must confront terrible personal and professional choices forced upon him in the aftermath of the 1917 Bolshevik Revolution.

Unable to adopt the steely confidence of the "new man" of the Soviet era, sensitive and dreamy, Zhivago drifts rather passively through life, falling into a passionate affair with Lara that separates him from his family, unable to decide between the two great loves of his life. Compassionate, generous, and charismatic, the indecisive Zhivago has few of the qualities of the positive Socialist Realist hero, for he shuns confrontation and violence, even in the service of socialist ideals. Pasternak's beautifully crafted prose, full of delicate symbols and imagery that form intricate and recurring patterns, is also saturated with Christian motifs, and Zhivago himself is closely associated with the character of Christ. The novel ends with a set of poems, supposedly written by Zhivago. The first is entitled "Hamlet," and draws a striking parallel between Shakespeare's guilty, passive prince and the life of Zhivago: "I love your preordained design / And am ready to play this role. / But the play being acted is not mine. / For this once let me go."[30]

In 1956, encouraged by the improving cultural climate following Stalin's death, Pasternak submitted *Doctor Zhivago* for publication to the leading literary journal *Novy mir,* but it was rejected for its "nonacceptance of the socialist revolution." For a time, it appeared that an abridged version might be published in the USSR, but then the novel was forbidden altogether. In November 1957, the Italian publisher Feltrinelli published *Zhivago* in Russian, and an English translation appeared in 1958. It was in large part the publication of *Zhivago* that led to the awarding of the Nobel Prize for Literature to Pasternak in 1958.

In the eyes of the Khrushchev regime, the publication of a work abroad by a Soviet writer that had been prohibited for publication at home was tantamount to an act of treason. The Kremlin also viewed the awarding to Pasternak of the Nobel Prize as provocative and anti-Soviet, and informed him that if he went to Stockholm to receive it, he would not be allowed to return to the USSR. Already ill and in his late 60s, Pasternak chose to remain at home, and became the focus of enormous international attention and publicity. The entire incident became a powerful symbol to the world of the continuing repression of artistic and creative freedom in the USSR.

Pasternak died not long afterward of lung cancer. Although his funeral was not officially announced or celebrated, thousands attended, and his gravesite at Peredelkino remains today a site of pilgrimage. The same year that he died, Ivinskaya was again arrested and was imprisoned for two more years. *Doctor Zhivago* became a bestseller in the West, but remained banned in the USSR until 1988, when it was finally published along with other long-banned books as part of the new policy of *glasnost* introduced by Mikhail Gorbachev.

David Lean faced a formidable challenge in reducing the sprawling complexity of Pasternak's lengthy novel to a manageable screenplay. The action occurs over a very long span of time, beginning in 1902 with the death of Zhivago's mother and the suicide of his father when he is ten years old and ending in the early 1950s, years after Zhivago's death in 1929. In between, Zhivago lives through the Revolution of 1905, World War I, the revolutions of 1917, and the Civil War, marries Tonya, moves to the Urals with her, and then abandons her after he reconnects with Lara, whom he came to know when they served together in a medical unit during World War I. Although Pasternak employs a third-person narrative, it is very close to Zhivago's point of view. Coincidences play a central role in the novel—Zhivago and Lara begin their affair after they meet again by chance in the library of the Urals city of Yuriatin, for example, in 1919. Some critics have found these coincidences far-fetched and arbitrary, but they aptly reflect the unsettled and catastrophic conditions of life in Russia during this period.

In contrast to Tolstoy in *War and Peace,* Pasternak avoids mentioning real historical events or figures (such as Lenin and Trotsky). Instead, he keeps the focus on his fictional characters and their lives, creating what Isaac Deutscher has called "a parable about a vanished generation."[31] *Doctor Zhivago* could even be called an "anti-political novel," an eloquent defense of the individual, of consciousness, and of the enduring value of artistic perception. For the most part, Pasternak pointedly refrains from making value judgments about Communism and the Soviet regime. None of the novel's characters are completely evil, although they may possess (like Lara's husband Pasha Antipov, who later takes the revolutionary name Strelnikov) mistaken and dangerous ideas.

Lean's first and only choice for screenwriter was Robert Bolt, a fellow Englishman who had received an Academy Award nomination for his script for *Lawrence of Arabia.* That the director and the screenwriter (along with most of the cast members) were British gave *Doctor Zhivago* a strong British flavor; they approached the material more objectively and less ideologically than an American crew might have been expected to. Lean's *Doctor Zhivago* is for the most part lacking in the us-versus-them thinking characteristic of most of Hollywood's Cold War era films about Communism and the USSR. True, the committed Communists for the most part come off rather badly. The tenants who after the Revolution commandeer the former Zhivago mansion in Moscow are an intimidating assortment of

FIGURE 23.

Doctor Zhivago. MGM 1965. Lobby card. Courtesy of the Margaret Herrick Library, Academy of Motion Picture Arts and Sciences.

FIGURE 24.

Doctor Zhivago. Julie Christie does the first scene in *Doctor Zhivago*. Here, young British actress as top feminine role of Lara, heroine of Boris Pasternak's novel, alights from a Moscow tram as director David Lean (fourth from left) and camera crew watch filming on spectacular Moscow street setting near Madrid, where Carlo Ponti is producing the multi-million-dollar film for MGM. Courtesy of the Margaret Herrick Library, Academy of Motion Picture Arts and Sciences.

surly and raffish types responding like puppets to a barking and humor-less political supervisor. They treat Zhivago and his family with a wither-ing contempt calculated to evoke powerful sympathy in the viewer, who has by now strongly sided with the courteous and courtly hero. And Zhivago's involuntary stint as a doctor with a group of bloodthirsty Bolshe-vik partisans does little to create positive feelings for the ideals of the Revo-lution. But the film retains Zhivago's political ambivalence and artistic fatalism, his helplessness in the face of overwhelming historical turmoil.

Bolt shared Lean's enthusiasm for the novel and for the film project, and was soon making suggestions about the visual style of the film:

> An ocean of daffodils. A man, tiny, stands in it. What's he doing? (we hold the "meaningless" shot long enough to raise the question.) Close shot the man; just standing. We move round to see his face; crying per-haps? No, just standing and looking. His POV; the daffodils again, the birch leaves, the white birch branches, we hurl the camera through them, we race, we are drunk, the shafts of black and white drop behind us, we soar, we return, we skim the daffodils and settle at the man's broken-booted feet, ascend slowly to his face. He is as before, but we have the poet's *mind* for a minute.[32]

Daffodils are an important unifying symbol in the finished film. After Zhivago and Tonya have moved to the family's estate at Varykino in the Urals, they plant daffodils in the field in front of their house. And it is with a shot of a daffodil dissolving into Lara's face that Lean and Bolt show us the sensual and joyful reunion between Lara and Zhivago at the library. Bolt and Lean also tried to retain other important recurring poetic sym-bols from the novel, such as a burning candle. Both men felt a heavy re-sponsibility to create a film worthy of the novel and of Pasternak.

Bolt and Lean agreed that the love story between Lara and Zhivago had to be the spine of the film. In a letter to Lean, Bolt wrote, "I suppose it's the old story of the woman falling not for the man but the artist, not realizing that only the man and not the artist can return her love."[33] In this sense, they envisioned a film about a universal theme, not just about Russia.

One of Bolt's biggest challenges was to handle the abrupt leaps in time that occur in the novel, and in particular the last sections (after Zhivago's death), which deal with the daughter of Lara and Zhivago, born after they were separated and whom Zhivago never knew. Being respectful of Paster-

FIGURE 25.

Doctor Zhivago. Julie Christie, about to begin her first scene for David Lean's film of Boris Pasternak's *Doctor Zhivago,* poses for the usual make-up and hair test for her role of Lara, heroine of the widely discussed novel. Courtesy of the Margaret Herrick Library, Academy of Motion Picture Arts and Sciences.

nak's text, they did not want to eliminate these chapters, but feared that the audience would lose interest once Zhivago and Lara had disappeared from the story. So they decided to use the minor character of Zhivago's half-brother Yevgraf (Alec Guinness) as a narrator, "half in and half out of the story."[34]

In the novel, the mysterious figure of Yevgraf, a devout but humane Communist, acts as a sort of guardian angel to Zhivago, coming to his assistance at crucial moments. In the film, he continues to protect Zhivago's legacy after his death in 1929, understanding his importance as a poet. Yevgraf, now a distinguished general in the Soviet security forces, locates the young woman he believes to be Tonya, the daughter of Zhivago and Lara (played with winning vulnerability by Rita Tushingham) and tells her about Zhivago, in a series of extended flashbacks. Yevgraf's narration serves to provide the film with necessary continuity; otherwise it would become a series of disconnected episodes.

The film opens at a vast construction site at a hydroelectric plant, sometime soon after the death of Stalin. Yevgraf, now a distinguished general, has tracked down Tonya, who works there as a laborer along with other young women orphaned or displaced during the Revolution and Civil War. She was separated from her parents as a child and has only dim recollections of them. At the film's end, we are still left somewhat uncertain whether or not she is in fact Zhivago's daughter; she has no documents and there is no certain proof (in this era before DNA testing). But as she bids farewell to Yevgraf, Tonya (her name is the same as that of Zhivago's first wife) is seen walking away with a balalaika slung over her shoulder, and her boyfriend tells us admiringly that she has a special gift for music. She has inherited her father's artistic disposition.

For Bolt and Lean, one of the main problems was how to make a film about a man who has no conventional heroic traits (unlike the fearless warrior hero of *Lawrence of Arabia*) and whose main accomplishment was to write great poetry. Hollywood has made few films about poets, and even fewer successful ones. They decided to concentrate the dramatic energy in Zhivago's relationship with Lara, which reaches its climax in the scene at the abandoned house at Varykino, "where the revolution is closing in on them, where the fearful cold is closing in on them," as Bolt wrote in a letter.

"What they were doing is in practical terms nonsense, if not highly irresponsible. The only justification of it is the intensity of their love for

FIGURE 26.

Doctor Zhivago. Cast members walking down the Moscow street set with director
David Lean. Left to right: Tom Courtenay, Alec Guinness, Geraldine Chaplin,
Lean, Julie Christie, Omar Sharif, Ralph Richardson, Rod Steiger. Courtesy of
the Margaret Herrick Library, Academy of Motion Picture Arts and Sciences.

each other. We hope to have shown by this time that they are unusually mature people. So we're hoping that the audience will now believe that this was a kind of *Tristan and Iseult* situation, a great, grand passion. And we have tried to arrange this sequence so that the climax of it shall be the writing of this poetry. In that way we hope to make poetry the crown of the film."[35]

If the romance between Zhivago and Lara was to be the driving force in the film, finding the right actors to play these roles was essential. Among the actors considered for Zhivago were Paul Newman (MGM's choice), Max von Sydow, Burt Lancaster, and Peter O'Toole (star of *Lawrence of Arabia*), none of whom seemed right to Lean. Omar Sharif was originally under consideration for the role of the revolutionary Strelnikov, but one of Lean's associates gave him the idea of casting him as Zhivago, reminding him that "not all Russians are blond."[36] By then, the impossibly handsome Sharif had proved his ability to play characters of various nationalities, including Armenian (*The Fall of the Roman Empire*), Arab (*Lawrence of Arabia*), and Mongolian (*Genghis Khan*), but it was with the Russian role of Zhivago that Sharif would be forever after most closely identified. That Sharif's son Tarek also appeared in the film as Zhivago at the age of eight, in the intensely emotional early scene of his mother's funeral, heightened the sense of dramatic truth.

Producer Carlo Ponti hoped that Lean would choose his wife, Sophia Loren, to play the role of Lara, an idea that repelled the director, since he felt that the siren Loren could not possibly portray a young virgin. Having diplomatically eliminated Loren from the running, Lean considered and rejected Yvette Mimieux, Jane Fonda (because of her strong American accent), and Sarah Miles before taking a look at the upcoming 24-year old English actress Julie Christie in John Schlesinger's *Billy Liar*. In her he found exactly the right combination of sexual allure and innocence that the role required; her genteel British accent also played well within the context of Russian middle/upper class society in the early twentieth century.

As Tonya, Zhivago's first wife, Lean originally wanted Audrey Hepburn (who had not long before played Natasha in King Vidor's *War and Peace,* a rather similar character), but in the end he went along with Ponti's choice, 20-year old Geraldine Chaplin, daughter of screen legend Charlie Chaplin. Her presence on the set immediately added to the glamour and buzz around the project. Rod Steiger, a veteran as a screen heavy (he had recently played the title character in *Al Capone*) was cast as the predatory Komarovsky, lover to both Lara and her mother, and Tom Courtenay as the uncompromisingly idealistic revolutionary Strelnikov. Both Steiger and Chaplin avoided the sort of broad American diction that had compromised Henry Fonda's performance as Pierre in King Vidor's *War and Peace*. Wisely, Lean did not instruct any of his actors to employ a "Russian" accent in English, which usually results in an alienating feeling of cultural displacement.

Since Pasternak's novel was banned in the USSR, and the logistics of dealing with the Communist regime were so difficult, shooting the film in Russia was never a real option. After briefly considering Yugoslavia, which was rejected because of the country's complicated bureaucracy, Lean and Ponti decided upon a location in Spain, near Madrid. Here they built an enormous set replicating pre-Revolutionary Moscow. For help in painting Russian street signs, they hired as a technical advisor Andrew Mollo, the son of a Russian émigré from London, who became indispensable to the production. He also provided historical photographs to assist costume designer Phyllis Dalton in her work, especially on the uniforms of soldiers and partisans. In time, the production budget swelled from $7 to $15 million as Lean struggled to get every detail right. It took close to a year, from late December 1964 to early October 1965, to shoot *Doctor Zhivago*.

The elaborate "Ice Palace" for the crucial scene at Varykino, where Zhivago and Lara seek refuge from the revolutionary chaos and he begins writing his "Lara" poems, was a studio set. In order to achieve the special glittering effect of the snow and ice in the interior, one of the film's most memorable visual moments, members of the crew threw hot candlewax, freezing water, and a special spray on the set, then added a layer of mica chips. For the scene of the Red Army charge across a frozen lake, filmed in the middle of Spanish summer, Lean did something similar to what Sergei Eisenstein had done for the "Battle on the Ice" sequence in *Alexander Nevsky* (also filmed in midsummer). "It was just a great big field," explained Lean's veteran property master Eddie Fowlie. "I spread it all with cement and in certain places I put down sheet iron. I used an awful amount of crushed white marble on top, thousands of tons of it, which we ironed out with steamrollers, so the horses were able to slide on that in a more natural way."[37]

One of the problems encountered in Spain was insufficient snow cover for the numerous scenes that take place in winter. In March 1965, a small crew was sent to Finland to get location shots. They were located not far from the Russian border in the far north. It was there that many of the shots of trains were done, using equipment supplied by Finnish railways.

That *Doctor Zhivago,* a story about the impact of the Russian Revolution, was shot in Finland and Spain is ironic, for both countries had a special and fraught relationship with the USSR and Communism. Until the Russian Revolution, Finland had been a province of the Tsarist Empire, but became an independent country in December 1917. In 1939–1940, in the so-called Winter War, Finland was invaded and overrun by Soviet forces during the period that the German-Soviet nonaggression pact was in force. After World War II, Finland (which nevertheless retained its independence and fought on the side of the Nazis) was forced to sacrifice a piece of its territory to the USSR. In Spain, many Soviet citizens and Communist sympathizers from all over the world had fought in the Spanish Civil War against General Franco during the 1930s, which ended in defeat for the Communists in 1939. Since then, the Communist Party had been outlawed. During the shooting, the Spanish extras enthusiastically joined in on the revolutionary songs sung during the Moscow street demonstrations, including the *Internationale,* long banned in Franco's Spain.

Lean and his editor Norman Savage edited *Doctor Zhivago* at the MGM studios in Culver City, a first for a British production. They worked very fast and under considerable pressure, since MGM executives were eager to release the film by the end of the year, so that it could receive consideration for the Academy Awards. In only two months, working nearly nonstop, they cut more than 31 hours of film to 192 minutes. (The version shown at the premiere in December ran 197 minutes.) This made the film shorter than *Lawrence of Arabia* (221 minutes) but considerably longer than *The Bridge on the River Kwai* (161 minutes), and one of the longest—and most expensive—Hollywood features ever made.

Lean had decided to ask Maurice Jarre—the French composer of the Oscar-winning score for *Lawrence of Arabia* on their first collaboration—to write the music, despite some hesitation on the part of MGM's music director, who wasn't sure Jarre could do snow as well as sand. A classically trained composer who had studied with Arthur Honegger and worked with Pierre Boulez, Jarre chose a romantic-folksy-symphonic style for *Zhivago* that not only proved emotionally appropriate but added enormously to the film's artistic and commercial success. His score also features one of the great movie themes of all time: "Lara's Theme," a swelling and simple tune scored for balalaikas (Lean was very keen on balalaikas) and orchestra that serves as the primary leit-motif for Zhivago's love for Lara and their grand passion.

Not long after the release of the film, lyricist Paul F. Webster (1907–1984) wrote words for the theme. Recorded as a song in 1966 by Ray Coniff, it soon became a mega-hit and one of the most durable pop movie tunes in history, and has been interpreted by a who's who of singers over the decades. Except for the mention of snow, the rather generic lyrics have nothing to do with Russia, instead recalling the song "Somewhere" from the musical *West Side Story,* another drama of forbidden love:

Somewhere, My Love, there will be songs to sing
Although the snow covers the hope of spring.
Somewhere a hill blossoms in green and gold,
And there are dreams—all that your heart can hold.
Someday we'll meet again My Love
Someday, whenever the spring breaks through
You'll come to me out of the long ago
Warm as the wind, soft as the kiss of snow.
Til then, My Sweet, think of me now and then;
God speed, My Love, til you are mine again.

Even though it was written by a Frenchman for a film produced by a British crew, "Lara's theme" also became synonymous in the coming decades with the image and idea of Russia. In the James Bond film *The Spy Who Loved Me,* for example, it is the tune that plays in the music box belonging to the Russian spy Anya Amasova. And when I visited Moscow for the first time in the summer of 1970, the dance band in the Hotel National played "Lara's Theme" for me and my American friends, glancing over at us with a knowing wink, since both the novel and the film *Doctor Zhivago* were at the time banned in Russia.

Jarre's score does not use any imported folk songs or folk material, but balalaikas figure heavily in the orchestration throughout, sometimes producing eerie plucked sounds that brilliantly convey a sense of wintry desolation, loneliness, and nostalgia. As was the custom for big-screen epics in this period, there is an overture heard at the beginning (we see the word "overture" on the screen against a plain background) and another musical interlude at intermission, giving the film the feeling of a high-culture event. The Tsarist anthem ("God Save the Tsar") is heard at several crucial dramatic moments early on, and the *Internationale* as revolutionary fervor increases, in a technique familiar from Tchaikovsky's *1812 Overture*. A male chorus singing a sort of dirge without words is occasionally heard, especially in scenes of war. For the important opening scene of the funeral of Zhivago's mother, Jarre uses an excerpt from the Russian Orthodox funeral liturgy, the heart-rending *"Vechnaya pamyat'"* ("Eternal Memory"), establishing a strong emotional atmosphere at the outset. Waltzes and sleigh-riding music complement the vividly staged social settings.

Jarre's score has few rivals as an emotional and dramatic (if not entirely authentic) evocation of cinematic Russianness, even if many Russians I have talked to tend to dismiss it as *"klyukva"* ("kitsch"). The hugely successful original sound-track album bears this description on its rear flap: "Music depicting the spectacle of armies changing history. . . . The epic of a grand, romantic age giving way to a new and violent order. . . . The drama of young lovers, far from the chaos, alone and silent." After I saw the film in early 1966, I ran out and bought the album and played it endlessly, reliving favorite scenes in my mind.

The initial reception of *Doctor Zhivago* was not what Lean had been hoping for. After the New York premiere at the Capitol Theatre on December 22, 1965, the reviews were mixed, with some decidedly negative. In the *Herald-Tribune,* Judith Christ called it "ultimately tedious epic-type soap opera." In the *New York Times,* Bosley Crowther couldn't seem to make up his mind, praising the production values and photography ("the décor and color photography are as brilliant, tasteful and exquisite as any ever put on the screen") but criticizing the script for reducing "the vast upheaval of the Russian Revolution to the banalties of a doomed romance."[38] Crowther found the "strange passivity" of the major characters inappropriate for a film, even if true to the spirit of the Pasternak novel.[39] Even so, Crowther did include *Zhivago* on his list of runners-up for the Ten Best Movies of 1965: "this massive but mundane illustration of the Boris Pasternak novel is distinguished mainly for its superlative scenic qualities and good acting by Julie Christie."[40]

Richard Schickel, in a laudatory review in *Life,* was more perceptive, noting that the film succeeds because Lean "has created the visual equivalent of Boris Pasternak's novel. . . . Lean simply refuses to refute his material for idle effect."[41] For the first few weeks after its release, *Doctor Zhivago* attracted very small audiences, but Robert O'Brien put up the money to keep it in the theater, and by the fourth week, according to Lean, "you couldn't get a seat. . . . *Zhivago* made more money for me than all my other films put together." In the end, the film grossed more than $200 million worldwide, and produced significant additional income from television and video sales.[42]

As a representation of the USSR, *Doctor Zhivago* broke new ground in several respects. It was the first major Hollywood film since World War II, and the first in color, to be set entirely in Russia and the USSR. It did not demonize Communism and Communists, showing that they could be both bad and good, like members of the Russian artistocracy, and like all people. The major characters do not conform to ideological stereotypes. *Zhivago* also attempted to convey the complexity of recent Russian history, and clarified some the complex factors that led to the Russian Revolution.

But perhaps most important, *Zhivago* humanized Russia and Russians for the American audience in a way that no other previous Hollywood film had done. One of the most effective celluloid love stories ever made, *Doctor Zhivago* opened a window onto Russia for a generation of Americans on the brink of the profound political and social transformations of the late 1960s. It created the impression that Russians—even if they had much worse luck with governments and the weather—were in the end not so terribly different from Americans. They, too, just wanted to be able to make love, not war.

To Defect or Not to Defect

"I'm not a hero—I'm just a dancer."
Nikolai Rodchenko (Mikhail Baryshnikov) in *White Nights*

Just before the filming of *Doctor Zhivago* began, in October 1964, Nikita Khrushchev was removed from power in the Kremlin amid intense secrecy and mystery, heightening curiosity in America about the future course of Soviet-American relations. That Khrushchev was ousted without violence, and allowed to live out his life in Russia in relative comfort until his death in 1971, was a sign of progress in the context of Soviet history. In the past, when leaders fell from grace, they were annihilated. The unpredictable but colorful Khrushchev was replaced as Communist Party First Secretary by the bland bureaucrat Leonid Brezhnev (1906–1982), who would retain that position for eighteen years.

Economically and culturally, the Brezhnev years were a period of apparent stagnation, with renewed repression of political and artistic dissidents, and pervasive corruption in the production and economic sphere. And yet the full-scale terror of the Stalin era was not reinstated, and various kinds of cultural, educational, and economic contact with the West were continued and in some cases expanded. Indeed, some historians argue that underneath the stagnation, important social and political changes were occurring that would make possible the cultural revolution that would unfold in the mid-1980s.

During the Brezhnev era, American-Soviet relations generally improved, until Soviet forces invaded Afghanistan in December 1979. During the late 1960s, tension rose over the Vietnam War on the one hand and the 1968 Soviet invasion into Czechoslovakia on the other, but President Nixon and Brezhnev steadily pursued a policy of détente that reached its apex at their summit meeting in Moscow in May 1972. Brezhnev made a return visit to the United States in June 1973—but without the Hollywood confab requested by Khrushchev. In June 1974, not long before he was forced to resign over the Watergate affair, Nixon travelled again to the USSR. Under his successor, Gerald Ford, the Helsinki Agreement of Human Rights was signed on August 1, 1975, hailed at the time as an important recognition that human rights should be extended to all peoples everywhere, even behind the "Iron Curtain." And yet, soon after, it became clear that the Soviet government was still severely restricting the emigration of Jews (and other religious groups) seeking a freer life abroad, which became a source of continuing friction in the superpower relationship. Arms control also remained a divisive issue.

When Soviet forces entered Afghanistan in December 1979 to subdue a recently instated rebel government unfriendly to Moscow, the period of détente came to an abrupt end. President Carter retaliated by canceling American participation in the upcoming Moscow Olympics. In the November 1980 elections, Ronald Reagan, a longtime staunch anti-Communist and former movie actor, defeated Carter after accusing him of being too soft on the USSR. From 1980 to 1985, when Mikhail Gorbachev ascended (in March 1985) to the post of First Secretary, after Brezhnev's death and two brief reigns by the aging insiders Yuri Andropov and Konstantin Chernenko, Soviet-American relations were at their most hostile since the Cuban Missile Crisis. In a famous speech delivered in March 1983, Reagan denounced the USSR as the "evil empire." The atmosphere was poisoned further when in September 1983 Soviet fighters shot down a Korean Airlines passenger jet near the island of Sakhalin.

Not long after Gorbachev came to power, however, it became obvious that he had a very different sort of agenda than his predecessors. Frankly admitting the drastic domestic problems facing the USSR, and advocating a reordering of priorities, he entered into an active disarmament dialogue with Reagan. The two leaders met for four high-level summits between 1985 and 1988. By now, news of a new Soviet movement of openness—*glasnost*—and reconstruction—*perestroika*—was reaching the United States. Public opinion toward the USSR radically changed, especially after Gorbachev's visit to the United States in late 1987.

"Gorby-mania" swept the country. Reagan and Gorbachev took a friendly stroll together on Red Square in May 1988, and the Soviet media was allowed greater freedom than at any time since the 1920s. On Pushkin Square, a short walk up Gorky Street from the Kremlin, large and boisterous crowds gathered daily under the seemingly indifferent gaze of policemen for loud public discussion of the *bolnye voprosy,* the burning issues of the day: nationalism, racism, industrial efficiency, corruption, pollution, the gulag, the extravagance of Raisa Gorbachev's wardrobe. Radio and television broadcasts vied to reveal the most disturbing atrocities committed by Stalin—and even by Lenin. Newspapers and magazines bulged with historical confessions and rehabilitations. The USSR engaged in an unprecedented cacophony of political, moral, economic, cultural, and historical soul-searching.

The spirit quickly spread to the non-Russian Soviet republics and to the Communist-controlled countries of Eastern Europe. Independence movements flourished. On November 9, 1989, the Berlin Wall was breeched in a massive outpouring of public sentiment. Communist regimes throughout the countries of the Warsaw Pact began to topple. In June 1991, Gorbachev was awarded the Nobel Peace Prize. Among many members of the Communist Party at home, however, Gorbachev's reforms were much less popular. In late August 1991 a group of right-wing hardliners opposed to *glasnost* and *perestroika* attempted to remove Gorbachev from power, but failed. The processes set in motion could no longer be stopped. On December 25, 1991, the unthinkable happened: the USSR was officially—and peacefully—dissolved as a nation and political entity. The Cold War was over.

★   During the last twenty-five years of the existence of the USSR, Hollywood continued to produce films about Russia, although they generally possessed less artistic interest and (at least until the Soviet invasion of Afghanistan) less ideological focus. The rise of the peace movement in the late 1960s, and the atmosphere of détente in the 1970s, created an attitude of ambivalence and uncertainty toward Russia. As we have seen, throughout the 1960s, major Hollywood features dealing with the USSR tended to project the message that Americans and Russians (taken to mean citizens of the USSR, although Russians in fact constituted only one-half of the Soviet population) were equally victimized by the dynamics of the Cold War and the arms race. This was also the message conveyed on the popular television series *The Man from U.N.C.L.E.,* about a team of American and Russian secret agents who work together (as in the James Bond films) to thwart the evil intentions of THRUSH, an international conspiracy bent on global destruction.

FIGURE 27

The Russians Are Coming, The Russians Are Coming. United Artists 1966.
The cast members on location in Mendocino. Standing, left to right: Eva Marie
Saint, Jonathan Winters, Theodore Bikel, Alan Arkin, Carl Reiner. Seated, left
to right: Roman Karman, director Norman Jewison, Natalie and Ievaz
Chekidze. Courtesy of the Margaret Herrick Library, Academy of Motion
Picture Arts and Sciences.

The "Russia" film most obviously influenced by the peace movement of the 1960s is the madcap comedy *The Russians Are Coming, The Russians Are Coming* (1966). Directed by Norman Jewison, it was adapted by screenwriter William Rose from a novel by Nathaniel Benchley, *The Off Islanders*. A Soviet submarine runs aground on a sandbar off the coast of a Massachusetts island when the captain's curiosity to get a closer look at American soil leads him to neglect his piloting duties. The philosophical but autocratic captain (played with gusto by popular actor/folk singer Theodore Bikel) commands his Lieutenant Rozanov (Alan Arkin) and a team of seven men to look for a boat that can push them free.

After going ashore, the first house they come to is a summer cottage occupied by a perpetually annoyed vacationing New York playwright Walt Whittaker (Carl Reiner), his wife Elspeth (Eva Marie Saint), and their two children. They are terrified when they realize Arkin, speaking in English with a comically heavy accent and broken syntax, and his partner Alexei Kolchin (the dreamy, blue-eyed John Phillip Law, a gentle pacifist), are Russians, and imagine the very worst. But Arkin and his men prove absurdly incompetent, nearly as incompetent as the locals attempting to mobilize a response under the crazed leadership of police office Norman Jones (Jonathan Winters), who keeps on repeating hysterically, "We've got to get organized!" Meanwhile, back at the Whittakers' house, the children's babysitter Alison Palmer (Andrea Dromm) is falling for Alexei, and they are taking a romantic walk on the beach and talking about peace and love.

The submarine crew finally manages to float free of the sandbar on its own and sails the craft into the picturesque town harbor, filled with fishing boats. As they approach, guns are raised on both sides, but the captain emerges and momentarily pacifies the situation, explaining that they only want their eight men back and will depart peacefully. Just as the situation threatens to explode, a small boy, who has climbed to the top of the church steeple so as to have a better look at the action, falls, catching his shirt on a pole from which he dangles. Instantly Russians and Americans are united by an instinctual desire to save the child, and forget their ideologically driven hostility. They form a human pyramid and the noble Alexei climbs to the top of the steeple to rescue the boy as cheers resound all around. The townspeople are so grateful that they help the Soviet submarine to leave the harbor by forming an escort of fishing boats. Despite his infatuation with Alison, Alexei does not defect, but takes away a happy memory of a beautiful girl he met in America. In the last sequence, the town drunk rides his tired old mare down the street, rousing the neighbors like a modern-day Paul Revere as he yells, "The Russians are coming, the Russians are coming!"

Jewison's satire in *The Russians Are Coming* is broad, aimed at Cold War paranoia and stereotypes. Much of the humor is verbal, originating in the attempt of Lt. Rozanov and Alexei to express themselves in English to the stunned and provincial locals. "Just to keep absolutely good behaved," Rozanov warns the bemused Whittaker family. "One small noise you are dead." Rozanov's strange pronunciation of the word "boat" as "bot" is a running gag. When Rozanov and his men scheme to seize a cabin cruiser to help them move their sub, they attempt to disguise themselves as locals. Rozanov teaches them a phrase to repeat to anyone they may encounter, thinking it is idiomatic English: "Egermency. Egermency. Everybody to get from street." In an unusual attempt to maintain a sense of authenticity, Jewison has all of the members of the submarine crew speak in Russian with each other, translated into English subtitles.

Native New Yorker Alan Arkin managed to cultivate a decent command of Russian, and was nominated for an Oscar for this bilingual role of a Soviet sailor trying to do his duty and still retain humanity. The islanders (played by such Hollywood veterans as Brian Keith, Paul Ford, and, as the overwhelmed telephone operator, Tessie O'Shea), are cranky and eccentric New Englanders who don't take kindly to strangers, let alone to Russians, but are capable of thinking independently. Their previous contact with Russians has been limited to scary images from the media; in the flesh, as individuals, they prove to be far less dangerous.

In the score he assembled for *The Russians Are Coming,* Johnny Mandel uses popular patriotic songs to symbolize the culture clash, in a technique that recalls the music of New England composer Charles Ives. For the opening credits, "Yankee Doodle Dandy" and the Russian "Song of the Volga Boatmen" (*"Ey, ukhnem"*) are juxtaposed with images of the American and Soviet flags. The popular Soviet World War II marching song *"Polyushka, polye"* (also used in *Jet Pilot*) is also heard throughout. When the Russians approach a church during Sunday morning service, they hear the strains of the hymn "Onward, Christian Soldiers," and an organ piece by Handel that one of the sailors immediately recognizes with a happy smile.

The Soviets/Russians in *The Russians Are Coming* do not encounter American consumerism, do not express dissatisfaction with their country or society, and exhibit no desire to remain in the United States. Even the submarine's captain, however, is curious about the other superpower and cannot resist the chance to take a closer look. (The film's opening shot is of the captain's eye looking through the periscope at the Massachusetts shoreline.) This theme is also explored some years later in another submarine film, *The Hunt for Red October,* but with considerably different results. Like *Doctor Strangelove, The Russians Are Coming* finds absurdity in the anti-Soviet paranoia of the Cold War years. Its protagonists are little people who are merely pawns in the international power game. That this message resonated well with the times seems evident, since the film was nominated for three Academy Awards, for best picture, screenplay, and best actor. Notably, no Russian émigré actors were cast in any of the major roles.

By now, the Russian émigrés who had come to Hollywood in the 1920s and '30s were well past their prime, and since emigration from the USSR had almost completely ceased by 1950, none had arrived to take their place. By the early 1970s, Michael Chekhov, Akim Tamiroff, Vladimir Sokoloff, Mischa Auer, and Maria Ouspenskaya had all passed on.

★   The features of Hollywood's representation of life in nineteenth-century Russia (adaptations of novels in which tortured leading characters seek spiritual meaning, happy peasants breaking spontaneously into song and dance, violent sexual attraction, love of warfare) had by the 1970s become so standardized and clichéd that they became the object of parody in a comedy directed by Woody Allen: *Love and Death* (1975).

Here, Allen pays homage to and also mocks the novels of Tolstoy and Dostoyevsky, as well as the films and distinct editing style of Soviet director Sergei Eisenstein (particularly in his classic film *Battleship Potemkin*), who was by far the best-known Soviet director in Hollywood. Later, Allen claimed he got the idea to film *Love and Death* on the spur of the moment, when he "just happened" to come across a Russian history book on the shelf. The action is set during the same time as the action of Tolstoy's *War and Peace,* when Napoleon is invading Russia, although characters, themes, and situations from Dostoyevsky's novels, especially *Crime and Punishment* and *Brothers Karamazov,* also appear. Initially, Allen was going to call the protagonist (played by Allen himself) Pierre Bezuhkhov (the hero of *War and Peace*), but changed his mind later, instead calling him Boris Grushenko. The object of Boris's affections is Sonya, a woman whose promiscuity is evident to all but Boris, played by Diane Keaton in her third role in an Allen film. Filming took place in Paris and in Hungary, where Allen used soldiers from the Soviet occupation army for the battle scenes. For the music, Allen uses various pieces by Sergei Prokofiev, including music Prokofiev wrote for the films *Alexander Nevsky* and *Lt. Kije,* as well as the *Scythian Suite* and the very familiar march from the opera *Love for Three Oranges.* The light, ironic quality of Prokofiev's music perfectly suits the mood of Allen's script and direction.

Numerous specific and familiar scenes from Russian literature are parodied in *Love and Death.* Among them are the scene when Anna Karenina goes to the opera as a divorcee, scandalizing society; the narration by Father Zossima in *Brothers Karamazov* about the youthful duel that led him to renounce violence and start a new way of life; Raskolnikov's philosophical conversations with Sonya in *Crime and Punishment;* and Pierre's trip to the front during the decisive battle of Borodino from *War and Peace.* In the leading role as the anti-hero and cowardly jokester Boris, who also acts as the film's narrator, Woody Allen wears thick black-rimmed glasses that clearly mark him as an American living in 1975—as does his strong New York accent. His glasses are a symbol of the way the film looks at the nineteenth-century past through the lens of the American present, questioning American preconceptions about Russia and Russian images of America. The film's very title, *Love and Death,* reflects both the titles of Russian novels known to Americans (especially *Crime and Punishment* and *War and Peace*) and the extremes of existence that in 1975 were occupied by the United States on the one hand and the USSR on the other.

But Allen forces us to examine our prejudices about Russia, and the way we receive them from film, by mixing references to Russian and American culture, and to 1812 and the present day. Cheerleaders dressed like those at an American football game, their sweaters emblazoned with "Russia," cheer on the Russian troops at Borodino, and dead officers worry about tax refunds on unused wedding rings. As Ronald LeBlanc has observed, Allen "seeks in his film to convey a serious message about the human condition, while at the same time poking fun not only at the message itself but also at some of the artistic vehicles traditionally used to convey it. As a parody of the Russian philosophic novel and the Hollywood film epic, *Love and Death* thus combines serious metaphysical concern with rich comic form."[1] Allen makes us realize that Hollywood's image of nineteenth-century Russia is very much a manipulated product, not a given reality, despite his claims that he had no serious intellectual ambitions for the film: "It came as I was writing. I just started to write it and I came upon something and thought, 'This would be funny.' And one thing led to another."[2]

★ One of the most intensely publicized and romanticized narratives of the Soviet-American relationship in the 1970s was the defection of prominent Soviet creative artists (writers, dancers, musicians) to the West. These incidents splashed across front pages and television screens with an irresistible combination of glamour, mystery and high-level superpower intrigue. For Hollywood producers, this new narrative was like catnip to a cat. In no time, artists' defection stories were finding their way to the silver screen, where they also acted as powerful pro-American propaganda.

Since the spectacular and dramatic defection of ballet dancer Rudolf Nureyev in 1961 (he jumped into the arms of a French customs official at a Paris airport just as the touring Kirov Ballet was preparing to fly to London), numerous other prominent Soviet dancers, musicians, and writers had either chosen to defect in pursuit of artistic possibilities or had been expelled for their alleged dissident political activity. Another ballet dancer, Natalia Makarova, defected in 1970, followed by Mikhail Baryshnikov in 1974 and Alexander Godunov in 1979. (Godunov's defection became front-page news when his wife, Ludmila Vlasova, also a dancer, was detained on the plane at JFK airport by American officials who wanted to determine that she was returning to Moscow voluntarily.) Superstar cellist Mstislav Rostropovich and his wife, opera singer Galina Vishnevskaya, left the USSR in 1974, not long after their close friend, Nobel Prize—winning author Alexander Solzhenitsyn, had been forced to emigrate. Solzhenitsyn eventually settled in a small town in Vermont. Poet Iosif Brodsky was forced to emigrate in 1972; having eventually mastered English, he went on to be chosen as the Poet Laureate of the United States and to receive the Nobel Prize for Literature.

All of these incidents received extensive coverage in the American media, and became a potent symbol of the repressive nature of the Communist regimes that ruled the USSR and Eastern Europe. Since many of these defectors (Solzhenitsyn, Baryshnikov, Godunov, Brodsky) chose to settle in the United States, their presence on American soil was also hailed as an affirmation of the American way of life and of our belief in the importance of personal and artistic self-expression. In addition to the artists who emigrated either voluntarily or involuntarily, thousands of Jews (for the most part secular and nonreligious) seeking to escape pervasive anti-Semitism and eager to enjoy a better standard of living were allowed (after enduring protracted delays and humiliation) to leave the USSR in the late 1970s. This wave peaked in 1979, when 51,000 Jews emigrated, but this number dropped dramatically after the Soviet invasion of Afghanistan. Many of these eventually found their way to the United States and remained there.

In *Moscow on the Hudson* (1984), it is not a superstar but a lowly saxophonist in the orchestra of a touring Soviet circus who defects. Paul Mazursky (already known for such hits as *Bob and Carol and Ted and Alice* and *An Unmarried Woman*) both wrote and directed this upbeat feature, a loving celebration of the contribution of immigrants from all nations and cultures to the melting-pot of New York City. Robin Williams, just beginning his career as a film actor, was cast in the leading role of Vladimir Ivanov, the saxophonist from Moscow who somehow finds the courage to break with his past and grab onto the American dream.

After a brief opening sequence set on a New York bus some time after Ivanov's defection, as he helps a recent immigrant with directions, the story flashes back in time to the drab, dreary, and repressive Soviet Moscow of the Brezhnev years. To represent Moscow, Mazursky used the streets of Munich, populated by Russians, for the most part Soviet film and television actors who had recently defected, many of them as Jews seeking religious freedom in the West. (Munich had a large Russian émigré community, since it long served as the headquarters for Radio Free Europe, which employed many Russians with a background in media and journalism.)

The most prominent among recent Soviet actor defectors appearing in *Moscow on the Hudson* is Savely Kramarov (1934–1995), a highly successful comedian and comic actor with an enormous and loyal following, who was featured in more than forty films in Russia but left to start a new career in the west in the early 1980s. His role as the circus' Party watchdog Boris in *Moscow on the Hudson* launched him in Hollywood; he subsequently appeared in *2010*, *Armed and Dangerous*, *Red Heat*, *Tango and Cash*, and even (as a Russian sailor) in *Love Affair,* in small character roles, usually as a Russian speaking English with a strong accent. As Vladimir's crazy and independent-minded grandfather, Mazursky cast Alexander Beniaminov (1903–1991), who had been appearing in films in Russia since the early 1930s but elected to leave his homeland for greener pastures in the late 1970s. Elya Baskin (born 1950), in the role of the circus clown Anatoly, Vladimir's best friend, also came to the United States in the late 1970s. After *Moscow on the Hudson,* he developed a busy career in film and television, and appeared (also as a Russian) in *Air Force One* and *Austin Powers: International Man of Mystery,* among other features.

In the Moscow section of the film, the characters speak primarily in Russian, with on-screen subtitles (as in *The Russians Are Coming*). Robin Williams (like Alan Arkin) therefore had to learn to speak credibly in Russian, which he for the most part is able to carry off. Since he and his friend Anatoly know they are soon to be going on tour with the circus to the United States, they also speak to each other in English, for practice. Most of the Moscow scenes are shot inside, in crowded apartments. With so many recent defectors on hand in the cast, Mazursky was able to create a strong feeling of authenticity.

Particularly amusing is the scene of the political indoctrination by the vigilant Boris of the members of the circus before their departure for New York, as he warns them of the horrible decadence and capitalist degradation they will encounter there. We see that Vladimir's life in Moscow was not unhappy (he has a loving girlfriend and family and friends), but that he is a free spirit who feels oppressed by the rigidity and limitations of Soviet life—just like his grandfather, who had come to the attention of the authorities for his tirades against the hypocrisy of the government. Vladimir is also warned by Boris that the authorities are aware that his friend Anatoly has expressed a desire to defect, and demand that he report on him during the tour. When Vladimir's girlfriend learns that he is going on tour to America, she begs him, during sex, to bring her back designer jeans, becoming increasingly excited as she recites the labels—"Jordache, Calvin Klein." Despite their declared ideological superiority, average Soviet citizens prove entirely susceptible to the lures of consumerism—a fact I had occasion to observe during my own visits to the USSR in the 1970s and '80s.

The scene shifts to New York, cutting from a shot of Vladimir playing his saxophone in Moscow for the circus animals, who nod appreciatively, to the view from a bus window cruising down a Manhattan street. Vladimir and Anatoly are dumbstruck when they see the abundance, variety, and vitality of life in New York. They share a room at the Howard Johnson's motel and stare in wonder at the lights down Broadway. They attend a reception given in their honor at Lincoln Center, where Vladimir converses with a Marxism professor from Columbia. He is surprised she studies Marxism, since "in Russia all Marxists have beards and whiskers." "Even the women?" asks the lady professor. "In Russia, especially the women," Vladimir retorts.

Anatoly continues to threaten to defect, but seems hesitant. The moment of truth comes during their thirty-minute group visit to Bloomingdale's, their last stop in America before they go to the airport and back to Moscow.

In this brilliantly choreographed sequence, Mazursky takes the theme of ideological conversion through consumerism seen in so many Hollywood films about Soviet citizens encountering western culture (*Ninotchka, Jet Pilot, Silk Stockings*) and raises it to a new level of humor and visual symbolism. Music is an important element in the comedy here. As the circus performers rush toward the department store entrance, anxious not to waste a single moment of their allotted time, they are accompanied by a rousing, up-tempo march, the popular Soviet song "It's Possible," extolling the marvels of the USSR, composed by Arkady Ostrovsky (1914–1967), the Irving Berlin of Soviet music, whose many songs were especially popular during the 1960s. (His cheerful 1962 children's song "May There Always Be Sunshine" is one of the most recognizable Soviet songs ever written.) The conflict between the intention of the music and the scene of the performers dashing madly about the store displays, ripping clothes from the rack, gets to the heart of the empty optimism with which Soviet leaders attempted to sell their policies of deprivation and sacrifice for the sake of the common good.

When the wildly vigilant Boris, followed like sheep by the circus performers who are afraid of making a wrong move, penetrates into this temple of capitalism, surrounded by glittering bottles of perfume and sparkling watches, he, too, is overwhelmed by the abundance and choice. The camera closes in on Savely Kramarov's thin, contorted face as he exclaims with a mixture of admiration and disdain, "What decadence!"

While trying to buy jeans for his girlfriend back in Moscow, Vladimir makes the acquaintance of a pretty salesgirl at the perfume counter. It happens that she, too, is a recent immigrant, from Sicily, who has come to New York for greater opportunities. As Anatoly dithers, trying to find the right moment to defect as time is running out, Vladimir (who has not previously expressed any desire to defect) is having a crisis of faith. He whispers in the ear of the gay salesman in the jeans department that he wants to defect, and the process is set in motion as the salesman summons the security guards, who come to Vladimir's defense. A crowd gathers, and suddenly the news media (with well-known New York news anchor Kaity Tong) is on hand to record the event. Even the desperate pleas of Boris, who gets down on his knees, fail to dissuade Vladimir from his sudden decision to defect. A New York City policeman chimes in: "This is New York. The man can do what he wants!"

Anatoly, however, has failed to find the courage to act. He shuffles sheepishly back onto the bus with the others, and they start off for the airport as Vladimir waves from the sidewalk, bittersweet tears of joy and sadness running down his face.

After the scene in Bloomingdale's, and the disappearance of Boris and Anatoly from the film, *Moscow on the Hudson* loses momentum. Vladimir finds a home with the black extended family of the Bloomingdale's security guard who has befriended him. As a saxophonist with a deep love of jazz, Vladimir feels at home in black culture, and from his communal Moscow experience finds entirely natural the idea of sharing a bed with the grandfather. That a black family is the first to welcome him makes a strong statement about the solidarity of outsiders. He courts and falls in love with the perfume salesgirl. After fits and starts, they are finally united. In the film's final scene, as Vladimir strolls near the Plaza Hotel, he buys a hot dog and recognizes the street vendor as his old antagonist Boris, who has also fled the USSR. "Can I say thank you?" this latest convert to capitalism asks Vladimir with a crooked smile.

Moscow on the Hudson is one of the most lyrical films ever made about the immigrant experience in America. It is Mazursky's loving tribute to the strength of the American dream, its ability to inspire acts of courage in its pursuit. As the film progresses, Vladimir's identity as a Russian becomes less important, as he merges with the thousands of other foreigners-turned-Americans. But the message also comes across loud and clear that

Soviet citizens—especially artists—would be happy to escape their prison of a country if they could.

★ When the dancers Nureyev, Baryshnikov, and Godunov defected, they did so in order to dance more freely, to pursue creative opportunities closed to them in the USSR. It did not take long for Hollywood producers to recognize the box-office appeal of their personal odyssey. Partly as a result of the tours made by the leading Soviet ballet companies to the United States under the guidance of impresario Sol Hurok, American interest in ballet and ballet dancers had grown explosively in the 1960s and 1970s. First Nureyev, and then Baryshnikov, quickly became stars on a scale that the American dance world had never seen before. Nureyev found a perfect partner in Margot Fonteyn at the Royal Ballet in England and turned into an international phenomenon. Soon after his defection, Baryshnikov joined American Ballet Theatre in New York as a soloist, and became, in the words of *New Yorker* dance critic Joan Acocella, "a celebrity, a dream-boat."[3]

In 1977, Nureyev and Baryshnikov were both featured in leading roles in major feature films. Nureyev was cast as the silent movie star Rudolf Valentino in *Valentino,* produced in England and directed by Ken Russell. Baryshnikov appeared as (more or less) himself in *The Turning Point,* produced and directed by Herbert Ross for 20th Century Fox. During the late 1930s, when the Ballets Russes companies were touring the United States, it was the female stars (Tamara Toumanova, Vera Zorina) who made the move into film and Broadway. In the 1970s, however, it was the male Russian ballet stars who were elevated to the status of heroes of popular culture. Their success helped to change the way the American public regarded the role of men in the world of dance.

Baryshnikov developed a much more successful career as a film (and television) dramatic actor than Nureyev. Nureyev's homosexuality, which he did not attempt to hide, scared producers, who did not believe he could succeed with the wide public as a leading man. In 1970, Tony Richardson cast Nureyev for a film he was planning to make about the legendary Russian ballet dancer Vaclav Nijinsky (with whom Nureyev had always closely identified). Playwright Edward Albee was to have written the screenplay. Nureyev wanted the film to include a performance of the ballet *Jeux,* choreographed by Nijinsky to music of Debussy in 1913 for three dancers, two female and one male, depicting the male's flirtation with both women during a game of tennis. According to Nijinsky's diary, however, the real subject of the ballet was homoerotic attraction between three men, reflecting the desire of his patron Serge Diaghilev to have three-way sex with Nijinsky and another boy.

For Richardson's film, Nureyev wanted to stage *Jeux* as Diaghilev had conceived it, for three male dancers, but the idea was too kinky for producer Harry Saltzman and the project was cancelled. In 1980, Saltzman did produce a serious and underrated film about Nijinsky for Paramount, directed by Herbert Ross and starring George de la Pena as a conflicted man struggling with his bisexuality.[4]

When in the mid-1970s Ken Russell began preparing to shoot a film about the silent film star Rudolf Valentino, he planned to cast Nureyev in a small role as Nijinsky. But upon further reflection, Russell decided that Nureyev "had the requisite sexual glamour and mystery essential to the starring role."[5] Nureyev considered this to be an important opportunity, and took a three-month break from dancing to make the film, co-starring with French actress Leslie Caron (as Russian silent film star Alla Nazimova) and American pop singer Michelle Phillips (as Natacha Rambova, Nazimova's lover and Valentino's second wife).

Nureyev excels in the scenes where he dances, but his dramatic performance falls rather flat, especially in his labored scenes with Phillips. Although both stars agreed to do a nude sex scene that leaves nothing to the imagination, their beautiful bodies generate no electricity. Nureyev's obvious difficulty in attempting to speak English with an Italian accent robs his performance of naturalness and spontaneity. As in most of Ken Russell's films (he also made a lavish, overstuffed film about Tchaikovsky, *The Music Lovers,* in 1970, starring Richard Chamberlain as the tortured composer), the sets and costumes consistently upstage the actors. Most of the critics found little to admire in *Valentino,* although Pauline Kael of the *New Yorker* singled out Nureyev for praise. "Seen up close, Nureyev has a camp devil loose in him; he has the seductive, moody insolence of an older, more cosmopolitan James Dean, without the self-consciousness. His eagerness to please would be just right for frivolous, lyrical comedy, and he could play cruel charmers—he has the kinky-angel grin. . . . He's a showman through and through."[6]

But *Valentino* was a commercial failure, and producers, ever mindful of middle America, were reluctant to take another chance on Nureyev, who had also developed a reputation for flamboyant unconventional sexual behavior. Besides a charming and funny duet with Miss Piggy in *Swine Lake* on *The Muppet Show*, and several appearances on television song-and-dance specials, Nureyev only made one more film after *Valentino*. In *Exposed* (1983), he plays opposite Nastassja Kinski (here, a high-fashion model), in the role of a famous violinist who has a double life as a terrorist who is shot at the end. But this film, too, failed to find an audience, and brought an end to Nureyev's career as a movie actor. Nureyev did remain very much in the public eye as a dancer, choreographer, and jet-setter until his death from AIDS in 1993.

Baryshnikov has had better luck on screen. His film and television career began in 1977—just two years after he defected in Canada during a tour with dancers from the Bolshoi Ballet—with his memorable portrayal of the sexy and egotistical Russian dancer Yuri Kopeikine in Herbert Ross's *Turning Point*, and has continued for nearly thirty years.

In *The Turning Point*, Baryshnikov plays the star male dancer of a New York–based ballet company closely modeled on the real American Ballet Theatre, with which "Misha" (as he become known) in fact danced from 1974 to 1978. (He later served as the company's artistic director.) In the screenplay, the circumstances of Kopeikine's defection from Russia are not mentioned, and Ross avoids political or ideological commentary. Kopeikine's primary plot function (besides dancing brilliantly in the numerous rehearsal and performance scenes) is to seduce and then cast aside a new arrival to the company, an aspiring dancer who also happens to be the daughter of a former company member, Deedee (Shirley MacLaine). Twenty years earlier, Deedee chose marriage and motherhood over a dance career and now lives in Oklahoma with her husband (also a former dancer in the company) and three children. As the film opens, she is reunited with Emma, her best friend from her dancing days, an aging former star played with subtlety and power by Anne Bancroft, who has come to Oklahoma on tour with the company. At the post-performance party, Kopeikine is seen playing the guitar and singing a song (by the Soviet balladeer Vladimir Vysotsky, a famous dissident with a passionate following) to a rapt circle of admirers.

Soon the action shifts to New York. Deedee's daughter (the real-life dancer Leslie Browne) Emilia is pursuing her dream of ballet stardom. She catches Kopeikine's rapacious eye, and before long they are dancing (what else?) the love scene from Prokofiev's *Romeo and Juliet*. In one of the great dance sequences on film, Prokofiev's swelling music leads them passionately forward as the editing cuts deftly from the rehearsal hall to the bed in Yuri's apartment, from performance to reality. Baryshnikov plays the role of the roué well, pouting and temperamental, as he continues to beguile the susceptible Emilia with irresistible Russian come-on lines like "I'm homesick." But Yuri never stays with a conquest for very long, and soon he is breaking her heart. (After he dumps Emilia, Deedee scornfully calls him "that horny little Russian.")

In his own highly publicized love life, Baryshnikov behaved not unlike Kopeikine, especially in his early years, as recorded by dancer Gelsey Kirkland in her best-selling book *Dancing on My Grave*.[7] Baryshnikov's off-stage romantic exploits only added to his aura and charisma, and gave the dance world a welcome injection of testosterone. Deedee's husband Wayne even remarks after he sees Kopeikine dance that "he is finally going to make it respectable for men to dance in this country."

In the end, Kopeikine at least in part redeems his caddish conduct with Emelia by helping her prepare for her big debut in the company gala, sending her on stage with a big smile and a kiss, telling her "Dance well." He is a team player, focused on the matter at hand, a star comfortable in his own skin, tossing off the leaps in the solo from *The Corsaire* with joyful energy and *esprit de corps*. It was Baryshnikov's convincing, athletic performance as Kopeikine that turned him into "an electronic-media ballet star, the first one in history," and helped create the dance boom of the late 1970s and 1980s.[8] Baryshnikov also brought back to Hollywood the tradition of Russian dramatic training, combining complete control of body movement with psychological truth, a discipline he had learned well in Soviet ballet schools.

Baryshnikov is not the only Russian ballet star in *The Turning Point*. Alexandra Danilova, a legendary dancer with the Ballets Russes and one-time companion of George Balanchine, appears in the cameo role of the former ballerina and teacher Mme. Dakharova. Impeccably coiffed and dressed at all times, she dispenses tea, cakes, and invaluable advice on dancing and life in English, French, and Russian ("*Eez goot, yes, eez vari goot!*") to her wide-eyed disciples, representing the link to the Russian imperial ballet tradition that has been reinvented on American soil by several generations of émigrés. So taken is Emilia with Dakharova and with the Russian atmosphere she has absorbed at the company that she mischievously assumes the identity of a recently arrived Russian émigré dancer with two down-home American boys she meets at a bar. "I need artistic freedom," she proclaims with a heavy accent as she downs countless cocktails, dazzling the out-of-towners and entertaining herself in this new glamorous role.

In *White Nights* (Columbia, 1985), Baryshnikov again plays a dancer who seems very much like himself. Here, however, the story (by James Goldman and Eric Hughes) crackles with political and ideological intrigue, reflecting the high level of tension in the Soviet-American relationship that prevailed in the mid-1980s. En route with his manager to an engagement in Japan, superstar Russian defector dancer Nikolai Rodchenko ends up back in the USSR—and in the custody of villainous KGB colonel Vladimir Chaiko—when the plane is forced to make a crash landing on a Siberian airfield.

Injured, taken to a hospital, and then held hostage in a remote town when his identity is discovered, Rodchenko is introduced to a black American tap dancer (Raymond Greenwood, played by dancer Gregory Hines) who some years earlier sought political asylum in the USSR during the Vietnam War. Greenwood has married his former interpreter (Isabella Rossellini, playing Russian in her first major film role), the lovely Darya, and is performing in *Porgy and Bess* in dingy Soviet culture clubs, frustrated and isolated, now a captive in the USSR, his moment in the limelight over. "I was big news while they needed me," he tells Rodchenko with bitter regret.

Chaiko (the impressively malevolent Polish actor Jerzy Skolimowski) orders Greenwood and Darya to help him in persuading Rodchenko to remain in the USSR and resume his dancing career, hoping to repair the humiliation that Soviet culture has endured in recent years with the highly publicized defection of major performing artists. Chaiko is a standard screen villain, a stereotype of the unfeeling and inhumane Soviet military/secret police. Under Soviet law, Rodchenko is a criminal, since he was tried and condemned in absentia eight years ago as an enemy of the Soviet state.

The action moves to Leningrad, where Rodchenko was a star with the Kirov Ballet (as in real life) before his defection. His apartment has been left just as it was when he lived there. There he reencounters the ballerina Galina Ivanova, his former girlfriend, now the head of the company, played by English actress Helen Mirren. Although she was raised in England, Mirren's father was Russian, the son of a Tsarist officer who happened to be abroad at the time of the Russian Revolution and remained there. This heritage gave Mirren a special feeling for the imperial traditions of the Kirov (formerly Mariinsky) Theatre—even if she did not grow up speaking Russian.

After Rodchenko's defection, Galina was partially blamed for his action, and encountered new difficulties in her career—just like the real person on which her character is based, the Kirov star ballerina Irina Kolpakova, who was on tour with Baryshnikov when he defected in Toronto in 1974. Having managed to restore her position, she views Rodchenko's unexpected return with mixed feelings of alarm and excitement. She accuses him of selfishness and lack of feeling for those he left behind. "I'm not a hero—I'm just a dancer," he replies.

One of the film's most successful moments shows Galina working out choreography on stage as she listens to a tape of the banned underground singer Vladimir Vysotsky singing his popular song *"Koni"* (*"Horses"*). As an artist, she is drawn to Vysotsky's bold and truthful lyrics, despite his dangerous anti-Soviet sentiments. She shows Rodchenko sketches for costumes for a planned evening of ballets choreographed by George Balanchine. As an émigré and American citizen, Balanchine, creator of the New York City Ballet, was for many years treated as a non-person in the USSR and his work was virtually unknown there. But Rodchenko reminds her that, for him, dancing Balanchine is no longer new—"I did it, I danced Balanchine, but you are still waiting." Rodchenko also realizes that he, too, has become a non-person in the USSR when he secretly pays a visit to a classroom filled with aspiring dancers and not a single one of them has ever heard of his name, now erased from Soviet dance history. This was exactly what happened to the names of all those artists who defected from the USSR—Nureyev, Makarova, Rostropovich, Vishnevskaya, Ashkenazy. They became non-people.

White Nights ends like an action thriller, with an extended chase scene. Greenwood finally decides to help Rodchenko escape. After much wall climbing, running, and reckless driving, Rodchenko and Darya reach the American consulate and freedom, but Raymond had to be left behind. In the last scene, at the Soviet border, amid romantic mist and barbed wire, Raymond is traded by Chaiko for a Soviet citizen (most likely a spy), reunited with the pregnant Darya (her baby will now be born in freedom in the West), and allowed to leave the USSR.

Because of its extremely anti-Soviet content, *White Nights* could obviously not be filmed in Russia. The scenes in Siberia were shot in Finland, as were most of the scenes set in Leningrad, since the architecture of Helsinki (as other filmmakers, including Warren Beatty, had already discovered) is strikingly similar to that of the former Russian imperial capital. But the director Taylor Hackford also makes extensive use of stock footage of Leningrad shot separately. In some scenes (the car rides through the city streets), shots of the car interior are primitively superimposed on the stock footage. Only a few years later, by the early 1990s, it would become possible for Hollywood directors to shoot Russia films on location, regardless of anti-Soviet content, and they would not have to resort to such old-fashioned editing tricks.

Despite its shortcomings (the screenplay progresses by fits and starts), *White Nights* attempts with a reasonable degree of honesty and seriousness to treat the issue of artistic and political defection. In the character of Raymond, the film raises the issue of racism in both the United States and the USSR and explains the very real appeal that the idea of the classless socialist utopian society promised by Communism held for many American blacks. (Chaiko is happy to use Raymond for his own purposes, but expresses intense racial prejudice, privately calling him "that black-ass.") The film's ending resoundingly upholds the superiority of the American way of life, as confirmed with a double defection: Rodchenko's re-defection and Raymond's reversal of his decision to seek a better life in the USSR. In this way, *White Nights* conforms with the virulent anti-Soviet messages proclaimed by action films of the mid-1980s such as *Rocky IV, Rambo III,* and *Red Dawn.*

White Nights also proved that Baryshnikov really could act as well as dance. In the coming years, he would appear again as a dancer in another film directed by Herbert Ross (*Dancers,* 1987) and as a jailed former Soviet spy—opposite Gene Hackman—in a thriller set in newly unified Germany (*Company Business,* 1991). So unhappy was this last experience, however, that Baryshnikov stayed away from movies for more than a decade.

In 2004, Misha made a dramatic comeback as the character Aleksandr Petrovsky in the final five episodes of the mega-hit television series *Sex and the City.* Here, he plays the same sort of roué and heartbreaker he had previously portrayed, this time a self-centered Russian artist with hypnotic sexual appeal before whom the usually cynical and relentlessly perky Manhattan columnist played by Sarah Jessica Parker dissolves into a girlish puddle. Petrovsky's Russian identity operates here on a post-ideological level; his character represents sophistication, intellectual depth, artistic sensibility. Parker even abandons her New York life to follow him (briefly) to Paris, where he proceeds to shower her with gifts, but neglects and belittles her among his highbrow friends. In the end, however, she prefers her life in the Big Apple to the pretentious Petrovsky and Paris.

In the same year that *White Nights* was released, dancer Alexander Godunov made his screen debut in *Witness*. Baryshnikov and Godunov had been friends since childhood; both studied at the ballet school in Riga, Latvia. Like Yul Brynner, Godunov was born in the Soviet far east, on the Soviet island of Sakhalin. In 1971, he joined the Bolshoi Ballet, and became one of its leading dancers.

After the defection of Baryshnikov in 1974, Godunov was watched very carefully by Soviet authorities, who feared that he would follow his friend's example. But Godunov was allowed to tour with the Bolshoi to the United States in 1979, and, with Baryshnikov's encouragement, decided (in August 1979) to remain in New York, although his wife elected to return to Moscow and was never allowed to join him in the United States. Almost immediately, Godunov was invited to join American Ballet Theater, at the time directed by Baryshnikov. The two friends had a serious falling out in 1982, however, and Godunov was fired from ABT, leaving him with very bitter feelings about both Baryshnikov and the world of ballet. Henceforth, Godunov put most of his energy into his film career. He moved to Los Angeles, and became part of the Hollywood scene through his well-publicized relationship with sexy star Jacqueline Bisset. Godunov's promising film career came to a premature end in 1995, when he was found dead in his West Hollywood home. Since Godunov was known to be a prodigious drinker (like so many of his Russian countrymen), it was long rumored that alcohol and/or drugs were involved in his death, but officially he expired of natural causes.

Unlike Baryshnikov and Nureyev, Godunov refused to take the role of a dancer on film. He also shunned Russian roles. In only one of his seven films—*The Zone*, released after his death—does he even take the role of a Slav (Lothar Krasna, a tyrannical magnate of nuclear processing). Instead, he accepted parts that required him to create characters far outside his own experience.

In *Witness*, one of the most highly regarded films of the 1980s, directed by the unorthodox Peter Weir, Godunov is cast as a Pennsylvania Amish farmer, Daniel Hochleitner, who is courting the young neighboring widow Rachel Lapp (Kelly McGillis). Godunov speaks few lines. Many of them are delivered in the Pennsylvania Dutch dialect, derived from German, in which the members of the Amish community converse among themselves. When he does speak in English, primarily to John Book (Harrison Ford), a Philadelphia cop hiding out from corrupt drug-running cops, Godunov's foreign accent sounds perfectly appropriate. In the opening scenes of *Witness*, Godunov is prominently featured, as he carefully sets out to win Rachel's affection after her husband's death. His stoic, smiling expression, erect posture, and simplicity of physical gesture create a strong and unique impression. The scene of the barn raising, where Hochleitner and Book compete to impress Rachel with their carpentry skills, reveals Godunov as an actor of considerable subtlety and grace, as he deftly scales the wooden barn frame, balancing on the beams. For some critics, in fact, Godunov's performance was the most memorable in the film—a high compliment considering the competition.

That a recent Russian/Soviet defector would be chosen to play Amish is ironic, for the Amish are staunch pacifists who believe that the taking of any human life is one of the worst of all sins. Amish men are exempt from military service because of their religious convictions. The refusal of the Amish to accept the modern world and their choice to live largely in isolation from technology also bears a strong resemblance to the beliefs espoused by the Old Believers, religious dissidents who broke away from the Russian Orthodox Church in the 1600s and remained remarkably vital through the centuries, especially in areas of Siberia. (Some members of Old Believer sects sought religious asylum in the Russian-held territory of Alaska, Washington, and Oregon through the mid-nineteenth century.) Could it be that Godunov's awareness of this aspect of Russian Orthodox tradition helped him to understand more completely the mind of Daniel Hochleitner, who radiates a kind of existential calm and communal assurance?

Unfortunately, none of the subsequent films in which Godunov appeared were on the same level of artistic ambition as *Witness*. Having demonstrated his ability to play a German-speaking character, Godunov took Germanic roles in *The Money Pit* (eccentric maestro Max Beissart) and then in the 1988 action hit *Die Hard,* as the German terrorist Karl, who participates in taking hostages in a Los Angeles office tower. Gunslinging Karl is the opposite of the pacifist Hochleitner. It disturbed Godunov that Hollywood producers were so much more enamored of the violent and robot-like terrorist, and that they wanted him to keep repeating that image in future films. "Producers said things like, 'You will play the guy who comes in with a long coat and machine gun and kills everybody in the room. And use that same expression on your face you used in *Die Hard.*'"⁹ Godunov turned down many roles of that sort. In the mystical film *Rune-stone* (1990) he plays the clockmaker Sigvaldson, and in *North* (1994) reprises (alongside Kelly McGillis) the character of an Amish Dad, almost as a joke.

Like Nureyev, Godunov dealt with personal demons and did not easily find a place for himself in American culture. Both were known for their self-destructive behavior, and both died long before their time. Of the three Russian male dancer defectors, Godunov showed the greatest talent as a film actor, and we can only wonder what he might still have given us.

★   The United States may have been winning the war of artistic defectors during the 1960s and '70s, but when it came to the exciting new arena of space exploration, the USSR proved to be a much more formidable opponent. In the highly competitive "space race," the Soviets had a head start, and continued to impress the entire world with their accomplishments after the stunning 1957 launch of the satellite Sputnik, including putting the first man in space (Yuri Gagarin) in 1961, and the first woman in space (Valentina Tereshkova). Soviet success in this complex technological field did a great deal to challenge American stereotypes about Russian backwardness, and stimulated both fear (of Communist domination of the new frontier of outer space) and unprecedented investment in similar research in the United States. The lavishly funded American "Apollo" program to land a man on the moon by 1970—a goal established by President John Kennedy in 1961—began to show impressive results by the late 1960s, with the orbiting of the moon by a three-man American craft in 1968.

But it was the landing of a manned lunar module on the moon carrying American astronauts from the Apollo XI mission on July 21, 1969, that gave supremacy—and bragging rights—back to the United States. When they placed an American flag in the moon's surface, it represented not only a triumph for American technology and organization, but also a valuable symbolic victory in the propaganda struggle of the Cold War.

Not so long after, however, the USSR and the United States began to co-operate in space, having decided mutually that celestial objects should not "belong" to any one nation. Both superpowers sent up space stations that remained for long periods of time in orbit, serving as a base of operations for research and exploration missions. In 1975, at the height of détente, Soviet and American space stations even accomplished a docking maneuver that allowed the crews to move from one machine to another. This initiated a long period of collaboration that lasted beyond the collapse of the USSR.

Not surprisingly, the exploration of space and the search for signs of life beyond earth became in both countries a major preoccupation of popular culture, including film. MGM released *Forbidden Planet*, "the first modern science fiction film to be made by a major studio," in 1956.[10] Many more followed. But the film that best captured the sense of wonder and infinite potential of the space race of the 1960s was Stanley Kubrick's *2001*, made in England and released by MGM in the United States in spring 1968, just a year before the American landing on the moon. Kubrick worked very closely with British writer Arthur C. Clarke in developing the screenplay for *2001*, which was rewritten numerous times as new developments in space flight continued to unfold at a rapid pace.

Russian/Soviet characters occupy a small but significant place in *2001*. Although the space exploration programs of the United States and the USSR were engaged in fierce competition in the mid-1960s when they were putting the film together, Kubrick and Clarke foresaw that, in the future, the two superpowers would work together in this field. (They wrongly assumed, like so many of us, that the USSR would still exist in the year 2001.)

When the American David Bowman (Keir Dullea) sets off on a long mission on the spacecraft Discovery to discover the origin and purpose of a mysterious monolith found by an earlier mission near the planet of Jupiter, he stops at a space station en route. There, he converses at length with two Russian scientists—Dr. Smyslov (Leonard Rossiter) and Elena (Margaret Tyzack)—about the monolith and its function. They offer him all the information they have, as colleagues engaged in the same work, and do not operate as ideological or military opponents. Thus, *2001*, one of the most influential films of the Cold War period, portrays a post-ideological world in which Americans and Russians are allies in a search for knowledge and understanding that transcends the struggle between Communism and capitalism.

In his "sequel" to *2001*, *2010*, released in 1984 by MGM-UA, director-writer-producer Peter Hyams brings the Soviet/American relationship into much sharper focus. The Russians want to find out what happened to Bowman and the spacecraft Discovery nine years earlier, in a search for more information about the monolith. But they need the cooperation of the Americans, owners of Discovery and creators of the HAL computer that malfunctioned on board, terminating the mission. So the Russians propose to send a new mission to Jupiter with several Americans as invited participants, and their proposal is accepted.

As the mission progresses, however, the political relationship on earth between the United States and the USSR (still in business here, nearly twenty years after its real collapse as a nation) badly deteriorates because of a conflict off the coast of Honduras (reminiscent of the 1962 Cuban Missile Crisis). The world is threatened by the prospect of total war. Even so, the scientists in space continue to work together, trying to unravel the secret of the failed Discovery mission by reactivating HAL: "We are scientists—our governments are enemies, we are not." Finally, they receive a cosmic message from the planet of Europa, which gives to earth a second sun, with the warning: "Use them together, use them in peace." In a gesture reminiscent of the pacifist conclusion of *The Day the Earth Stood Still*, then, *2010* concludes with an affirmation of the importance of peace between the superpowers. In 1984, when *2010* was released, during the Soviet occupation of Afghanistan and with virulent anti-Communist rhetoric emanating from President Ronald Reagan—who was even proposing to militarize space through a new "Star Wars" program of missiles to be fired from satellites—this was a message that reflected the anxieties of the moment.

Three of the Russian members of the crew of in *2010* are played by Russian émigré actors—Savely Kramarov, Oleg Rudnik, Elya Baskin—who also appeared as Russians in *Moscow on the Hudson*, released the same year. But the principal Russian role, that of hardened air force officer Tania Kirbuk, is given to Helen Mirren, playing Russian for the first time. There is a significant amount of dialogue in Russian, without any subtitles. Maxim

Brajlovsky (Elya Baskin) and his American engineer colleague, played by John Lithgow, also engage repeatedly in jokes involving the proper use of confusing English language idioms—"piece of cake," "easy as pie"—which serve to humanize their relationship.

As in so many films of the Cold War era, the Russians and Americans in 2010 are shown to be natural friends who are mere pawns in the dangerous ideological game played between the governments of their countries.

✦✦✦ 7 ✦✦✦
Worst of Enemies, Best of Friends

"Get away from me, you crazy Russian!"
Humphrey Bogart (Rick) in response to the kiss of
Leonid Kinskey (Sascha) in *Casablanca*

––––––––––

The 1980s were a very confusing decade in Soviet-American relations, beginning in tense hostility but ending with the euphoria of *glasnost* and the melting of the Iron Curtain. The decade began badly, as the Soviet invasion of Afghanistan in late 1979 gave way to an extended brutal occupation. Especially in the early years of his new presidency, the longtime anti-Communist Reagan led a virtual crusade against the "evil empire" of Communist states controlled by the Soviet Union. "Let us pray," he said in 1983, "for the salvation of all those who live in totalitarian darkness, pray that they will discover the joy of knowing God."[1] In speeches, he fanned fears of Soviet aggression launched in the countries of Central America and the Caribbean (especially Nicaragua, El Salvador, and Cuba) against the United States.

Reagan also promoted the development of a new system of satellite-based missiles (Star Wars) that would further escalate the arms race. Reagan's rhetoric, and a climate of renewed xenophobia and repression in the USSR during the brief reign of Yuri Andropov as General Secretary, led to heightened anti-Soviet sentiment in the United States that did not take long to find expression in the movies. A new genre even arose and flourished in the 1980s: the anti-Soviet action film. Characterized by what Strada and Troper have called "Cold War vigilantism," these films no longer make a distinction "between the Soviet system and the Russian people."[2]

The earliest, and perhaps most important, example of this product is *Red Dawn*, released in August 1984 by MGM-UA/Valkyrie Films. (It was almost a requirement that the films in this genre use the anti-Communist branding word "red" in the title—*Red Dawn, Red Heat, Red Scorpion*). Directed by John Milius, *Red Dawn* brings to vivid visual life the fears—repeatedly articulated by President Reagan—of an invasion of the United States by an army combining Soviet and Central American forces bent on ideological domination, replicating the model already used in Afghanistan. The film opens with a series of on-screen titles in lurid yellow (accompanied by creepy horror-movie music by Basil Poledouris) setting the stage for a perfect storm of Communist aggression: "1) Soviet Union suffers worst wheat harvest in 55 years. 2) Labor and Food Riots in Poland. Soviet troops invade. 3) Cuba and Nicaragua Reach Troop Strength goals of 500,000. El Salvador and Honduras fall. 4) Greens Party gains control of West German Parliament. Demands withdrawal of nuclear weapons from European soil. 5) Mexico Plunged into Revolution. 6) Nato Dissolves. United States Stands Alone."

The setting for the playing out of this apocalyptic scenario is a small town in Colorado; the music suddenly changes to an imitation of Copland's score for the film *Our Town*. After omniscient shots of Main Street (in a tongue-in-cheek nod to Sergei Eisenstein, *Alexander Nevsky* is playing at the town movie theater), the camera leads us to a monument erected to Teddy Roosevelt the Rough Rider. On its pedestal are inscribed his words: "Far better it is to dare mighty things than to take rank with those poor timid spirits who know neither victory nor defeat." *Red Dawn*'s Teddy Roosevelt is a former high school quarterback, Jed Eckert, played by Patrick Swayze in his first major role, three years before *Dirty Dancing* made him a mega-star. Just moments after Jed drops off his younger brother and a friend at high school, the town is attacked by paratroopers bearing lethal weapons with which they proceed to strafe the history class of poor Mr. Teasdale, who had (not coincidentally) just been lecturing on the savage combat tactics of the Mongols. Mr. Teasdale is one of the first to die. Jed returns to rescue his brother and a few others in his pickup truck, and they manage to elude enemy fire, escaping to the nearby mountains with a few supplies. There they organize a heroic guerilla resistance force against the Soviet/Central American army that has already occupied a large portion of the United States, from Texas to Wyoming. They call themselves "Wolverines"—the name of the high school team on which most of them played.

For Jed and his buddies (who include Jennifer Grey as Toni, in a dress rehearsal for her later pairing with Swayze in *Dirty Dancing*), World War III is really a lot like football. They even have hazing rites, like drinking the blood of a freshly killed deer. "It's really not that bad," the dazed initiate keeps repeating, a buck's blood dripping from his chin.

Red Dawn offers some of the most virulent anti-Soviet (and anti-Russian) imagery ever seen in a major Hollywood feature. The Russian officers and soldiers who run the occupation are without exception crude, lascivious, and inhumane. Having adorned the walls of the town's buildings with propaganda posters and portraits of Lenin and Brezhnev, they send the innocent townsfolk (including Jed's father) to "re-education camps" where they are subjected to nonstop Communist indoctrination behind high barbed-wire fences. Those who offer any resistance are shot—even as they bravely sing "America, the Beautiful" in defiance. The Russian soldiers also insult and sexually assault the local girls. The two Russian officers in charge of the occupation, Col. Strelnikov (a name stolen from *Doctor Zhivago*) and General Bratchenko (played by William Smith and Vladek Sheybal, respectively) leer malevolently as they converse in bad Russian (translated in subtitles).

In contrast, the character of Col. Ernesto Bella, the Central American commander, a Castro clone played by Ron O'Neal, who speaks Spanish, Russian, and English, is developed much more sympathetically. He attempts to persuade the Russians that it would be wiser to attempt to "win the hearts and minds" of the local population rather than to abuse them, but his opinion is rejected as absurd and weak. Bella also reflects upon the fact that he was once also a partisan, like the Wolverines, but now "I'm just a policeman"—an observation that the Soviet general does not find amusing. And in the end, the compassionate Bella cannot bring himself to shoot at Jed when he is carrying the body of his wounded brother, Matt. (Matt is played by teenager Charlie Sheen, wearing faux Mongol attire, in his first movie role.) The message is clear: the Russians (not the Cubans/Nicaraguans) are the real villains here, incessantly marching and strutting to their national anthem and to the *Internationale,* having themselves photographed against the background of the beautiful American scenery that they are intent on conquering.

That the anti-Soviet insurgency is led by a bunch of teenaged jocks implies that the American adults have somehow lost their ideological bearings and resolve—and also makes clear who was the intended audience for *Red Dawn.* All the fathers can do is stand behind barbed wire and tell their sons to take revenge. The only adult on the team is a pilot who was shot down and joins up with the Wolverines in the mountains. Until he is killed in a later skirmish, he provides hard-bitten "wisdom" to the group. In response to the big question of why World War III has started, he uses a simple tough-guy metaphor: "It's a fight between the two toughest kids on the block . . . maybe they forgot what war was like." He also points out that the "green" European powers, America's alleged allies, have refused to provide help.

The hypernationalistic sentiments of *Red Dawn* reappeared in another action feature released in 1985, *Rocky IV.* For the fourth installment in the Rocky series, Sylvester Stallone took the franchise abroad to capitalize, so to speak, on the tense superpower relationship of the early 1980s. After his boxing buddy Apollo Creed (Carl Weathers) dies following a defeat in a match held in the United States with fearsome Soviet champion Ivan Drago (Dolph Lundgren), Rocky vows to avenge his death by challenging Drago on his own home turf in Russia. To prepare, he trains at a special secure facility in Siberia. Held before a hostile crowd of crude and blood-thirsty Russians, the match is an obvious allegory for the struggle between the enemies of the Cold War. Predictably, Rocky stumbles at first before the brute strength of Drago (cheered on by his wife and training partner Ludmilla, played by a pumped-up Brigitte Nielsen), but then recovers to pummel his rival, the pride of Soviet boxing.

The Siberian scenes of *Rocky IV* were shot in Wyoming, in Jackson Hole and at Grand Teton National Park, which explains why Siberia, renowned for its endless flat expanses, suddenly seems to have sprouted high mountains. But those mountains also give Rocky the chance to climb up high so the camera can show him at the peak of his powers and majesty. Like *Red Dawn, Rocky IV* trades in the most primitive stereotypes of Russian cruelty and brutality. It takes a patriotic American underdog everyman-turned-champ like Rocky to teach those nasty repressed Soviets a lesson.

A few years later, Stallone also enlisted his Rambo character in the struggle against Soviet aggression. In *Rambo III* (1988), John Rambo, who had started out as an underappreciated Vietnam green beret vet wreaking havoc on morally flabby Americans, is lured out of retirement in a Buddhist monastery in Thailand into action against the Soviet occupiers in Afghanistan when his old Marines buddy and officer Col. Trautman (played again by Richard Crenna) is taken captive there in a failed secret mission. "I'm no tourist," Rambo tells the rebels in his characteristically sullen

manner when he arrives. In no time, he has made fast friends with the locals and they are aiding him in hot pursuit of his buddy, who is being tortured with insane Nazi-like glee in a rotting fortress by the Soviet Regional
Commander Col. Zaysen—played with manic wide eyes by French actor
Marc de Jonge. (Conveniently, Zaysen speaks excellent English, although
his subordinates must converse in bad subtitled Russian.)

Having proved himself to the Afghans by excelling at their traditional
horse-riding games, Rambo and his new friends storm the fort (manned
by drunken soldiers and vicious German shepherds) and liberate Trautman. Zaysen's increasingly desperate, obsessive pursuit of Rambo with an
attack helicopter becomes cartoon-like in the closing minutes, something
like the fox's doomed pursuit of the roadrunner.

In *Rambo III,* Stallone does at least give us a single sympathetic Russian.
He is a defector named Yuri who has come over to the side of the Afghans
in disgust at the tactics employed by the Soviet army against the local
population. But Yuri does not survive until the film's end. By the time he
has liberated Trautman and the Afghans who were being held and tortured
in the fortress, Stallone has become a soulmate of his Afghan comrades,
sharing their struggle against imposed foreign rule in the time-honored
American tradition. Just before the closing credits, this point is made ex-
plicitly with a title: "This film is dedicated to the gallant people of
Afghanistan." As in the earlier Rambo films, Rambo here symbolizes the
power of American individuality—he always "goes it alone" and fights for
freedom and decency, often against the wishes of the cowardly and excessively bureaucratic American political and military establishment. In this
installment, it is the Russians who sit at the other end of the spectrum,
consumed with a mistaken Communist ideology that they impose upon
other defenseless peoples. *Rambo III,* like *Rocky IV* and *Red Dawn,* lacks any
of the humor or irony about the demonization of the Russian "other" expressed in films of the 1960s such as *The Russians Are Coming, The Russians
Are Coming.* In these films, the Russians really are coming, and they are
coming to kill us.

Another Russia film released in the same year (1988) as *Rambo III* did
move cautiously in a less ideological direction, reflecting the changing
political climate in Gorbachev's USSR. *Red Heat,* directed by Walter Hill
and starring The Terminator and current governor of California, Arnold
Schwarzenegger, also broke ground in an important way: it was the first

major Hollywood feature (not including such artificial American-Soviet projects as the 1976 fairy-tale flop *The Bluebird*) to be filmed—in part—on location in Russia. With censorship collapsing, the government searching for foreign currency, and the borders opening, it had at last become possible for American producers to make movies dealing with contemporary Russian life in Russia itself. After a surprising opening that features Arnold (as police captain Ivan Danko) wrestling in the buff in the snow with gangsters, the scene changes to Red Square—yes, real Red Square this time, not a set in Finland or Spain—and we hear an excerpt from Sergei Prokofiev's *Cantata for the Twentieth Anniversary of October,* a gigantic piece for chorus and orchestra written in an attempt to please Stalin. (The rest of the film's bland score was composed by James Horner in his pre-*Titanic* days.) As is so often the case with Hollywood films about Russia, the letters of the credits are reversed to look like Cyrillic (especially the reversed capital R). Then we are in a smoky cabaret where someone is singing the underground songs of Vladimir Vysotsky, and everyone, even Arnold, is speaking in (heavily accented) Russian.

Significantly, the villains in *Red Heat* are not Russians, but Georgians. And it is drug dealing, not Communism, that makes them bad. Sadistic Victor "Rosta" Rostavili (Ed O'Ross) leads a cocaine-dealing operation that leaves behind a trail of violence and mayhem. One of Rosta's recent victims is Yuri, Danko's police buddy. This makes Danko very angry. So angry that Danko decides to pursue Rosta to Chicago, where the crook has fled to continue his work in the international drug trade. Danko, it turns out, is not as dumb as he looks: he learned English in the army in language school in Kiev, and is an accomplished chess expert as well. In Chicago, Danko pairs up in an odd couple with the wisecracking and foul-mouthed police detective Sgt. Art Ridzik (James Belushi), who takes to calling the robot-like hulk Danko "Gumby."

As the film progresses, Belushi overcomes his hostility toward the "Commie" Danko and they become an efficient team, proving that former ideological enemies can work together for a common international cause. Like Rambo, Danko is operating on his own, without the approval of his superiors back home. In a funny cameo appearance, comedian Savely Kramarov (from *Moscow on the Hudson*) turns up as an official from the Soviet embassy in Washington to upbraid Danko for his flaunting of the rules. "My government does not like to do laundry in public," Danko explains to his bemused American partner. After numerous bloody shoot-outs, a bus chase that brings mayhem to Chicago traffic, and the inevitable baseball game (a celebration of the fundamental American values for which the good guys are fighting), Danko finally guns Rosta down. But Danko is no dissident or defector—he's on the first plane back to Moscow as soon as his job is done.

Red Heat for the most part avoids ideology. Like *Gorky Park,* this is fundamentally a cop buddy flick that shows that good cops are the same the world over. Danko does not spout Communist rhetoric. The only time he expresses a political sentiment is when he turns on the television in his Chicago hotel and sees porno—"Capitalism," he remarks with disgust. But *Red Heat* also admits that there is drug traffic in the USSR, although, significantly, it is carried on by members of an alien non-Russian minority group, even more "other" than the Russians.

Red Scorpion, released in 1989, turns the anti-Soviet action film into a conversion narrative. Here, Nikolai, a Russian KGB agent (Dolph Lundgren) sent to kill an anti-Communist black revolutionary in Africa, switches sides and helps the rebels because he cannot accept the brutal tactics used by the Russian and Cuban forces against the local population. In *Rambo III,* the Soviet defector Yuri had to die, but in *Red Scorpion,* the defector triumphs, and the audience sees that Soviet soldiers, now enlightened by the democratization of *glasnost,* are able to tell right from wrong after all and still survive.

★   Parallel to the anti-Soviet action films of the 1980s ran another stream of films that humanized Russians. As the decade progressed, and the news of Gorbachev's stunning political reforms began to effect public opinion in the United States—culminating with Gorbachev's highly publicized "Gorby-mania" visit to the United States in December 1987 and Reagan's stroll with Gorbachev across Red Square in May 1988—Hollywood producers and directors began to feel the need to present a kinder, gentler vision of the evil empire. At the same time, these films convey a certain confusion about what the Soviet Union is up to, and how the West should respond to the apparent thawing of the Cold War.

Although *Gorky Park,* the film adaptation of Martin Cruz Smith's 1981 blockbuster crime novel (praised by *Penthouse* magazine as "the most extraordinary overview of Soviet Russia since *Doctor Zhivago*") was released in 1983, before Gorbachev's rise to power, it prefigures the new attitudes of the *glasnost* era in presenting Russians as being "just like us." In his novel, Smith is fascinated with the "strange love" between the two superpowers. Smith's hero, Arkady Renko, is in many ways an American sort of character—a loner, a renegade, an average guy. A plodding, disheveled, proletarian and devoted police detective, he is the anti—James Bond. Renko also rejects the careerism of his wife, an ambitious Communist Party member, and attempts to retain his moral integrity while living in a pervasively corrupt system that protects the privileges of the Party elite.

The screenplay by Dennis Potter makes numerous significant changes to Smith's novel. The character of Renko's wife is eliminated, as is an important subplot involving Communist Party loyalty and an attempted Party coverup of an incident in Leningrad in 1943. Ideology plays almost no role in the film; the motivations are profit and greed. Renko's ordinariness is emphasized by the casting of William Hurt, an actor familiar to audiences for his very American appearance, manner, and voice. (In the same year that *Gorky Park* was released, Hurt also starred in *The Big Chill*.) Director Michael Apted wisely instructed Hurt not to use a Russian accent; instead, he speaks with his usual flat American intonation, thereby reducing the perception of cultural difference. Renko also teams up and works very effectively with the American cop (played by Brian Dennehy, the quintessential American tough guy) who comes to Moscow to investigate the murder of his idealistic brother. They immediately find a common language as two regular-guy underdogs out to uphold justice, truth, and their professional honor.

In *Gorky Park*, there are bad guys on both sides of the superpower divide, but what unites them is privilege, entitlement, greed, and disregard for human life. On both sides, there are fierce turf wars between different agencies: the KGB versus the Moscow police, the CIA versus the FBI. Jack Osborne (Lee Marvin) is an American businessman dealing in the illegal export of sables to the West. He recruits Russians to help him in his dirty business by promising them that he will get them out of the USSR. When he realizes his operation is about to be uncovered by Soviet authorities, he savagely murders his accomplices. Brought in to investigate this murder, Renko stumbles across a highly sophisticated network of corruption that links Osborne to the highest echelons of the KGB, including his own superiors. Imprisoned in cages, the sables are like the citizens of the USSR, kept behind iron fences and barbed wire.

The conflict in *Gorky Park* is less about ideology than about class—the privileged KGB brass and wealthy corrupt capitalists against the common man's representative, Renko. We see how the Cold War has created a self-perpetuating economic system in which many players (the military, the spy agencies, unscrupulous "businessmen") can prosper. To the very end, Renko retains his personal and professional integrity, although he becomes deeply disillusioned by "the chasm between what is said and what is done" in his country. Renko is also willing to sacrifice his own happiness in order to save the woman he loves, Irina, from the clutches of Osborne's villainy. At the end, he even delivers her (and the captive sables) safely to freedom in the West, but returns dutifully to Moscow and reports for work the next day. It is his work and his Russian patriotism, not ideological commitment, that draw him home. Unlike Ninotchka, he cannot be lured abroad even by love or champagne or hats: "A Russian—I could never be anything else."

Gorky Park was filmed in Finland and Sweden, one of the last major Hollywood dramatic features set in the USSR to be filmed elsewhere. Tchaikovsky's *1812 Overture* turns up here again, this time used to clever dramatic purpose: it is the climactic loud moments of the *1812 Overture* (broadcast over a loudspeaker at the skating rink) that drown out the sound of the shooting in Gorky Park. Along with music from Tchaikovsky's *Swan Lake,* this theme returns repeatedly as an emotional leit-motif. *Gorky Park* does not attempt to conceal the shabbiness and shortages endemic in the life of the average Soviet citizen, but its message concerns human nature more than political systems.

★ A more explicit response to *glasnost* and the improving American-Soviet relationship is the comedy *Russkies* (1987), a remake of the classic sixties film *The Russians Are Coming, The Russians Are Coming.* As its title indicates, *Russkies* (produced by New Century Entertainment Corporation) is a critique of popular American anti-Soviet attitudes. The screenplay, by Alan Jay Glueckman, Sheldon Lettich, and Michael Nankin, tells the story of three Soviet sailors who are shipwrecked off the coast of Key West during a mission to pick up a secret surveillance device that has been illegally provided to them by a profiteering American military supplier. The young operator, Mischa Pushkin (bearing the name, not coincidentally, of Russia's most celebrated poet to convey his idealistic Russian patriotism) is discovered hiding out near shore by a group of three adolescent buddies. Initially, the three boys, who have been consuming a steady diet of anti-Soviet comics and films (*Red Dawn* among them) treat Mischa (the handsome Baryshnikov clone Whip Hubley) as a dangerous enemy. (One of the boys, Danny, is played by Joaquin Phoenix in one of his earliest roles.)

Gradually, however, their attitudes change to friendship as they come to know the appealing Mischa better, and he proves himself a loyal and helpful buddy. One of the boy's sisters also develops a crush on Mischa when she treats him for a minor wound at a hospital where she works. The most anti-Soviet and hostile of the three boys finds it impossible to overcome his perception of Mischa as an enemy, however. As it happens, his father is a Hungarian émigré who fled Hungary after the Soviet invasion of 1956, and has passed on his hatred of Russians to his son, who has become obsessed with one particular anti-Soviet cartoon action figure. That cartoon figure even visits local carnivals, where he flies above the crowd with a jet propulsion pack, further inflaming anti-Soviet sentiment among the kiddies. But we discover later that the man inside the action figure suit is nothing but a drunk.

In the highly improbable rescue-over-the-ocean denouement, Mischa saves the hostile boy from drowning as his Hungarian father looks on with gratitude. As in *The Russians Are Coming, The Russians Are Coming,* it takes the plight of an endangered child to bring the two hostile sides in the Cold War together on a local level. Mischa and his two bumbling Soviet comrades (who "look like Shriners," says one of the disappointed boys, hoping that Soviets would look more menacing) are successfully reunited with a Soviet submarine sent to fetch them. The profiteering arms dealer is punished. The Americans have been converted to view Mischa as a friend and sympathetic fellow human, and the boys have learned that comic books and films can distort the truth about perceived ideological enemies. In the film's last scene, safely back on dry land in American suburban comfort, the three boys are shown reading together an excerpt from Tolstoy's *War and Peace,* one that celebrates the glory of friendship and nobility of character. "Sometimes the worst of enemies can become the best of friends," reads the advertising blurb for *Russkies,* a hymn to the new possibilities opening up under *glasnost.*

The rapidly shifting ideological terrain in U.S.-USSR relations also forms the background for the thriller *Little Nikita* (1988), directed for Columbia by Richard Benjamin with a witty and humorous flair. Combining plot features from several earlier films (*The Turning Point, Gorky Park*), *Little Nikita* stars young River Phoenix (Joaquin's brother) as Jeff Grant, an apparently normal San Diego teenager who wants to attend the Air Force Academy. But his plans are disrupted when FBI agent Roy Parmenter (Sidney Poitier), conducting a routine background check, discovers that Jeff's parents are "sleepers"—Soviet agents who have long been living undercover in the United States in the expectation that some day they will be "activated" from Moscow. "Your parents are Russian spies," Parmenter tells an understandably confused Jeff, whose notion of himself as an all-American kid has just been shattered.

Jeff's mother, Elizabeth (Caroline Kava), it turns out, was a Russian dancer who went on tour in the United States at age 17, picked up English quickly, and has been able to learn to blend seamlessly into American life. Jeff's realization of the truth, when he finds his parents' Soviet passports at home under a cactus, is conveyed symbolically through cross-cutting with a sequence from the ballet *Sleeping Beauty,* the scene of the Prince awakening the princess with a kiss. (The Kirov Ballet just happens to be on tour in San Diego.)

Meanwhile, a fierce battle is raging between Parmenter and Soviet undercover agents. Parmenter is out to avenge the death of his partner, killed years earlier by the unscrupulous Scuba, then a Soviet agent but now working against the USSR. Another Soviet agent (Karpov) is also out to get Scuba, whose name comes from his habit of killing his victims on the water. This puts Parmenter and Karpov on the same side, like Danko and Ridzik in *Red Heat.* Karpov even longs for the good old days of the Cold War: "I remember when we used to fear the CIA, instead of the media," he grouses.

The various plot lines of *Little Nikita* converge in another border-crossing scene, a furious chase and shoot-out at the gateway between Mexico and the United States near San Diego. Parmenter and Karpov (Richard Bradford) finally kill Scuba, and Jeff is reunited with his parents on the American side. Karpov flees to Mexico. Now free of their onerous "sleeper" obligations, Jeff's parents can finally live for real the normal, happy, suburban American life they have until now only been pretending to lead.

Like the Prince's kiss in *Sleeping Beauty,* this film tells us, *glasnost* has awakened the Soviet population from its long enforced Communist slumber, enabling them to express their true feelings at last after decades of dissembling.

★ After decades of playing a spy working for the Western side in the Cold War, and most often making Russians look silly, Sean Connery changed his image in 1990 when he took very different roles in two major films dealing with the USSR: *The Hunt for Red October* and *The Russia House.*

In *The Hunt for Red October,* a film adaptation of Tom Clancy's 1984 best-selling novel, Connery also plays Russian on the big screen for the first time in his career. (He was Vronsky in a 1961 television version of *Anna Karenina.*) Actually, the character Connery plays in *The Hunt for Red October* is only half Russian, on his mother's side. The other, more important, half of his background is Lithuanian. Soviet Navy Captain First Rank Marko Ramius is the son of a high-ranking Party official who became famous for his heroic acts during World War II in Lithuania, when he helped to enforce Soviet occupation of what had been an independent country. As Clancy writes, "Marko's father had been a true Soviet hero—and Marko was deeply ashamed to be his son."[3] Ashamed, because his father had helped to enforce brutal Soviet rule against the wishes of the Lithuanian population, and to wipe out Catholicism. For years, Marko harbored profound doubts about Communism and the Soviet system, but he kept them to himself, rising through the ranks of the Soviet Navy, eventually being awarded with the command of the newest and most technologically advanced Soviet submarine, the Red October, equipped with a nearly silent propulsion system that allowed it to elude American sonar detection.

But the death of Ramius's beloved wife at the hands of an incompetent drunken Soviet doctor have pushed him over the brink of concealed dissidence into open rebellion. In a plot he has developed with a few other officers, Ramius has decided to highjack the Red October and take it to the United States, where he will ask for political asylum. "The rage he had almost unknowingly suppressed throughout his life had burst forth with a violence and passion that he had struggled to contain. A lifetime of self-control had enabled him to conceal it, and a lifetime of naval training had enabled him to choose a purpose worthy of it."[4]

Clancy's techno-thriller appeared in 1984. By the time the film adapta-

FIGURE 28

The Hunt for Red October. Paramount 1990. Sean Connery as Captain Marko
Ramius. Courtesy of the Margaret Herrick Library, Academy of Motion Picture
Arts and Sciences. Photo by Bruce McBroom.

tion was released in early 1990, the situation in the USSR had profoundly changed. In their screenplay, Clancy and his collaborators (Larry Ferguson and Donald Stewart) are careful to provide the information at the outset that the action occurs in November 1984, "shortly before Gorbachev came to power." The film opens at the Soviet submarine base at Murmansk with the launching of the gigantic Red October, the new pride of the Soviet fleet. Ramius/Connery stands on deck chatting about the weather in Russian with fellow officer and conspirator Captain Borodin (Sam Neil) as we hear music (by Basil Poledouris) that sounds like a combination of Russian Orthodox liturgical chant and Soviet patriotic anthems, with Russian words.

When the action shifts later to the sub's cabin, Ramius continues to speak in Russian with the enemy he is about to exterminate, the Political Officer Putin. (Not to be confused with another Putin, the very real Vladimir Vladimirovich, who would a few years later rise from the KGB to succeed Yeltsin as President of the Russian Federation.) Putin is reading aloud from a book by J. Robert Oppenheimer, father of the atomic bomb, that he has found among Ramius's papers. The passage (from a Hindu text) concerns Armageddon—the destruction of the world—and makes Putin suspicious. Why has Ramius marked this passage? As Putin reads, director John McTiernan has the camera come in close, and then draw away, as the language in which Putin is reading changes from Russian to English, in a notably creative solution to the Russian/English language problem always encountered in Hollywood films about Russians.

This scene of Putin reading from Oppenheimer is missing in Clancy's novel, and gives the film an additional antiwar and anti-nuclear message. In the novel, Ramius's motivations are primarily personal, involving his own inability to continue to exist under the moral oppression of the Soviet system. He is also disaffected with his own role in the Cold War, "a war with no battles." What exactly Ramius intends to do when he arrives in the United States is not entirely clear. In any case, his defection is motivated by moral concerns, not lust for consumer goods or romance, like Captain Borodin, who wants to live in Montana and have an RV.

The suspense in *Hunt for Red October* revolves around the reaction of the American CIA and military, and of the Soviet navy, to Ramius's behavior. The Soviet ambassador tries to convince the Americans that Ramius plans to shoot missiles at the United States, so that the U.S. navy will destroy

Ramius and prevent him from escaping with the Red October. On board the Red October, Ramius and his conspirators fake a radiation leak in order to evacuate the crew and leave them free to carry out their plan. With the help of the Soviet submarine specialist Jack Ryan (Alec Baldwin), the Americans are able to devise a plan that allows the Red October to slip away up a river in Maine, where Ramius first inhales the air of freedom—and U.S. intelligence gets the Red October, which is reported lost in official reports.

Ideological conversion and defection sit at the center (again) of the plot of *Hunt for Red October*. In some ways, the film felt dated when it appeared in 1990, at a time when the real physical and ideological barriers between East and West were fast disappearing, many Soviet citizens were traveling abroad, and the very survival of Communism appeared already in jeopardy. One can almost feel an incipient nostalgia for the Cold War in *The Hunt for Red October*, for a time when there was a stark clarity in American-Russian relations. The smart casting of Connery as Ramius contributes to this disorientation—what is the world coming to if James Bond is switching sides?

In *The Russia House*, released the same year as *The Hunt for Red October*, Connery returns to somewhat more familiar ground, playing a jazz-loving English publisher (Barley Scott Blair) asked to help the British secret service obtain information about a mysterious Russian dissident scientist and author whose manuscript (concerning the weaknesses of Soviet military technology) has been offered to Barley for publication. Based on a 1989 novel by the master of the Cold War spy genre, John le Carre, *The Russia House* was adapted for the screen by another Cold War connoisseur, playwright Tom Stoppard. Both le Carre and Stoppard bring to the project an acute understanding of how *glasnost* and *perestroika* have undermined old certainties, and a deep compassion for the plight of Soviet citizens, facing a new world for which they feel unprepared. Both writers also understand that the powerful and elaborate infrastructure of superpower spying that has been built up for nearly fifty years is not going to disappear without a struggle. There are many people on both sides—the "grey men"— who have invested heavily in the status quo and need the game to continue.

Initially resistant to the idea of working for the secret service, given his love for Russians and their culture, Barley finally yields only with misgivings. His job is to clarify the origin of the secret manuscript written by a certain Dante (German actor Klaus Maria Brandauer) and to ascertain Dante's intentions. Dante's go-between is the appealing but wary Katya Orlova (Michelle Pfeiffer). In time, Barley falls in love with Katya, and his allegiances shift to her and to Russia. He refuses to complete his assignment for the British secret service—something James Bond would never have done. Barley's complicated relationship with Katya (and her family) unfolds to the accompaniment of a seductive, urban bluesy score by Jerry Goldsmith that captures the sense of depression and anxiety that prevailed in Moscow at the time. The film was shot on location in Moscow and Leningrad, the first major Hollywood feature to be shot almost entirely (the other locations are London and Lisbon) in the USSR.

Like so many earlier films, *The Russia House* ends with the Russian heroine—Katya—fleeing to the West, in this case to Lisbon, Barley's new home. But the fact that Barley chooses his love for Katya over his allegiance to England indicates a new twist in the usual conversion narrative. Usually it is the female Russian protagonist who defects to the West, through love for an American or European. But here the male protagonist converts (emotionally and ideologically, if not geographically) in the other direction. Katya symbolizes the Russian culture and values Barley cherishes, and he must have her. Dante, meanwhile, has been apprehended by the KGB and is in prison somewhere. Yes, Russia is changing, this film tells us, but much remains the same. In its depiction of the lives of ordinary Soviet citizens, *The Russia House* represents a significant advance, achieving a new level of realism possible only with on-location shooting and cooperation.

★ By the 1980s, most of the Russian émigrés who had come to work in the Hollywood film business in the 1920s and '30s had passed on. The ideological hostility and severe travel restrictions of the Cold War years had also prevented the arrival of new talent from Russia, with a very few exceptions: dancer defectors Nureyev, Baryshnikov, and Godunov—and director Andrei Konchalovsky.

Konchalovsky's story is an unusual one. On both sides of his family, Konchalovsky (born in 1937) was descended from the Russian/Soviet cultural elite. Konchalovsky's grandfather, Pyotr Konchalovsky (1876–1956), was a well-known artist of the Stalin era, who painted portraits of numerous famous people, including composer Sergei Prokofiev. His mother was a writer and great-granddaughter of the Russian painter Vasily Surikov. His father, Sergei Mikhailkov, headed the Soviet Writers' Union and wrote the lyrics to the Soviet national anthem. Through his well-connected father, Konchalovsky met numerous leading figures in the Soviet film industry, and he began studying directing at the most prestigious Soviet film school, the All-Union State Film Institute (VGIK) in Moscow, during the vibrant Thaw period after Stalin's death. (Konchalovsky's brother Nikita also became a film director, but uses his father's name Mikhailkov and has worked only in Russia.) Konchalovsky filmed his first full-length feature, *The First Teacher* (1965), in Kirghizia and quickly established himself as an accomplished and serious director capable of bending (but not breaking) the rules of Socialist Realist filmmaking. In *Asya's Happiness* (1967), however, Konchalovsky went too far for Party censors in his sympathetic treatment of the story of an unwed mother. The film was banned for twenty-one years, and reemerged to critical acclaim only in 1988. Konchalovsky's nostalgic and wistful film adaptations of two Russian literary classics, Turgenev's novel *A Nest of Gentlefolk* (1969) and Chekhov's play *Uncle Vanya* (1970), firmly established his reputation abroad and led to his first trip to the United States in 1969, for a screening of *A Nest of Gentlefolk* at the San Francisco Film Festival.

In his 1998 memoirs, *Ugly Truths,* Konchalovsky writes that even though he had already travelled to several cities in Europe by then, America—especially California in the late 1960s—"fell on me like a ton of bricks." He was taken to a raucous Jefferson Airplane stadium concert and witnessed the social and sexual revolution of the late 1960s at close range. "Yes, this world smelling of marijuana and the ocean astonished me with its deafening freedom and high decibel level. And there were other, more trivial revelations. You could buy chicken liver in the grocery store, in a separate package, fresh, in a container. And the radio played in stereo. The radio! . . . When I told my friends about this in Moscow, they all nodded their heads, but I think that they really didn't believe me about the chicken liver. They thought I was exaggerating."[5]

Konchalovsky's American friend Tom Luddy, a film curator and historian, introduced him to prominent producers and directors, including Milosz Forman, an émigré who had begun his career in Communist Czechoslovakia. Konchalovsky returned to Moscow laden with gifts for all the Party officials and bureaucrats who had approved his visit abroad, hoping that the experience would be repeated but fearful that—like so many other Soviet artists—he would never be allowed to leave Russia again. But Konchalovsky was fortunate: he managed to get to America almost every other year on various film-related trips. "Every time I went to America, it gave me the sensation of being on a binge. Not only because I really did do a lot of drinking there, but because the whole time I would experience a feeling of hyper-stimulation."[6]

Back in Moscow, Konchalovsky continued to work productively and provocatively. His 1974 feature *Romance of Lovers* takes innovative liberties with the melodrama format. But it was his epic *Siberiade* (1978), starring Konchalovsky's brother Nikita, that firmly established Konchalovsky as an important independent artistic voice. A family saga that stretches from 1900 through the 1970s, *Siberiade* addresses difficult questions of progress, change, and spirituality in a traditional and remote rural environment. It won a "Special Jury Prize" at the Cannes Film Festival, and was widely seen by important Hollywood actors, directors, and producers.

Soon afterward, Konchalovsky arrived in Hollywood with a group of French colleagues who were trying to promote a new project. For the first time, he came "not as the member of a Soviet delegation, but just as a normal person."[7] His legal status was uncertain, and he found that most people in Hollywood regarded him with suspicion, since the only Soviet citizens who were living abroad at that time were "dissidents or KGB agents."[8] But Konchalovsky had fallen in love with the freedom and expanse of America, and with the intoxicating possibilities of Hollywood, and was determined to stay, even after the French project collapsed. It took him some time before he learned that filmmaking in Los Angeles was completely different from the game he had mastered in Moscow.

"I was full of the typical Soviet conceptions of Hollywood. I am a famous director. I have many friends and acquaintances here. So they will help me get set up. . . . I was living according to the rules of Mosfilm. I thought that all I had to do was to hang around some offices, drink tea and conduct pleasant conversation. . . . It turned out that it was not quite that simple! It turned out that no one knew anything about me here. Cannes, Venice, prizes, reviews—no one here had heard anything about all that. Who are you? What films have you directed? I had to tell everything about myself all over again."[9]

Just as Konchalovsky was about to lose hope, he found a savior in

Shirley MacLaine. MacLaine and her brother, Warren Beatty, were long-time afficianados of Russian culture; Beatty's film *Reds* was about to be released. Konchalovsky invited MacLaine to a screening of his *Siberiade,* and she was immediately enthralled not only with the film but also with its attractive and slightly exotic creator. The next day they had dinner at a French restaurant on Sunset Boulevard, discovered they were soulmates, and within a matter of days, Konchalovsky was sharing MacLaine's bed at her house in Malibu. Through MacLaine, he met many of Hollywood's movers and shakers, although eventually he found his financial and social dependence upon her oppressive, especially when he began to realize that her friends considered him nothing more than a "star-fucker, a handsome, appealing Russian." For most of Shirley's Hollywood friends, he discovered, "Russia was something extremely unfamiliar and remote."[10] Their affair ended and Konchalovsky was out on the street with nothing in his pocket.

By now, however, Konchalovsky had managed to cultivate other Hollywood stars who believed in his talent, including John Voight and Jill Clayburgh. Having worked with Nastassya Kinski and Keith Carradine in *Maria's Lovers* (1984), he went on to direct Voight in *Runaway Train* (1985), based on an Akira Kurosawa screenplay. Voight portrays an escaped convict who commandeers a train and drives it through the Alaska wilderness. Like *Siberiade, Runaway Train* explores the struggle of man against nature, and the moral aspects of the relationship between prisoners and their jailers that also preoccupied such major Russian writers as Dostoyevsky (*Notes from the House of the Dead*) and Tolstoy (*Resurrection*). Suspenseful, fast-paced, and sharply edited, *Runaway Train* was a commercial and critical success, and received three Oscar nominations, for best actor (Voight), supporting actor (Eric Roberts), and editing. The following year, Julie Andrews, Alan Bates, and Max von Sydow appeared in Konchalovsky's *Duet for One,* an intelligent story of a cellist stricken with a debilitating disease, based on the real-life story of English cellist Jacqueline Du Pre.

Shy People (1987), starring Clayburgh and Barbara Hershey, a quirky and highly personal story of family roots set in the Louisiana bayou, was less successful, although esteemed for its offbeat atmosphere by some critics. The screenplay, co-authored by Konchalovsky, examines the destructive impact of the oil business on the environment, one of the main concerns of *Siberiade*. In 1989, Konchalovsky directed Whoopi Goldberg and James Belushi in the road movie *Homer and Eddie*. By the end of the 1980s, then, Konchalovsky had proven that he could make competitive (if small-scale) Hollywood features with major talent, and still retain something of his original voice and style.

Then Konchalovsky encountered Warner Brothers and Sylvester Stallone. The pairing of action-hero Stallone—who had recently starred in several of the most virulently anti-Soviet Hollywood films ever made (*Rambo III, Rocky IV*)—with the urbane Russian *auteur* Konchalovsky is surely one of the oddest in recent Hollywood history. But Konchalovsky was eager to make a "blockbuster." When his agent called and said that Warner Brothers studio wanted to talk to him about directing Stallone's new project, Konchalovsky, knowing of Stallone's reputation of abusing directors, was hesitant, although intrigued. The film was *Tango and Cash*, a story of two cops (Stallone and Kurt Russell) who are jailed on a false murder charge and escape to take revenge. The film was to be produced by mega-producer John Peters, and Konchalovsky was given repeated assurances that Stallone would not interfere with the director's work.

As he describes at length in his autobiography, *Ugly Truths*, Konchalovsky soon discovered that working at a major studio like Warner Brothers with a superstar like Stallone and a major budget placed severe limitations on the director's creative freedom. For the first time, he was confronted with the power of such activities as merchandising and the endless required nurturing of multitudes of ancillary personnel attached to such a high-profile production. For Konchalovsky, used to a much more spontaneous and director-centered kind of filmmaking, it was an alien and nearly impossible task to cater to so many different constituencies. Peters soon began telling Konchalovsky how and what to film, undermining his authority and confidence. A "parallel group" was formed to shoot extra scenes, without Konchalovsky's control. A fierce struggle broke out between the film's financial backers and Peters, who decided to outflank them by offering up Konchalovsky as a scapegoat for cost overruns and production delays. Konchalovsky was fired from *Tango and Cash* and replaced with Albert Magnoli, best known for directing *Purple Rain*, although Konchalovsky was credited as director when the film was released. Thanks to Stallone's fame, *Tango and Cash* did achieve a respectable commercial success.

Konchalovsky's "humbling" experience working on *Tango and Cash* brought an end to the Hollywood period of his career.[11] Just like Sergei Eisenstein in the 1930s, Andrei Konchalovsky in the 1980s found, as a director trained in the Soviet system where the director was the ultimate figure of respect and authority, that working in Hollywood required skills he did not possess. Konchalovsky could deal with political objections to his films, but the endless interference in the creative process of the "money people" in Hollywood was to him intolerable and depressing. He came to understand that, although there was no ideological censorship in America, there was another kind of censorship. "It took me a while, but eventually I became convinced that Hollywood also has a Central Committee of the Communist Party of the Soviet Union—but in a mirror image. Hollywood is a collection of people who are very pretty, or trying to be pretty—tanned, well-groomed, manicured, and frightened to death."[12]

Fortunately for Konchalovsky, the debacle of *Tango and Cash* coincided with the impending collapse of the USSR and the old system of Soviet filmmaking. Like many others who had been living in quasi-legal émigré status abroad, Konchalovsky was invited back and encouraged to participate in reconstructing Russian culture. For his next major film, distributed by Columbia but filmed entirely in Moscow, *The Inner Circle,* Konchalovsky returned to his Soviet/Russian roots. It is the story of Stalin's projectionist, Alexander Ganshin, who was still working around Goskino in the late 1960s when Konchalovsky met him. Ganshin's story had always fascinated Konchalovsky, and now that it had become possible to treat the "Stalin theme" more openly, thanks to *glasnost* and *perestroika,* the director decided to bring it to the screen.

As he describes in his second book of memoirs, *Sublime Deceit,* Konchalovsky wanted in *The Inner Circle* to raise deeper questions about the relationship of ordinary Russians to Stalinism, and how people like Ganshin (named Ivan Sanshin in the film) ennabled Stalin to develop and maintain his emotional power over the population. Konchalovsky wrote the screenplay himself, with help from Anatoly Usov. Tom Hulce plays Sanshin as an ordinary guy thrust into an extraordinary situation. When he is suddenly summoned to replace Stalin's former projectionist, Sanshin is overcome with awe and fear. Even as he witnesses the brutal persecution and extermination of his Jewish neighbors in a crowded communal apartment, Sanshin maintains his admiration for and abject devotion to Stalin. Only his wife (Lolita Davidovich) and their elderly neighbor, a retired professor (Fyodor Chaliapin, Jr.) question Sanshin's complicity in Stalin's crimes. "Who do you love better? Me or Comrade Stalin?" she screams at him. The film opens in 1939, and ends on the day of Stalin's funeral in March 1953, when thousands of people were crushed in the streets as they expressed their grief over the leader's passing.

As Sanshin, Hulce unfortunately adopts a fake Russian accent, although most of the other actors in the film (including Bob Hoskins as Beria) speak in clear American English. For Stalin, Konchalovsky chose the Russian actor Aleksandr Zbruyev. Although he does not closely resemble Stalin physically, Zbruyev does convey the quiet but terrifying charm with which Stalin dominated all those around him. Konchalovsky's slow and atmospheric direction proved problematic for American audiences, and the film was not a commercial success. But *The Inner Circle* is a noble and valuable attempt to make sense of the nightmare of Stalinism. For Konchalovsky, the cult of Stalin was a product of the Russian mentality, but the Russian nation has been unwilling to accept responsibility. Instead, he believes, Russians have wanted to shift all the blame for the excesses of the Soviet period onto those who were in power, like a slave who upon receiving his freedom immediately begins cursing his liberator.[13]

It seems entirely fitting that *The Inner Circle* was released on Christmas Day, 1991—the same day that the Soviet Union officially ceased to exist.

Show Me the Real Moscow

"You are in Russia—everything is complicated."
The Saint

In the fifteen years since the collapse of the USSR in December 1991, the number of big-budget "Russia films" produced in Hollywood has declined significantly. With the termination of the Cold War and the apparent "victory" of American capitalism over Soviet Communism, one of the major themes (either overt or covert) of movies since World War II vanished. Ironically, it also now became possible for American studios to film freely on location in Russia for the first time in history. It was no longer necessary to fabricate Russia at great expense somewhere else—Spain, Finland, Alaska. This is not to say that filming in Russia was easy for Americans. The breakup of the Soviet bureaucracy and the emergence of primitive private enterprise led to disorganization and rampant corruption. At the same time, the Soviet film industry entered a prolonged period of crisis as the huge studios that had dominated the production of feature films saw their budgets slashed as a result of the precipitous decline in state funding and the new economics of film distribution.

The political and economic situation in Russia also remained extremely volatile. Gorbachev, seen as a hero in the West but a villain at home, was succeeded by Boris Yeltsin, in the new office of President of the Russian Federation. Yeltsin remained in power for eight years, throughout the 1990s. For most Russians, this was a difficult and depressing period, as they saw the value of their money plummet, and they lost many of the social benefits they had been guaranteed under the Communist system. Unemployment soared as inefficient enterprises cut back production or closed down altogether. The delivery of electricity and other public services was frequently disrupted. Various insurgent groups also challenged Yeltsin's power. In October 1993, Yeltsin's long struggle against the newly appointed parliament came to a climax when rebels occupied the seat of power, the so-called White House, and raised the Communist red flag. Yeltsin ordered the building stormed by government troops. CNN broadcast live the burning of the White House to a fascinated but disturbed American public. Hopes of a peaceful transition from Communism to American-style democracy and free enterprise went unfulfilled.

The intelligentsia celebrated the removal of Communist censorship and the newly granted freedom to travel and even work abroad, but many segments of the Russian population felt intense nostalgia for the stable days of pre-*glasnost* Communism. New political leaders promoting nationalist, imperialist, and racist ideas emerged and gained large followings. One of the most successful was Vladimir Zhirinovsky, a crazy but exciting orator who advocated that Russia reclaim its nineteenth-century empire—including Alaska, Finland, and half of Poland. Semi-autonomous regions of the newly created Russian Federation populated primarily by non-Russians also began to express dissatisfaction with the Moscow government and to seek independence. In Chechnya, on the northern edge of the Caucasus, a war broke out in December 1994 between Russian forces and Muslim rebels demanding independence, and has raged sporadically ever since. The highly publicized brutality of this conflict severely damaged Russia's image in the United States, destroying much of the good will generated during the *glasnost* era. The news coming out of Russia, which heavily influenced the thinking of studio executives and producers, was not very encouraging. Yes, the Russians were now free. But free to do what?

With the collapse of Communism also came the highly publicized rise of the Russian mafia both at home and abroad. In the absence of reliable law and order, and with a proliferation of weapons among the general population, organized crime gained control over many sectors of the economy. The Russian drug trade portrayed in *Red Heat* continued to grow at an alarming rate.

It should not come as a surprise, then, that the first Hollywood film to be released after the death of the USSR deals with the Russian mafia and corruption. *Back in the USSR,* named for the famous Beatles song that could now—at last—be played at full volume anywhere in Russia, also introduced to the American mainstream movie audience a hot new Russian actress: Natalya Negoda. Born in 1964, Negoda came to international attention in 1988 when she starred in the Soviet film *Little Vera,* directed by Vasily Pichul. In its frank and angry outspokenness, this nihilistic, gritty portrait of domestic life in a dingy Ukrainian industrial city (Mariupol) enjoyed enormous popularity in the USSR, where it became a symbol of the soul-baring atmosphere of the *glasnost* era. Even in the United States, *Little Vera* attracted a great deal of attention, mainly for its in-your-face portrayal of numerous problems that the Soviet government had long tried to pretend did not exist under Communism: alcoholism, domestic violence, unwed motherhood, depression, even AIDS. Its portrayal of sexual activity is extremely graphic, violent, and unprecedented in Soviet film.

In *Little Vera,* Negoda plays the role of Vera, a young woman drifting through "a life without spiritual or even passionate materialistic values, a life in a vacuum, affected by the vestiges of stagnation and decay."[1] To escape an abusive home life dominated by her alcoholic father, she enters into a steamy relationship with the nonconformist Sergei, who rejects the values of her parents' generation and makes no attempt to hide his contempt for social norms or courtesy. Hopelessly torn between Sergei (with whom she is shown nude, having energetic and acrobatic sex) and her parents, she attempts to commit suicide—the ultimate antisocial act.

Little Vera made Negoda into an international celebrity, precisely at the moment when the American media was at the height of its romance with *glasnost* and the historic transformation of Russia under Gorbachev. She was "That Glasnost Girl," the emblem of the new openness and permissiveness. In May 1989, she appeared provocatively photographed in *Playboy,* becoming the first Soviet woman to be so honored. Mother Russia was taking it off. In 1990, Negoda was invited to be a co-presenter of the Oscar for Best Foreign Language Film. That portion of the ceremony was beamed live from Moscow via satellite to the international television audience, a glamorous image of the exciting changes taking place in the USSR. After decades of isolation, Russia was rejoining the international community, now an electronically linked global village.

In *Back in the USSR,* produced and written by Lindsay Smith (founder of the American/Soviet Film Initative) Negoda was cast in the leading role of Lena. By the time the film was released in early 1992, the furious pace of history had overtaken the project and the USSR no longer existed.

Lena is an aspiring clothes designer who works on the side as a prostitute and also for the mafia. She is hired by the mobster Kurilov (Roman Polanski, in a rare and wonderfully nasty acting job) to assist in the theft of a valuable icon from a monastery. As she leaves a hotel carrying the icon in a bag, she encounters an American tourist named Archer Sloan (Frank Whaley). He immediately takes a fancy to Lena, and follows her to Kurilov's establishment, a place called the War Club where rock music is played at deafening volume as an accompaniment to war newsreels. Naïve and inquisitive, Archer wants to make the most of his last night in Moscow. "Show me the real Moscow," he tells a taxi driver. Lena seems to be just the kind of tour guide he thinks he needs.

Before long, Archer is drawn into the web of violence and coercion surrounding Lena and the icon. He is beaten up by thugs in the employ of Kurilov, travels to the city of Mozhaisk with Lena in pursuit of the icon, and is accused by the bumbling American Embassy of murdering an Englishman who was actually taken out by his double-crossing Russian cronies. In this upside-down world, everyone is corrupt, including a museum curator, a fanatic nationalist who murders the priest (the film's only source of positive moral values) seeking to regain the stolen icon. Even one of the American Embassy's employees is working with Kurilov in an attempt, foiled at the last minute, to smuggle the icon out of the country. Despite her nefarious behavior, the film treats Lena with sympathy, as a helpless victim of the impossible circumstances of Russian life. She is "very unpredictable these days—like the whole country," says her boyfriend Georgi.

Back in the USSR was shot entirely in the USSR, and with a Russian crew. Its message—that Russia is a violent and chaotic place where very bad things can happen to innocent American tourists—certainly did little to improve the country's image, however. With Communism effectively dead, the plot lacks the driving force of the ideological conflict that had informed most of Hollywood's earlier films about Russia. No longer can the villainy of Russians be explained by the fact that they are Communists. What remains is a residual anxiety about Russians as members of an alien and chaotic culture, a fear of the unknown.

Nor did the film do much for Negoda's career. After *Back in the USSR,* in which she speaks heavily accented English, she made several television appearances, including one in 1993 on the show *Law and Order,* but she did not sustain an acting career in Hollywood, and slid into obscurity. The appeal of "That Glasnost Girl" proved to be no more durable than *glasnost* itself.

★ Perhaps the most memorable portrayal of contemporary Russia to come out of Hollywood in the 1990s is *The Saint* (1997). Val Kilmer stars as Simon Templar, known as the Saint, a sort of Robin Hood of crime, a beloved character created by Leslie Charteris that had already appeared in many different adaptations on television and on screen over the years. (The most popular of the Saints was Roger Moore, on television in the 1960s, in his pre–James Bond days.) A mercenary thief who works for hire, the Saint—rather like James Bond—takes great pleasure in the game of eluding his pursuers, employing numerous high-tech gadgets, incredible physical agility, silly disguises, a dry sense of humor, and a large libido. Wherever there is trouble, you can count on finding the Saint, outsmarting the rich and powerful.

And there is plenty of trouble in Moscow—it is "like Dodge City right now," a character tartly observes at the film's outset. The streets are filled with demonstrators angry because their homes are unheated and their salaries unpaid. Right-wing nationalists take advantage of the unrest to promote the restoration of the former glory of the Soviet Union, with support from the Orthodox clergy, even resurrecting the ancient ideology of Moscow as the Third Rome. They love to sing the anthem of the former Soviet Union: "Unbreakable union of free republics." The United States has become deeply unpopular because American policies toward Russia are blamed for the country's decline into poverty and humiliation.

Into this void steps Ivan Petrovich Tretiak (Croatian actor Rade Serbedzija), owner of Tretiak Oil and Gas, an energy monolith built through the hasty privatization of former state-owned enterprises. As a politician, Tretiak (modeled on Zhirinovsky) advocates the rearming of Russia, and opposes the democratically elected government of President Karpov (modeled on Yeltsin). As a businessman, he and his unsavory son Ilya (Russian actor Valeri Nikolayev in his first Hollywood film) are using their monopoly on the oil supply business to inflame the political situation to their financial advantage. They are also hiding huge supplies of heating oil.

Tretiak encounters the Saint as he is completing a heist of a computer chip from the Ministry of Foreign Affairs building in Moscow. One of the formidable "birthday-cake" style skyscrapers erected by Stalin, this fortress-like complex on Smolensk Square for decades symbolized Soviet might and inscrutability. To see the Saint crawling up and down its thick walls at will, violating this formerly sacred space, represents the ultimate collapse of Soviet authority and self-respect. It is also a first for Hollywood filmmakers, who could only have dreamed of gaining access to such a top-secret shooting location only ten years earlier. In *The Saint,* Moscow for the first time in a major Hollywood feature becomes just another location, demystified and deromanticized, a real physical space rather than an ideological construct.

Impressed with the Saint's abilities, Tretiak hires him to obtain a secret formula for cold fusion from a scientist in England. With cold fusion, Tretiak can produce huge amounts of power from a small quantity of water, further strengthening his political and financial position.

The action moves to England, where the Saint meets the scientist, the shy but sexy Emma (Elizabeth Shue), and sets about obtaining the formula. Like James Bond, he seduces her at the same time that he is gaining the information he needs. After she discovers the theft of her precious equation, Emma pursues the Saint to Moscow. "You are in Russia—everything is complicated," she is told. Soon she and the Saint have teamed up against the evil Tretiak father and son and are making their way through the seedy Moscow underground of overcrowded communal apartments, secret hiding places formerly used to elude the KGB, and labyrinthine tunnels. In the furious climax, they succeed in delivering the cold fusion mechanism to President Karpov, who stages a dramatic public exhibition of its magical capabilities on Red Square, thereby restoring himself to favor with the people and ensuring the demise of the Tretiaks.

In *The Saint,* the only Russian favorably portrayed is President Karpov (distinguished Russian stage actor Yevgeni Lazarev, a teacher at the Moscow Art Theater Studio School), who receives very little screen time. He represents the institution of American-style democracy. Everyone else is corrupt and out to make money. The country teeters on the edge of political and economic chaos, in a condition close to mob rule. As in the post-Soviet James Bond film *GoldenEye* (1995), order has vanished and the former Soviet military and government elite work only to enrich themselves. *The Saint* also stresses the rabid anti-Americanism of the Russian population and military, pandering to the patriotism of American audiences, particularly in a scene at the gate into the American Embassy, where a stalwart black Marine ("Back off! I said back off!") rescues Emma from the clutches of the Russian police. One of the inhabitants of the shabby communal apartment tells Simon and Emma with utter disdain, "You're not people. You're Americans." In *The Saint,* economic hardship has surpassed ideology as the reason for Russians to envy and hate the United States.

Air Force One, another major feature released in the same year as *The Saint,* conveys a similarly scary message about post-Communist Russia, and comes even closer to home. The villains here are "Russian ultra-nationalist radicals" who (with inside help) hijack Air Force One with President James Marshall (Harrison Ford) and his family aboard. They are demanding the release of the fascist President of Kazakhstan, General Radek, imprisoned for terrorist crimes after a coup carried out by a joint Russian-American force. The terrorists are headed by Ivan Korshunov, played by Gary Oldman, well known for his portrayal of bad guys—including Dracula in 1992. For Oldman, as for Bela Lugosi (in *Ninotchka*), the next logical career step after successfully playing monsters in horror movies was to take the demonic role of a nasty Russian. Not coincidentally, Oldman had also played the role of another presidential assassin, an infamous American with Soviet sympathies—Lee Harvey Oswald in *JFK.*

Like *The Saint, Air Force One* contains just one positive Russian character—the democratically elected President Petrov, who speaks fine (if slightly accented) English and even indulges in the distinctly Western (and humanizing) pastime of playing handball. The others are sadistic criminals who fanatically support Korshunov's platform: that Mother Russia will again become great, for the capitalists in the Kremlin to be shot in the street, for "our enemies to run and hide in fear at the mention of our name," and for Americans to "beg our forgiveness. . . . You have taken everything from us." As it happens, President Marshall also speaks a bit of Russian, thanks to his mother, a skill that helps him in the prolonged struggle to regain control of the plane from the terrorists.

In an elaborate scheme worked out between the American and Russian presidents, General Radek is released from prison (accompanied by an enthusiastic chorus of the *Internationale* sung by his prisoner fans, who also apparently yearn for the golden days of Communism) only to be gunned down by the Russian army. Korshunov is killed and thrown off Air Force One like refuse. Order is restored, but the threat to the United States from the newly independent former Soviet republics (supported by unscrupulous Russians intent on personal gain) remains. President Marshall promises to be vigilant to protect threatened Americans and Russian democracy.

Fear of the consequences of the breakdown of the Soviet military establishment propels another 1997 action film, too, *The Peacemaker.* This time the attractive American lady techie is Nicole Kidman, and George Clooney the upright representative of the American military. A maverick Russian general steals a missile from a trainwreck in a remote part of the country and plans to deliver it (for a large sum of money) to Bosnian Serb terrorists so they can detonate it at a UN Conference devoted to resolving the conflict in Bosnia. The only Russians portrayed positively here are two rustics living in the rural area where the train explodes. Most of the others sweat profusely and smoke far too many cigarettes.

★   Five years after *Air Force One,* Harrison Ford, rather like Sean Connery before him, switched sides to play a Russian character for the first time in his career. In *K-19: The Widowmaker* (2002), based on a real event that took place in 1961, Ford takes the leading role of Alexei Vostrikov, commander of a Soviet nuclear submarine on its doomed maiden voyage. His performance recalls that of Connery as Marko Ramius in *The Hunt for Red October,* but without the ideological soul-searching. Here, the conflict is a less compelling one—man versus faulty technology. Using previously classified and highly sensitive information about the malfunctioning of the submarine's nuclear power mechanism that became public only after the collapse of the USSR, director Kathryn Bigelow focuses on the interaction between members of the crew (including Liam Neeson as the stalwart Mikhail Polenin) as they face horrible illness and death in attempting to rectify the problem.

K-19 is more docudrama than feature, a tribute to the pioneers of nuclear-powered submarine technology on both sides of the Cold War. The film is also highly critical of the Soviet defense establishment, which was eager to place new technology into operation without sufficient testing and safeguards. Thirteen years earlier, a similar message had been conveyed in the underwater sci-fi adventure film *Leviathan* (1989). Here, an American crew discovers a mammoth abandoned Soviet underwater laboratory that has been leaking deadly germs from carelessly conducted germ warfare experiments.

Both *Leviathan* and *K-19* emerged from the extended aftermath of the 1986 disaster at the Chernobyl nuclear power plant in Ukraine, a huge international embarrassment for the Soviet leadership and system, and a demonstration of the destructive potential of atomic energy and biological warfare. This highly publicized incident served to undermine confidence in the ability of the Soviet government to monitor and control research in these and other areas.

Space Cowboys (2000), a rollicking comedy/adventure/sci-fi film directed by Clint Eastwood, also deals with the dangerous consequences of aging and faulty Soviet-era technology. When a Soviet communications satellite threatens to fall out of orbit and crash, NASA calls upon four retired and embittered American astronauts (played with gritty gusto by Eastwood, Tommy Lee Jones, Donald Sutherland, and James Garner) to fix the problem, since they are the only ones around who still understand the satellite's outmoded systems. But when they arrive at the satellite, the four aging Cold War buddies discover that the evil Russian rogue general Vostov (played again by Rade Serbedzija, in a reprise of his role in *The Saint*) is plotting—with the help of stolen NASA technology—to reactivate the satellite's missile-launching capabilities for his own sinister political intentions. In order to save the day, the brash Hawk Hawkins (Tommy Lee Jones), ill with terminal cancer, mounts the Soviet installation and rides it toward the moon, averting nuclear catastrophe and leaving life with a bang. The sequence pays nostalgic tribute to Slim Pickens's exhilarating bomb buckaroo ride at the end of *Doctor Strangelove*.

★   Despite Russia's impressive economic growth in the opening years of the new twenty-first century, its increased political stability under the leadership of President Vladimir Putin, and its emerging power as one of the world's largest suppliers of energy, major Hollywood films have continued to represent Russia as an unstable and dangerous place. In *The Bourne Supremacy* (2004), as in *The Saint,* a Russian oil tycoon (in this case, Yuri Gretkov, played by Czech actor Karel Roden) creates international mayhem and murder in his pursuit of supremacy in the oil business. He is assisted by double-dealing agents of the CIA, who helped him to divert $20 million in secret CIA funds to purchase oil leases. Super secret agent Jason Bourne (Matt Damon) was unwittingly enlisted to help the crooks as the result of brainwashing by a special CIA team (the Treadstone Project) later taken over by the double agents. Bourne was successfully programmed to kill the progressive anti-corruption Russian politician Neski and terminate his attempts to crack down on Gretkov. Only years later, as he emerges from a state of amnesia induced by his training, does Bourne realize what he has done.

Stricken with a guilty conscience, Bourne travels to Moscow to apologize to Neski's daughter for having murdered her parents. His confession scene in Irena Neski's apartment—a pre-fab box in the middle of an end-less housing project of identical buildings—seems intentionally to recall similar scenes from the novels of Fyodor Dostoyevsky (especially Raskol-nikov's confession to Sonya in *Crime and Punishment*). On the way, Bourne also takes revenge on Gretkov's hit man, the evil Kirill (played by New Zealand actor Karl Urban), smashed to smithereens in a crash at the end of what must be the most elaborate automobile chase scene filmed to date on the streets of the Russian capital. In *The Bourne Supremacy,* Moscow is a hyperkinetic metropolis, choked with traffic, providing anonymity and pleasure in its darkened nightclubs, a far cry from the puritanical and starchy city of *Ninotchka,* where the May Day parade was the most exciting leisure activity.

What is different about Moscow in *The Bourne Supremacy,* however, is that it has become just another of the film's European locations, not so different from London, Berlin, or Amsterdam. Crossing the border into Russia is no longer an ideological act. Director Paul Greengrass conveys a kind of nostalgia for the days of the Cold War in the film's dark atmosphere and its settings. Much of *The Bourne Supremacy* unfolds in Berlin, where the Cold War raged at its most intimate and where so many important Cold War films were set, but now the action crosses freely back and forth across the city's east and west, its wall now only a distant memory, like the scar from an old wound.

Corruption in high places—this time in the former Soviet military es-tablishment—also drives *Lord of War* (2005), directed by Andrew Niccol. Nicolas Cage stars as Yuri Orlov, the son of Ukrainian immigrants, who spent his childhood around their restaurant in a New York City Russian/ Ukrainian neighborhood. As an adult, using the knowledge of Russian, Ukrainian, and the former Soviet system that he learned from his parents, Yuri becomes involved in the extremely lucrative trade in illegal arms from Ukraine to third world countries, especially to corrupt and brutal regimes in Africa. His suppliers are military insiders (former Soviet brass) in Ukraine eager to profit by their access to deadly weapons. Rich and successful, Yuri achieves the American dream of a fancy Manhattan apart-ment and a supermodel wife (Bridget Moynahan). Yuri's life is haunted, however, by the evil of what he has done in order to succeed. He has made it to the top, but in the process he has lost his soul. *Lord of War* is an effec-tive cautionary antiwar tale about the American immigrant experience, and how the fall of the USSR affected the lives of the children of parents who left the USSR.

Turzanski, a former KGB agent (played by Geza Kovacs) now working for the Neo-Nazi dictator of a former Soviet republic, is the villain in *The Sentinel* (2006). Using a mole inside the secret service, he and his partners are planning to assassinate the American president at the Toronto G-8 summit meeting. They are foiled at the last minute through the strenuous efforts of the agent (Michael Douglas) who has been framed as the informer. "The KGB may be gone," Turzanski remarks darkly, "but we are still here."

Nostalgia for an even more distant moment in Russian history drives the recent romantic epic *White Countess* (2005). The last film produced by the legendary team of Ismail Merchant (producer) and James Ivory (director), *The White Countess* (with a screenplay by acclaimed writer Kazuo Ishigruro) tells the story of an extended family of Russian aristocrats who escaped the Russian Revolution for a life of genteel poverty in Shanghai in the late 1930s, on the eve of the Japanese invasion of the city. Featuring Vanessa Redgrave and Lynn Redgrave as snobbish, impractical relics of a vanished era, now forced to live off the prostitution of their younger relation (Natasha Richardson), *The White Countess* attempts without success to revive the spirit of *Doctor Zhivago*.

Of all the recent features representing Russia or Russians, the quirky independent film *Forty Shades of Blue* (2005) most clearly shows how the portrayal of Russians living in American society has lost its ideological charge. Winner of the Grand Jury Prize at Sundance Film Festival in 2005, *Forty Shades of Blue* (directed by Ira Sachs) is set in the music business in Memphis. Rip Torn plays Alan, a famous musician and producer. On a recent business trip to Moscow, Alan met a young Russian woman named Laura (Lara in Russian, like the heroine of *Doctor Zhivago*) who worked as the interpreter and guide for his delegation. He has brought her to live with him in Memphis, where she struggles to find an identity apart from her husband.

Adrift and isolated, Laura (played with astonishing subtlety and command by the fine Russian actress Dina Korzun) falls into an affair with Alan's adult son, afflicted with identity problems of his own. Alan's hip friends, used to mingling with all sorts of people, treat Laura's Russianness as something almost incidental. In a conversation with Alan's son, however, she confides that she doesn't feel she "has the right" to be unhappy considering the circumstances she came from in Russia, and that she finds Americans to be "incredibly spoiled." In Russia, she says, the ability to survive is something everyone learns naturally, and unhappiness is somehow irrelevant. But now that she has all the material comfort she could possibly desire, Laura feels completely empty, aimless, and depressed. The casually unfaithful Alan treats her with a kind of benevolent indifference, as a kind of exotic possession.

In the end, the Laura of the moody and provocative *Forty Shades of Blue* remains a mystery—a poetic, lyrical spirit, post-ideological and universal. Unlike Ninotchka, she does not need to be converted to or from anything and symbolizes nothing beyond her own vulnerable humanity. Having enjoyed many of the pleasures consumerism has to offer, she is still left spiritually hungry and searching for meaning.

★   So what Hollywood images of Russia might we expect to see on movie screens in years to come?

Since the end of the USSR, mainstream commercial producers and directors have proven reluctant to move beyond the sinister image of Russia and Russians that prevailed for nearly fifty years after World War II. In Hollywood, given the fantastic amounts of money expended on the production and promotion of a feature film, habit and tradition exercise enormous power. Throughout the industry, a certain nostalgia prevails for the old black-and-white good guy/bad guy world of Communism vs. Capitalism. James Bond's plainspoken boss M (a resplendent Judi Dench) seems to be speaking for many movie folks when she declares with exasperation in the critically praised and highly profitable 2006 *Casino Royale:* "God, I miss the Cold War." That much of *Casino Royale* is set in the formerly Communist Eastern bloc (Czech Republic and Montenegro), and that the film was produced in Prague, which has emerged since the early 1990s as a major new venue for high-profile Hollywood features, shows how the resurgent formerly Communist countries of Central and Eastern Europe have in the post-Communist era quickly moved to capitalize on their novelty and accessibility. They are reclaiming their place in the western world, no longer perceived as simply an extension of the USSR both ideologically and culturally.

As has always been the case, new Hollywood films dealing with the "new Russia" will continue to be generated by developments in Russian-American political and economic relations. That Russia is now a major energy supplier—especially in view of the pervasive instability in other nations upon which the United States has traditionally relied for oil and gas—has become a major factor affecting the image of Russia in the American media and popular culture. Under President Vladimir Putin, Russia has largely shed the image of confused helplessness it developed during the 1990s for one that is once again threatening and militarily powerful. The "Americanization" of Russia that many observers had naïvely predicted after the fall of Communism has failed to materialize.

The American media also remains obsessed with Russian espionage activity, as the case of the mysterious poisoning of the former agent Alexander Litvinenko in London in late 2006 made abundantly clear. It sounded just like old times when *Variety* announced in January 2007 that three Hollywood film projects dealing with the Litvinenko story were already in the works. Associated Press reported that Columbia Pictures agreed to pay $1.5 million for the film rights to a book about Litvinenko being "co-written by his widow and close friend."[2] Meanwhile, superstar Johnny Depp announced his intention to star as Litvinenko in a film to be made by his production company for Warner Brothers. The role of Litvinenko, a maverick crusader who left the KGB and defected from Russia to the West to fight for justice against his vicious former employers, seems tailor-made to appeal to the sensibilities of American audiences. And who better to portray Litvinenko than Johnny Depp, an actor popularly identified with the character of that marauding but tender pirate Jack Sparrow in *Pirates of the Caribbean?*

If Hollywood's movies about Russia and Russians have taught us anything, it is the importance of creative casting.

Notes

Introduction: Meeting Doctor Zhivago (pages 1–10)

1. Josef von Sternberg. *Fun in a Chinese Laundry* (New York: Macmillan, 1965), 242.

2. Randall M. Miller, ed. *The Kaleidoscopic Lens: How Hollywood Views Ethnic Groups* (Englewood, N.J.: Jerome S. Ozer, 1980), xi.

3. Ibid., 12.

4. Ibid., 11.

5. Richard Dyer. *The Matter of Images: Essays on Representations* (London: Routledge, 1993), 16.

Chapter 1: Romanovs and Revolution (pages 11–58)

1. Sergei Prokofiev, *Dnevnik (Diary) 1919–1933*, (Paris: sprkfv, 2002), 131.

2. Ibid., 134–135.

3. Gavin Lambert, *Nazimova: A Biography* (New York: Knopf, 1997), 231.

4. Prokofiev, *Dnevnik* 144.

5. George Martin Day, *The Russians in Hollywood: A Study in Culture Conflict* (Los Angeles: University of Southern California Press, 1934), 2.

6. Yuri Tsivian, "Leonid Kinskey, the Hollywood Foreigner," *Film History* 11 (1999), 180.

7. Day, *Russians in Hollywood*, 22.

8. John Russell Taylor, *Strangers in Paradise: The Hollywood Emigrés, 1933–1950* (New York: Holt, Rinehart and Winston, 1983), 98.

9. Harlow Robinson, *The Last Impresario: The Life, Times and Legacy of Sol Hurok* (New York: Viking, 1994), 95.

10. Erica Munk, ed., *Stanislavsky and America: An Anthology from the Tulane Drama Review* (New York: Hill and Wang, 1966), 144.

11. Lewis Milestone, and Donald Chase, *Milestones* (unpublished draft of uncompleted autobiography of Milestone), Margaret Herrick Library archives, 5.

12. Ibid., 255.

13. Ibid., 1.

14. Ibid., 9.

15. Lewis Milestone and Joel Greenberg, Interview with Milestone, Oral History Project of American Film Institute, Herrick Library archives.

16. Milestone and Chase, *Milestones*, 141–142.

17. Pat McGilligan, ed., "Lenore Coffee: Easy Smiler, Easy Weeper," in *Backstory: Interviews with Screenwriters of Hollywood's Golden Age* (Berkeley: University of California Press, 1986), 142.

18. Frank N. Magill, ed., *Magill's Survey of Cinema* (Engelwood Cliffs, N.J.: Salem Press, 1980), 1426.

19. Ibid., 1427.

20. Arthur Laurents, *Original Story By: A Memoir of Broadway and Hollywood* (New York: Applause, 2000), 106–107.

21. Ibid., 108.

22. Josef von Sternberg, *Fun in a Chinese Laundry* (New York: Macmillan, 1965), 264–265.

23. Steven Bach, *Marlene Dietrich: Life and Legend* (New York: William Morrow, 1992), 184.

24. Carolly Erickson, "The Scarlet Empress," in *Past Imperfect: History According to the Movies* (New York: Henry Holt, 1995), 89.

25. John Baxter, *The Cinema of Josef von Sternberg* (Zwemmer/Barnes, 1971), 131.

26. S. L. Bertenson, *V Khollivude s V. I. Nemirovichem-Danchenko 1926–1927* (In Hollywood with Nemirovich-Danchenko 1926–1927) (Monterey, Calif.: K. Arensburger, 1964), 3.

27. Ibid., 15–17.

28. Ibid., 32.

29. V. I. Nemirovich-Danchenko, *Izbrannye pis'ma v dvukh tomakh, t.vtoroi* (Selected Letters in Two Volumes, Vol. 2), (Moscow: Iskusstvo, 1979), 351.

30. Bertenson, *V Khollivude*, 90.

31. Nemirovich-Danchenko, *Izbrannye pis'ma*, 354.

32. Bertenson, *V Khollivude*, 131.

33. Ibid., 159.

34. Ibid., 164.

35. Sheila Benson, Review of *Reds*, *Los Angeles Times*, December 4, 1981.

36. Michael Strada, and Harold Troper, *Friend or Foe? Russians in American Film and Foreign Policy, 1933–1991* (Lanham, Md.: Scarecrow Press, 1997), 155.

37. Kurt Vonnegut, Jr., "A Gorgeous Movie—An Audacious Political Act," *Vogue* (April 1982), 315.

38. Carolyn Porter, Review of *Reds*, *Film Quarterly* (Spring 1982), 43.

39. Prokofiev, *Dnevnik*, 756–757.

40. Ronald Bergan, *Sergei Eisenstein: A Life in Conflict* (Woodstock, N.Y.: Overlook Press, 1999), 188.

41. S. M. Eisenstein, and Richard Taylor, ed. *Beyond the Stars: The Memoirs of Sergei Eisenstein*, trans. William Powell (London: BFI Publishing, 1995) 287.

42. Bergan, *Sergei Eisenstein*, 195.

43. Ibid., 210.

44. Eisenstein and Taylor, *Beyond the Stars*, 288.

45. Ibid., 286.

46. Eisenstein papers, Herrick Library archives.

47. Ibid.

48. Salka Viertel, *The Kindness of Strangers* (New York: Holt, Rinehart and Winston, 1969), 144.

49. Ibid., 145–146.

50. Sternberg, *Fun in a Chinese Laundry*, 45.

51. Eisenstein and Taylor, *Beyond the Stars*, 329–331.

52. Ibid., 333.

53. Frank Capra, *The Name Above the Title: An Autobiography* (New York: Da Capo, 1997), 161.

54. Brian Harvey, "Soviet-American 'Cinematic Diplomacy' in the 1930s: Could the Russians Really Have Infiltrated Hollywood?" *Screen* 46:4 (Winter 2005), 489.

55. Boris Pilnyak, *Okei: Amerikanskii roman* (Okay: An American Novel), in *B. Pilniak: Izbrannye proizvedeniia* (Leningrad, 1978), 532–536.

Chapter 2: *"Isn't There Some Russian in Your Background?"* (pages 59–114)

1. Herrick Library archives, *Soviet* project, MGM treatment 3855, MGM script file 1690.

2. MGM script file 1690, 2.

3. Ibid., 5.

4. MGM script file 4916.

5. Ibid.

6. Herrick Library archives, letter to Honorable Will H. Hays, dated February 3, 1933.

7. Ilya Erenburg, *Eve of the War, 1933–41*, trans. Tatiana Shebunina, in collaboration with Yvonne Kapp (London, 1963), 8.

8. Paul Kohner Collection, Archives of Stiftung Deutsche Kinemathek, Berlin.

9. Ibid.

10. Mark Spergel, *Reinventing Reality—The Art and Life of Rouben Mamoulian* (Lanham, Md.: Scarecrow Press, 1993), 154.

11. Production Code Administration file on *We Live Again*, Herrick Library, Academy of Motion Picture Arts and Sciences, Los Angeles, Calif.

12. Ibid.

13. J. D. Salinger, "Uncle Wiggily in Connecticut," *Nine Stories*, (Boston: Little, Brown, 1991), 23.

14. Walker Percy, *The Moviegoer*, (New York: Knopf, 1961), 165.

15. *Newsweek*, October 2, 1972, 47.

16. "Akim Tamiroff Dies After Illness," *Los Angeles Herald Examiner*, September 18, 1972.

17. "Tamiroff Calls Accent Key to His Success," *Paterson (N.J.) Call*, December 21, 1965.

18. Donald Hough, "Actors Don't . . . ," *This Week Magazine*, August 24, 1941, 6.

19. Paramount Studios official biography, 1940.

20. John L. Scott, "Tamiroff's Accent Pays Off," *Los Angeles Times*, September 7, 1958.

21. Ibid.

22. Mary Blume, "Tamiroff—International Actor but the Accent is Russian," *Los Angeles Times*, September 3, 1965.

23. Biography of Akim Tamiroff, Warner Bros. Studio, February 20, 1967.

24. Undated clipping, *Motion Picture Magazine*.

25. *Films in Review*, June/July 1962.

26. Erskine Johnson, "Stanislavski Pupil Raps 'Methods,'" *Los Angeles Mirror*, April 1, 1960.

27. Paul Weeks, "Actor Mischa Auer, Comedian Star of '30s, Dies in Rome," *Los Angeles Times*, March 6, 1967.

28. Studio biography, Herrick Library archives.

29. Sidney Howard and Sinclair Lewis, Screenplay of *Dodsworth*, Maria Ouspenskaya papers, Special Collections, UCLA Libarary.

30. Screenplay of *Waterloo Bridge*, Ouspenskaya papers, UCLA.

31. Homer Dickens, "Maria Ouspenskaya," *Screen Facts*, 1963(?), Ouspenskaya papers, UCLA.

32. Jerry Asher, "How Ugly Ducklings Can Find Happiness," *Screenland* 17:6.

33. Mayme Ober Peak, "Next to the Stars," *Boston Globe,* April 21, 1939.

34. Maria Ouspenskaya, Unpublished autobiographical fragment, Ouspenskaya papers, UCLA.

35. Promotional brochure for Maria Ouspenskaya School of Dramatic Arts, Ouspenskaya papers, UCLA.

36. Maria Ouspenskaya School of Dramatic Arts, 1940–41 brochure, Ouspenskaya papers, UCLA.

37. Tess Slesinger and Frank Davis, Revised final script of *Dance Girl Dance,* Ouspenskaya papers, UCLA.

38. Ibid.

39. John Franchey, "Meet the Madame," *Modern Screen,* November 1940.

40. Ouspenskaya letter to Paul Kohner, December 19, 1943, Paul Kohner Collection, Stiftung Deutsche Kinemathek, Berlin.

41. Ibid., letter of April 27, 1944.

42. Ibid., letter of Elizabeth Dickinson to Ouspenskaya, January 18, 1943.

43. Ibid., unsigned memo to Paul Kohner, April 4, 1941.

44. "Russian-born actress left estate of $358.32," *Daily News,* January 12, 1950, "Maria Ouspenskaya Estate Only $358.82," *Citizen-News,* January 13, 1950.

45. "It's the Accent That Confuses," *New York Times,* November 30, 1941.

46. "Gregory Ratoff Dies in Swiss Clinic at 63," *Hollywood Citizen News,* December 14, 1960.

47. "It's the Accent That Confuses."

48. Yuri Tsivian, "Leonid Kinskey, the Hollywood Foreigner," *Film History* 11, 178–179.

49. Ezra Goodman, "Reflections by Gregory Ratoff," unidentified source and date, Herrick Library clipping files.

50. Harlow Robinson, *The Last Impresario: The Life, Times and Legacy of Sol Hurok,* (New York: Viking, 1994), 167.

51. I. V. Nest'ev and G. Ia. Edel'man eds., *Sergei Prokof'ev: Stat'i i materialy,* (Moscow, Muzyka, 1965), 222–223.

52. *Motion Picture Daily,* October 16, 1936.

53. Letters from Joseph Breen to Louis B. Mayer, December 13, 1937, and February 3, 1939, Herrick Library archives.

54. Uncredited review of *Balalaika* in *Film Daily,* December 15, 1939; review by Frank S. Nugent in *New York Times,* December 15, 1939.

55. Uncredited preview article on *Balalaika, Variety,* December 14, 1939.

56. Uncredited review of *Balalaika, Variety,* December 20, 1939.

57. Scott Eyman, *Ernst Lubitsch: Laughter in Paradise* (New York: Simon and Schuster, 1993), 265.

58. "Memorandum for the files," written by Joseph Breen, May 13, 1938, Herrick Library archives.

59. Eyman, *Ernst Lubitsch,* 245.

60. Ibid., 247.

61. Ed Sikov, *On Sunset Boulevard: The Life and Times of Billy Wilder* (New York: Hyperion, 1998), 135.

62. Ibid.

63. Memo from Al Block of MGM to Joseph Breen, September 8, 1939, Herrick Library archives.

64. Review of *Ninotchka* by Frank S. Nugent, *New York Times,* November 17, 1939.

65. Letter from W. G. Van Schmus to Joseph Breen, quoted in letter from Breen to Bernard Hyman, December 4, 1939, Herrick Library archives.

66. Production Code Administration files, Herrick Library archives.

67. Letter from Joseph Breen to Louis B. Mayer, August 23, 1940, Herrick Library archives.

68. *Variety,* December 4, 1940.

Chapter 3: Temporary Comrades (pages 115–145)

1. For an enlightening discussion of this topic, see Neal Gabler, *An Empire of Their Own: How the Jews Invented Hollywood* (New York: Crown, 1988).

2. *New York Times,* March 8, 1943 and May 7, 1943.

3. Andre Bazin, "On *Why We Fight:* History, Documentation, and the Newsreel (1946)," trans. and ed. Bert Cardullo, *Film and History* 31.1 (2001), 60.

4. Ellen Schrecker, *Many Are the Crimes: McCarthyism in America* (Boston: Little, Brown, 1998), 320–21.

5. Kenneth Lloyd Billingsley, *Hollywood Party: How Communism Seduced the American Film Industry in the 1930s and 1940s* (Rocklin, Calif.: Forum, 1998).

6. Gregory D. Black and Clayton R. Koppes, *Hollywood Goes to War: How Politics, Profits and Propaganda Shaped World War II Movies* (New York: Free Press, 1987), 221.

7. *New York Times,* March 7, 1943.

8. Billingsley, *Hollywood Party,* 64.

9. William Wright, *Lillian Hellman: The Image, The Woman,* (New York: Simon and Schuster, 1986), 186.

10. Lillian Hellman, *An Unfinished Woman* (Boston: Little, Brown, 1969), 125.

11. Bosley Crowther, "The Ecstasies in *Mission to Moscow* Raise Doubts on Political Films," *New York Times*, May 9, 1943.

12. "Several Faults Are Found in *Mission to Moscow* Film," *New York Times*, May 9, 1943.

13. "V.F.W. Aide Defends *Mission to Moscow*," *New York Times*, May 19, 1943.

14. "*Mission to Moscow* Cards Banned by City Subways," *New York Times*, May 28, 1943.

15. "A Dramatist's Viewpoint on *Mission to Moscow*," *New York Times*, June 13, 1943.

16. "Asks Ban on *Mission to Moscow*," *New York Times*, June 16, 1943.

17. "Ambassador," *Time*, June 12, 1944.

18. William Darby and Jack DuBois, *American Film Music: Major Composers, Techniques, Trends 1915–1990* (Jefferson, N.C.: McFarland, 1990), 47.

19. Interview with Esa-Pekka Salonen, Los Angeles Philharmonic press office, December 7, 2000.

20. Dick Adler, "Rachmaninov in Beverly Hills," *Upbeat* (Los Angeles Philharmonic Magazine), October 10, 1989, 3.

21. Ibid., 2.

22. Otto Friedrich, *City of Nets: A Portrait of Hollywood in the 1940s* (New York: Perennial, 1987), 35.

23. Fred Karlin, *Listening to the Movies: The Film Lover's Guide to Film Music* (New York: Schirmer, 1994), 53.

24. Christopher Palmer, *The Composer in Hollywood* (London: Marion Boyars, 1993), 121.

25. Ibid., 127.

26. Tony Thomas, *Music for the Movies* (second ed.) (Los Angeles: Silman-James, 1997), 85.

27. "Two Beatings Charged by Actress," *Los Angeles Examiner*, June 1, 1938.

28. Vernon Duke, *Passport to Paris* (Boston: Little, Brown, 1955), 209.

29. Ibid., 367.

30. Michael Chekhov, *Put' aktera* (*The Actor's Path*) (Moscow: Tranzitkniga, 2003), 208.

31. Charles Marowitz, *The Other Chekhov*, (New York: Applause, 2004), 204.

32. Ibid., 213.

33. Ibid., 210.

34. Liisa Byckling, "Mikhail Chekhov v Khollivude: Razmyshleniia i pis'ma

Marku Aldanovu (Michael Chekhov in Hollywood: Notes and Letters to Mark Aldanov)" (Helsinki: Studia Slavica Finlandensia, 1991), 8.

35. Quoted in Marowitz, *The Other Chekhov*, 238.

36. Yuri Tsivian. "Leonid Kinskey, the Hollywood Foreigner," *Film History* (1999), 180.

37. Byckling, "Mikhail Chekhov," 17.

38. Ibid.

39. Marowitz, *The Other Chekhov*, 266.

40. "Ambassador," *Time*, June 12, 1944.

41. Ibid.

42. For more on Kalatozov's sojourn in Hollywood, see Golovskoi, Valerii, "Mikhail Kalatozov—poltora goda v Gollivude," *Kinovedcheskike zapiski* 77 (2006), 271–298.

43. David Niven, *Bring on the Empty Horses* (New York: Putnam, 1975), 156.

44. Ibid., 157.

45. Ibid., 159.

Chapter 4: Russians Don't Smile Like That (pages 146–176)

1. Michael J. Strada and Harold R. Troper *Friend or Foe: Russians in American Film and Foreign Policy, 1933–1991* (Lanham, Md.: Scarecrow Press, 1997), 92.

2. Otto Friedrich, *City of Nets: A Portrait of Hollywood in the 1940s* (New York: Perennial, 1987), 316.

3. Kenneth Lloyd Billingsley, *Hollywood Party: How Communism Seduced the American Film Industry in the 1930s and 1940s* (Rocklin, Calif.: Forum, 1998), 112.

4. Testimony of Ayn Rand, October 24, 1947, House Committee on Un-American Activities. Reprinted in Eric Bentley, ed., *Thirty Years of Treason: Excerpts from Hearings Before the House Committee on Un-American Activities, 1938–1968* (New York: Viking, 1971), 111–119.

5. Friedrich, *City of Nets*, 318.

6. Joel Greenberg, Oral History Project of American Film Institute, interview with Lewis Milestone, taped October 21, 1971. Herrick Library archives, Milestone papers, Files 171 and 172.

7. Ibid.

8. Jhan Robbins, *Yul Brynner: The Inscrutable King* (New York: Dodd, Mead and Co., 1987), 82.

9. Ibid., 83.

10. Ibid., 104.

11. Ibid., 105.

12. Ibid., 151.

13. Elia Kazan, *A Life* (New York: Anchor, 1989), 519.

14. Ibid., 524–525.

15. Raymond Durgnat, and Scott Simmon, *King Vidor, American* (Berkeley: University of California Press, 1988), 302–303.

16. *Variety,* August 22, 1956.

17. Charles Marowitz, *The Other Chekhov: A Biography of Michael Chekhov, the Legendary Actor, Director and Theorist* (New York: Applause, 2004).

18. *Variety,* December 12, 1962.

19. John Baxter, *The Cinema of Josef von Sternberg* (New York: A. S. Barnes, 1971), 162.

20. Letter from Joseph Breen to Harold Melniker of RKO, June 7, 1949, Production Code Files, Herrick Library archives.

21. Mark Spergel, *Reinventing Reality: The Art and Life of Rouben Mamoulian* (Metuchen, N.J.: Scarecrow, 1993), 215.

22. Ibid., 218.

23. Letter from Geoffrey Shurlock of Production Code Administration to Dore Schary, May 7, 1956, Production Code Files, Herrick Library archives.

24. Arthur Marx, *Goldwyn: A Biography of the Man Behind the Myth* (New York: Ballantine, 1976), 451–452.

Chapter 5: Not All Russians Are Blond (pages 177–215)

1. Review by Ann X. Smith, Newark *Star-Ledger,* April 16, 1953.

2. For a more detailed description and analysis of *Tonight We Sing,* see *The Last Impresario,* 318–333.

3. Murray Schumach, "Hollywood Stews About Luncheon," *New York Times,* September 15, 1959.

4. William Taubman, *Khrushchev: The Man and His Era* (New York: Norton, 2003), 430.

5. "Premier Annoyed by Ban on a Visit to Disneyland," *New York Times,* Sept.20, 1959.

6. Ibid.

7. Harrison Salisbury, "Premier Angered," *New York Times,* September 20, 1950.

8. Ed Sikov, *On Sunset Boulevard: The Life and Times of Billy Wilder* (New York: Hyperion, 1998), 458.

9. Leonard Maltin, ed., *Leonard Maltin's Movie Encyclopedia,* (New York: Plume, 1994), 899.

10. Peter Ustinov, *Dear Me* (Boston: Little, Brown, 1977), 270.

11. Ibid., 267.

12. Ibid., 270.

13. Ibid., 281.

14. Ibid., 309.

15. Review in *The Reporter,* May 9, 1961.

16. J. M. Roberts, *The Penguin History of the Twentieth Century* (New York: Penguin, 1999), 658.

17. Greil Marcus, *The Manchurian Candidate* (London: BFI, 2002), 16.

18. *Los Angeles Herald-Examiner,* November 23, 1962.

19. John Baxter, *Stanley Kubrick: A Biography,* New York: Carroll and Graf, 1997), 40.

20. Ibid., 176.

21. *New York Times,* February 16, 1964.

22. Ibid., March 1, 1964.

23. James Chapman, *Licence to Thrill: A Cultural History of the James Bond Films* (New York: Columbia Univ. Press, 2000), 272.

24. Ibid., 9, 274.

25. Steven Jay Rubin, *The James Bond Films: A Behind the Scenes History* (London: Talisman, 1981), 25.

26. Lars Ole Sauerberg, *Secret Agents in Fiction: Ian Fleming, John Le Carre and Len Deighton* (New York: St.Martin's, 1984), 160–161.

27. Thomas J. Price, "The Changing Image of the Soviets in the Bond Saga: From Bond-Villains to 'Acceptable Role Partners,'" *Journal of Popular Culture* 26.1 (Summer 1992), 30.

28. Chapman, *Licence to Thrill,* 255.

29. Kevin Brownlow, *David Lean: A Biography* (New York: St.Martin's, 1996), 499.

30. English translation by Jon Stallworthy and Peter France, in Jon Stallworthy and Peter France, *Selected Poems of Boris Pasternak* (Harmondsworth: Penguin, 1984).

31. Isaac Deutscher, "Pasternak and the Calendar of the Revolution," in Donald Davie and Angela Livingstone, eds., *Pasternak: Modern Judgements* (London: Macmillan, 1969), 240.

32. Brownlow, *David Lean,* 500.

33. Ibid., 501.

34. Robert Bolt, Screenplay for *Doctor Zhivago*, 12.

35. Brownlow, *David Lean*, 507.

36. Ibid., 513.

37. Ibid., 528.

38. Bosley Crowther, Review of *Doctor Zhivago*, *New York Times*, December 23, 1965.

39. Ibid.

40. Bosley Crowther, "The Ten Best Films of 1965," *New York Times*, December 26, 1965.

41. Richard Schickel, Review of *Doctor Zhivago* in *Life*, January 24, 1966, 62A.

42. Brownlow, *David Lean*, 542.

Chapter 6: To Defect or Not to Defect (pages 216–241)

1. Ronald D. LeBlanc, "*Love and Death* and Food: Woody Allen's Comic Use of Gastronomy," *Literature Film Quarterly* 17.1 (1989), 23.

2. Woody Allen, *Woody Allen on Woody Allen: In Conversation with Stig Bjorkman* (New York: Grove Press, 1995), 74.

3. Joan Acocella, "The Soloist," *Life Stories: Profiles from The New Yorker* (New York: Random House, 2000), 73.

4. Diane Solway, *Nureyev: His Life* (New York: William Morrow, 1998), 362–363.

5. Ibid., 409.

6. Pauline Kael, Review of *Valentino*, *New Yorker*, November 7, 1977.

7. Gelsey Kirkland, with Greg Lawrence, *Dancing on My Grave* (Garden City, N.J.: Doubleday, 1986).

8. Acocella, "The Soloist," 73.

9. "Alexander Godunov," IMDb website.

10. John Baxter, *Kubrick: A Biography* (New York: Carroll and Graf, 1997), 199.

Chapter 7: Worst of Enemies, Best of Friends (pages 242–263)

1. Catherine Evtuhov et al., *A History of Russia: Peoples, Legends, Events, Forces* (Boston: Houghton Mifflin, 2003), 778.

2. Michael Strada and Harold Troper, *Friend or Foe? Russians in American Film and Foreign Policy, 1933–1991* (Lanham, Md.: Scarecrow Press, 1997), 170.

3. Tom Clancy, *The Hunt for Red October* (New York: Berkley, 1984), 4.

4. Ibid., 27.

5. Andrei Konchalovsky, *Nizkie istiny* (Ugly Truths) (Moscow: Sovershenno sekretno, 1998), 186.

6. Ibid., 187.

7. Ibid., 189.

8. Ibid., 188.

9. Ibid., 203.

10. Ibid., 212–213.

11. Alessandra Stanley, "A Feel for Siberia and Walden Pond," *New York Times,* October 30, 1997.

12. Konchalovsky, *Nizkie istiny,* 190–191.

13. Andrei Konchalovsky, *Vozvyshayushchyi obman* (Sublime Deceit) (Moscow: Sovershenno sekretno, 1999), 244.

Chapter 8: Show Me the Real Moscow (pages 264–276)

1. Andrew Horton and Michael Brashinsky, *The Zero Hour: Glasnost and Soviet Cinema in Transition* (Princeton: Princeton University Press, 1992), 113.

2. "Depp to Make Film About Poisoned Ex-Spy," Associated Press wire service, January 13, 2007.

Selected Filmography

FILM (RELEASE DATE)	DIRECTOR
The Last Command (1928)	Josef von Sternberg
The Tempest (1928)	Sam Taylor, Lewis Milestone, Victor Tourjansky
Grand Hotel (1932)	Edmund Goulding
Rasputin and the Empress (1932)	Richard Boleslawski
The Scarlet Empress (1934)	Josef von Sternberg
We Live Again (1934)	Rouben Mamoulian
Anna Karenina (1935)	Clarence Brown
Crime and Punishment (1935)	Josef von Sternberg
My Man Godfrey (1936)	Gregory La Cava
Tovarich (1937)	Anatole Litvak
Balalaika (1939)	Reinhold Schunzel
Ninotchka (1939)	Ernst Lubitsch
Comrade X (1940)	King Vidor
Now, Voyager (1942)	Irving Rapper
King's Row (1942)	Sam Wood
Frankenstein Meets the Wolf Man (1943)	Roy William Neill
For Whom the Bell Tolls (1943)	Sam Wood
Mission to Moscow (1943)	Michael Curtiz
Days of Glory (1944)	Jacques Tourneur
North Star (1944)	Lewis Milestone
Song of Russia (1944)	Gregory Ratoff
Battle of Russia (1944)	Anatole Litvak
Spellbound (1945)	Alfred Hitchcock
Red Danube (1950)	George Sidney
All About Eve (1950)	Joseph L. Mankiewicz
The World in His Arms (1952)	Raoul Walsh
High Noon (1952)	Fred Zinnemann
On the Waterfront (1954)	Elia Kazan
Anastasia (1956)	Anatole Litvak

War and Peace (1956)	King Vidor
Jet Pilot (1957)	Josef von Sternberg
Silk Stockings (1957)	Rouben Mamoulian
The Brothers Karamazov (1958)	Richard Brooks
Touch of Evil (1958)	Orson Welles
Ocean's Eleven (1960)	Lewis Milestone
One, Two, Three (1961)	Billy Wilder
Romanoff and Juliet (1961)	Peter Ustinov
The Manchurian Candidate (1962)	John Frankenheimer
Taras Bulba (1962)	J. Lee-Thompson
From Russia with Love (1963)	Terence Young
Dr. Strangelove (1964)	Stanley Kubrick
Dr. Zhivago (1965)	David Lean
The Russians Are Coming, The Russians Are Coming (1966)	Norman Jewison
2001: A Space Odyssey (1968)	Stanley Kubrick
The Music Lovers (1970)	Ken Russell
Nicholas and Alexandra (1971)	Franklin Shaffner
Love and Death (1975)	Woody Allen
The Spy Who Loved Me (1977)	Lewis Gilbert
The Turning Point (1977)	Herbert Ross
Valentino (1977)	Ken Russell
For Your Eyes Only (1981)	John Glen
Reds (1981)	Warren Beatty
Gorky Park (1984)	Michael Apted
Red Dawn (1984)	John Milius
Moscow on the Hudson (1984)	Paul Mazursky
Witness (1985)	Peter Weir
White Nights (1985)	Taylor Hackford
Rambo, First Blood, Part II (1985)	Ted Kotcheff
Rocky IV (1985)	Sylvester Stallone
Runaway Train (1985)	Andrei Konchalovsky
2010 (1985)	Peter Hyams
Russkies (1987)	Richard Rosenthal
Little Nikita (1988)	Richard Benjamin
Rambo III (1988)	Peter MacDonald
Red Heat (1988)	Walter Hill

Leviathan (1989)	George P. Cosmatos
The Hunt for Red October (1990)	John McTiernan
The Russia House (1990)	Fred Schepisi
The Inner Circle (1991)	Andrei Konchalovsky
Back in the USSR (1992)	Deran Sarafian
GoldenEye (1995)	Martin Campbell
The Saint (1997)	Phillip Noyce
Air Force One (1997)	Wolfgang Petersen
The Peacemaker (1997)	Mimi Leder
Space Cowboys (2000)	Clint Eastwood
K-19: The Widowmaker (2002)	Kathryn Bigelow
The Bourne Supremacy (2004)	Paul Greengrass
Lord of War (2005)	Andrew Niccol
White Countess (2005)	James Ivory
Forty Shades of Blue (2005)	Ira Sachs
The Sentinel (2006)	Clark Johnson

Selected Bibliography

Acocella, Joan. "The Soloist." In *Life Stories: Profiles from The New Yorker*, ed.
David Remnick, 61–78. New York: Random House, 2000, 61–78.

Alexander, John T. *Catherine the Great: Life and Legend*. New York: Oxford
University Press, 1989.

Allen, Woody. *Woody Allen on Woody Allen: In Conversation with Stig Bjorkman*.
New York: Grove Press, 1995.

Anschel, Eugene, ed. *The American Image of Russia: 1775–1917*. New York:
Frederick Ungar, 1974.

Arenskii, K. *Pis'ma v Khollivud* (Letters to Hollywood). Monterey, Calif.:
K. Arensburger, 1968.

Bach, Steven. *Marlene Dietrich: Life and Legend*. New York: William Morrow, 1992.

Baxter, John. *The Cinema of Josef von Sternberg*. New York: A. S. Barnes, 1971.

———. *The Hollywood Exiles*. London: MacDonald and Jane's, 1976.

———. *Stanley Kubrick: A Biography*. New York: Carroll and Graf, 1997.

Bentley, Eric, ed. *Thirty Years of Treason: Excerpts from Hearings before the House
Committee on Un-American Activities*. New York: Viking, 1971.

Bergan, Ronald. *Sergei Eisenstein: A Life in Conflict*. Woodstock, N.Y.: Overlook,
1999.

Bertenson, S. L. *V Khollivude s V. I. Nemirovichem-Danchenko* (In Hollywood
with V.I. Nemirovich-Danchenko). Monterey, Calif.: K. Arensburger, 1964.

Billingsley, Kenneth Lloyd. *Hollywood Party: How Communism Seduced the
American Film Industry in the 1930s and 1940s*. Rocklin, Calif.: Forum, 1998.

Black, Gregory D., and Clayton R. Koppes. *Hollywood Goes to War: How Politics,
Profits and Propaganda Shaped World War II*. New York: Free Press, 1987.

Boyle, Peter G. *American-Soviet Relations: From the Russian Revolution to the Fall
of Communism*. London: Routledge, 1993.

Brownlow, Kevin. *David Lean: A Biography*. New York: St. Martin's Press, 1996.

Brynner, Rock. *Yul: The Man Who Would Be King: A Memoir of Father and Son*.
New York: Simon and Schuster, 1989.

Carnes, Mark C., ed. *Past Imperfect: History According to the Movies*. New York:
Henry Holt, 1995.

Chapman, James. *Licence to Thrill: A Cultural History of the James Bond Films.*
New York: Columbia University Press, 2000.

Chekhov, Mikhail. *Put' aktera* (The Actor's Path). Moscow: Soglasie, 2000.

_____. *Put' aktera, memuary* (The Actor's Path, Memoirs). Moscow:
Tranzitkniga, 2003.

Clancy, Tom. *The Hunt for Red October.* New York: Berkley, 1984.

Cohan, Steven, and Ina Rae Hark. *Screening the Male: Exploring Masculinities in
Hollywood Cinema.* London: Routledge, 1993.

Darby, William, and Jack DuBois. *American Film Music: Major Composers,
Techniques, Trends 1915–1990.* Jefferson, N.C.: McFarland, 1990.

Day, George Martin. *The Russians in Hollywood: A Study in Culture Conflict
(USC School of Research Studies No.4).* Los Angeles: University of Southern
California Press, 1934.

Dick, Bernard. *Hellman in Hollywood.* Rutherford, N.J.: Fairleigh Dickinson
University Press, 1982.

Duke, Vernon. *Passport to Paris.* Boston: Little, Brown, 1955.

Durgnat, Raymond, and Scott Simmon. *King Vidor.* Berkeley: University of
California Press, 1988.

Dyer, Richard. *The Matter of Images: Essays on Representations.* London:
Routledge, 1993.

Eisenstein, S. M., and Richard Taylor, ed. *Beyond the Stars: The Memoirs of Sergei
Eisenstein,* trans. William Powell. London: BFI Publishing, 1995.

Evtuhov, Catherine, David Goldfrank, Lindsey Hughes, and Richard Stites. *A
History of Russia: Peoples, Legends, Events, Forces.* Boston: Houghton Mifflin,
2004.

Eyman, Scott. *Ernst Lubitsch: Laughter in Paradise.* New York: Simon and
Schuster, 1993.

Filene, Peter. *Americans and the Soviet Experiment 1917–33.* Cambridge, Mass.:
Harvard University Press, 1967.

Fried, Richard M. *The Russians Are Coming! The Russians Are Coming!: Pageantry
and Patriotism in Cold-War America.* New York: Oxford University Press, 1998.

Friedrich, Otto. *City of Nets: A Portrait of Hollywood in the 1940s.* New York:
Harper and Row, 1986.

Fyne, Robert. *The Hollywood Propaganda of World War II.* Metuchen, N.J.:
Scarecrow Press, 1994.

Gabler, Neal. *An Empire of Their Own: How the Jews Invented Hollywood.* New
York: Crown, 1988.

Gaddis, John Lewis. *We Now Know: Rethinking Cold War History.* New York: Oxford University Press, 1997.

Geduld, Harry M. *Sergei Eisenstein and Upton Sinclair: The Making and Unmaking of "Que Viva Mexico!"* Bloomington: Indiana University Press, 1970.

Graham, Sheilah. *The Garden of Allah.* New York: Crown, 1970.

Hellman, Lillian. *An Unfinished Woman.* Boston: Little, Brown, 1969.

_____. *Scoundrel Time.* Boston: Little, Brown, 1976.

Henriksen, Margot A. *Dr. Strangelove's America: Society and Culture in the Atomic Age.* Berkeley: University of California Press, 1997.

Horton, Andrew, and Michael Brashinsky. *The Zero Hour: Glasnost and Soviet Cinema in Transition.* Princeton: Princeton University Press, 1992.

Kalinak, Kathryn. *Settling the Score: Music and the Classical Hollywood Film.* Madison: University of Wisconsin Press, 1992.

Karlin, Fred. *Listening to the Movies: The Film Lover's Guide to Film Music.* New York: Schirmer, 1994.

Klehr, Harvey, and John Earl Haynes. *The American Communist Movement: Storming Heaven Itself.* New York: Twayne, 1992.

Konchalovsky, Andrei. *Nizike istiny* (Ugly Truths). *Moscow: Sovershenno sekretno, 1998.*

_____. *Vozvyshaiushchii obman* (Sublime Deceit). Moscow: Sovershenno sekretno, 1999.

Lambert, Gavin. *Nazimova: A Biography.* New York: Alfred A. Knopf, 1997.

Laurents, Arthur. *Original Story By.* New York: Applause, 2000.

Maltin, Leonard, ed. *Leonard Maltin's Movie Encyclopedia.* New York: Plume, 1994.

Marcus, Greil. *The Manchurian Candidate.* London: British Film Institute, 2002.

Marmorstein, Gary. *Hollywood Rhapsody: Movie Music and Its Makers 1900 to 1975.* New York: Schirmer, 1997.

Marowitz, Charles. *The Other Chekhov: A Biography of Michael Chekhov, the Legendary Actor, Director and Theorist.* New York: Applause Theatre and Cinema Books, 2004.

Marx, Arthur. *Goldwyn: A Biography of the Man Behind the Myth.* New York: Ballantine, 1976.

Millichap, Joseph R. *Lewis Milestone.* Boston, Twayne, 1981.

Miller, Randall M., and Allen L. Woll. *Ethnic and Racial Images in American Film and Television: Historical Essays and Bibliography.* New York: Garland, 1987.

_____, ed. *The Kaleidoscopic Lens: How Hollywood Views Ethnic Groups.* Englewood. N.J.: Jerome S. Ozer, 1980.

Montagu, Ivor. *With Eisenstein in Hollywood*. New York: International Publishers, 1967.

Nemirovich-Danchenko, V.I. *Izbrannye pis'ma* (Selected Letters), *Vols. I and II*. Moscow: Iskusstvo, 1979.

Niven, David. *Bring on the Empty Horses*. New York: Putnam, 1975.

Palmer, Christopher. *The Composer in Hollywood*. London: Marion Boyars, 1993.

Pilnyak, Boris. *Okei: Amerikanskii roman* (Okay: An American Novel). In *B. Pil'niak: Izbrannye proizvedenia* (B.Pilnyak: Selected Works). Leningrad: Khudozhestvennaia literature, 1978.

Prokofiev, Sergei. *Dnevnik 1907–1918, Dnevnik 1919–1933* (Diary 1907–1918, Diary 1919–1933). Paris: sprkfv, 2002.

Radosh, Allis, and Ronald Radosh. *Red Star Over Hollywood: The Film Colony's Long Romance with the Left*. San Franciso: Encounter Books.

Rand, Ayn. *We the Living*. New York: Signet, 1996.

Roberts, J. M. *The Penguin History of the Twentieth Century*. New York: Penguin, 1999.

Robbins, Jhan. *Yul Brynner: The Inscrutable King*. New York: Dodd, Mead, 1987.

Robinson, Harlow. *The Last Impresario: The Life, Times and Legacy of Sol Hurok*. New York: Viking, 1994.

_____. *Selected Letters of Sergei Prokofiev*. Boston: Northeastern University Press, 1998.

_____. *Sergei Prokofiev: A Biography*. Boston: Northeastern University Press, 2002.

Rubin, Steven Jay. *The James Bond Films: A Behind the Scenes History*. London: Talisman, 1981.

Sayre, Nora. *Running Time: Films of the Cold War*. New York: Dial, 1982.

Schrecker, Ellen. *Many Are the Crimes: McCarthyism in America*. Boston: Little, Brown, 1998.

Senelick, Laurence, ed. *Wandering Stars: Russian Émigré Theatre, 1905–1940*. Iowa City: University of Iowa Press, 1992.

Sikov, Ed. *On Sunset Boulevard: The Life and Times of Billy Wilder*. New York: Hyperion, 1998.

Smith, Martin Cruz. *Gorky Park*. New York: Ballantine, 1981.

Solway, Diane. *Nureyev: His Life*. New York: William Morrow, 1998.

Spergel, Mark. *Reinventing Reality: The Art and Life of Rouben Mamoulian*. Metuchen, N.J.: Scarecrow Press, 1993.

Strada, Michael, and Harold Troper. *Friend or Foe? Russians in American Film and Foreign Policy, 1933–1991*. Lanham, Md.: Scarecrow Press, 1997.

Sternberg, Josef von. *Fun in a Chinese Laundry.* London: Secker and Warburg, 1965.

Swenson, Karen. *Greta Garbo: A Life Apart.* New York: Scribner, 1997.

Taubman, William. *Khrushchev: The Man and His Era.* New York: Norton, 2003.

Taylor, John Russell. *Strangers in Paradise: The Hollywood Emigrés, 1933–1950.* New York: Holt, Rinehart and Winston, 1983.

Thomas, Tony. *Music for the Movies* (2nd edition). Los Angeles: Silman-James Press, 1997.

Tiomkin, Dimitri (with Prosper Buranelli). *Please Don't Hate Me.* New York: Doubleday, 1959.

Ustinov, Peter. *Dear Me.* Boston: Little, Brown, 1977.

Viertel, Salka. *The Kindness of Strangers.* New York: Holt, Rinehart and Winston, 1969.

Walsh, Stephen. *Stravinsky, The Second Exile: France and America, 1934–1971.* New York: Knopf, 2006.

Whitfield, Stephen. *The Culture of the Cold War.* Baltimore: Johns Hopkins University Press, 1996.

Williams, Robert C. *Culture in Exile: Russian Emigrés in Germany 1881–1941.* Ithaca: Cornell University Press, 1972.

Zorina, Vera. *Zorina.* New York: Knopf, 1986.

Index

Continued from page iv

Library of Congress Cataloging-in-Publication Data
Robinson, Harlow.
Russians in Hollywood, Hollywood's Russians : biography of an image / Harlow Robinson.
p. cm.
Includes bibliographical references and index.
ISBN-13: 978–1–55553–686–2 (cloth : alk. paper)
ISBN-10: 1–55553–686–7 (cloth : alk. paper)
1. Soviet Union—In motion pictures. 2. Russia (Federation)—In motion pictures.
3. National characteristics, Russian, in motion pictures. 4. Motion picture producers
and directors—Soviet Union—Biography. 5. Russians—California—Los Angeles—
Biography. I. Title.
PN1995.9.S665R63 2007
791.43089'9171—dc22   2007027410